IMAGES
of America

BROOKFIELD

IMAGES
of America

BROOKFIELD

Marilyn Whittlesey

ARCADIA
PUBLISHING

ISBN 978-0-7385-0116-1

Published by Arcadia Publishing
Charleston, South Carolina

Printed in the United States of America

Library of Congress Catalog Card Number: 99-62315

For all general information contact Arcadia Publishing at:
Telephone 843-853-2070
Fax 843-853-0044
E-mail sales@arcadiapublishing.com
For customer service and orders:
Toll-Free 1-888-313-2665

Visit us on the Internet at www.arcadiapublishing.com

This book is dedicated to my husband, Richard,
and my daughters, Laura and Janet,
who have encouraged me in my many endeavors.

Contents

ACKNOWLEDGMENTS

Over the years, many people have shared their photographs, postcards, and memorabilia with the Brookfield Historical Society and with me. They have also shared the history of Brookfield in the hopes that we would pass it along to be shared and preserved for future generations. I would like to give a special thanks to the Brookfield Historical Society for giving me permission to use their photographs. I would also like to thank the following people for allowing me the use of their photographs and for their support on this project: Florence Crowell, Ray and Dorothy Waidelich, the Congregational Church of Brookfield, James Kellogg, Robin Rose, Sharon Brown, Richard Greene, Eleanor Loesch, Daniel Morehouse, Louise Henion, the Gurski Family, Mildred Reynolds, Ruth Ballard, Ethel Anderson, Joan Pierpont, Jean and John Stauffer, Stuart Terrill, and Bob Brown.

INTRODUCTION

This collection of images of Brookfield, Connecticut, is the culmination of over 30 years of my involvement in local historical research in various capacities as a church historian, historical society member, town historian, and contributing writer for the local news media. I have been very fortunate to know some of Brookfield's longtime residents. They have been willing to share their memories and many unique photographs that have been passed down through their families; they have made this book a very special and personal view into the past. The combination of photographs, memories, and the preservation of many early homes and buildings brings together the history of the town as it evolved with the arrival of early settlers, craftsmen, farmers, religious groups, societies, and schools. Later, the arrival of the automobile, trains, and planes brought Brookfield into the 20th century. I would like to pass on the history of the town that I have grown to love. As it is said, "A picture is worth a thousand words." I hope you enjoy seeing old Brookfield from before the turn of the century to about the 1940s.

The following brief history of the town provides a framework for the early development and growth of Brookfield. In the early 1700s, settlers began to move into this area, which was occupied by the Pootatuck Indians. As the settlers purchased the land from the Native Americans, factories and farms began to spring up. As more and more families settled here, a need for their own place of worship became important to them. They began to petition the General Assembly, asking for permission to establish a parish and to build their own meetinghouse. At this time, many of these families had to travel as far as 12 miles to attend church. Those who could afford to travel built Sabbath Day houses near the meetinghouse in Newtown. For many years, the petition was turned down. Finally, in 1752, the boundaries for a parish were set and winter privileges were granted to the settlers. From September to March, they could worship in a neighbor's home that was set aside for a parish. In 1754, the General Assembly finalized the boundaries and the Parish of Newbury was formed. Land had been taken from Newtown, New Milford, and Danbury. The name Newbury was formed by combining the names of these three towns. In 1757, the first Congregational Church building was built. On September 28, 1757, Rev. Thomas Brooks was ordained as the first settled pastor and the church meetinghouse was dedicated. Finally, in 1788, the Parish of Newbury was incorporated as the town of Brookfield, named after Reverend Brooks, who was still the pastor at that time.

The town was made up of farms, factories, businesses, and homes. As early as 1732, it was indicated in land records that iron furnaces had been set up at Half-Way Falls. This area became known as the Iron Works District of Brookfield. Soon factories lined the banks of the Still River using the river for power. Brookfield Center was the religious and governmental center of the area. The Congregational church was built here and was soon followed by the Episcopal church. The first town house was built in 1797, across the road from the churches. The rest of the town was made up of farms whose main crops were tobacco, corn, wheat, and beans. Later on, there were commercial orchards, dairy farms, cattle farms, and sheep farms. Most of the farms are gone now, and houses have been built on those fields that were cleared of stones. The stones have been used as foundations for homes, bridges, buildings, and walls.

As the town has grown and the old buildings and the way of life have changed, it is hard to visualize old Brookfield. Hopefully, this book will allow the reader to catch glimpses of the Brookfield that was, even as it continues to evolve as a suburban town.

—Marilyn S. Whittlesey

One

The Iron Works District

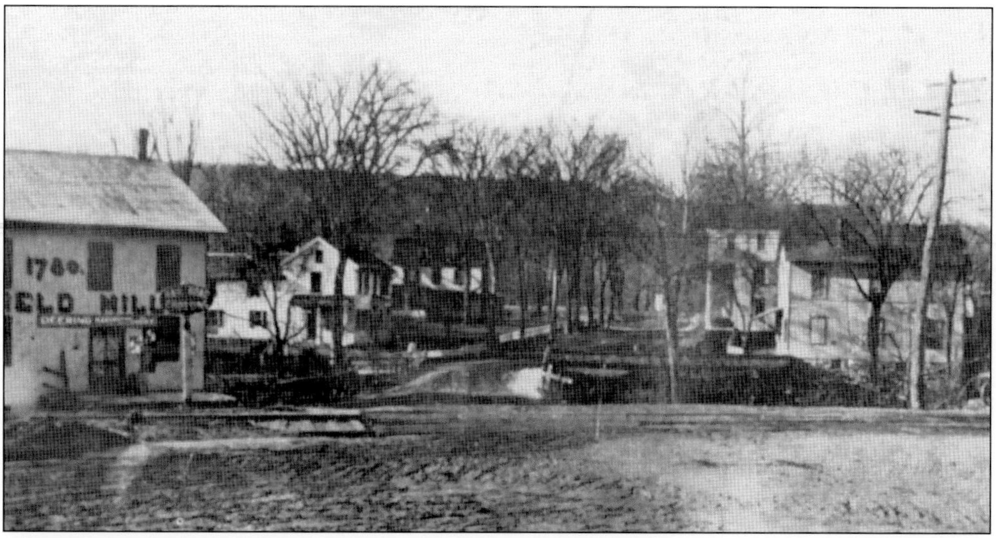

The Brookfield Iron Works were in existence by 1732. The owners were Peter Hubbell, Samuel Hathaway, and Joseph Ruggles. In 1733, the owners loaned Eleazer Hathaway £100 to work as a "skillful bloomer" in the iron works. Abel Barnum built the first gristmill in 1748. After being destroyed by fire, a new gristmill was built on the same site in 1780. When William D. Meeker was the miller, he completely rebuilt the mill. After crossing the bridge, there is the miller's house, built *c.* 1790. Just beyond the miller's house is the Hendrickson house. The house with the pillars contained a ballroom. The house across from the miller's house was originally built as a blacksmith shop. Around 1913, the tracks were moved away from the river to their present location. There were many different types of industry in the Iron Works. Some of the businesses that were located here were a cheese factory, an iron forge, sawmills, hat shops, a button factory, a shoe company, a shear shop, and a cigar company.

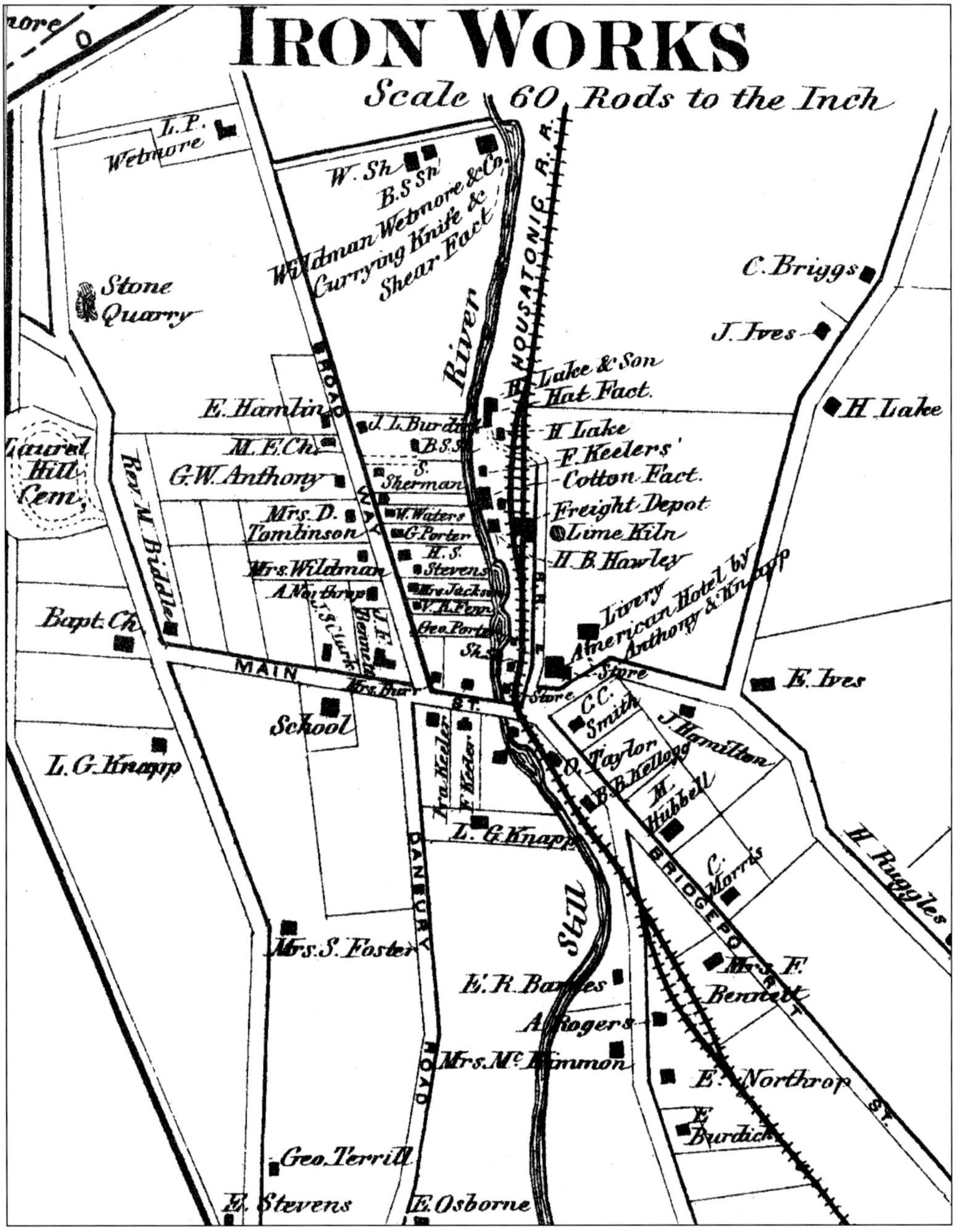

This is a *c.* 1867 map of the Iron Works District. The following people and businesses are listed in the directory: Anthony & Knapp; the American Hotel; Jesse James, blacksmith; Keeler, manufacturer of cotton batting; Lake & Son, manufacturer of hats; A. Northrop, manufacturer of lime; H.S. Stevens, manufacturer of carriages and wagons; and Wetmore, Wildman & Company, manufacturer of shears and currying knives.

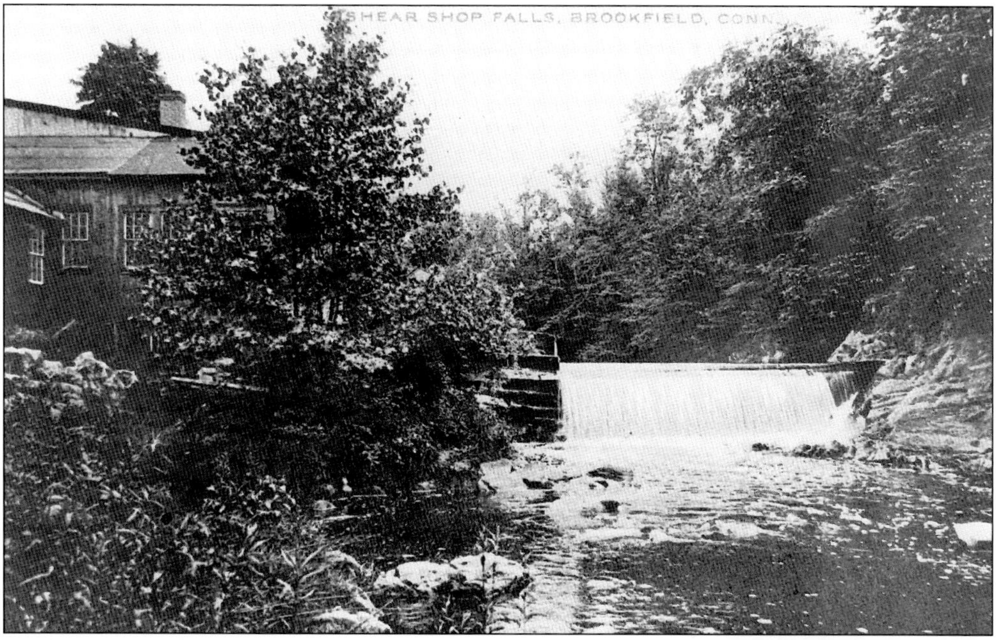

In 1837, Daniel Tomlinson built a dam along the Still River, along with a shop for making currier's knives. Over the years, this shop was enlarged and rebuilt. Treat, Wildman, & Wetmore built an addition to the shop. In 1854, Bennett & Wildman were manufacturing shears here. In 1882, John T. Bateman joined the firm.

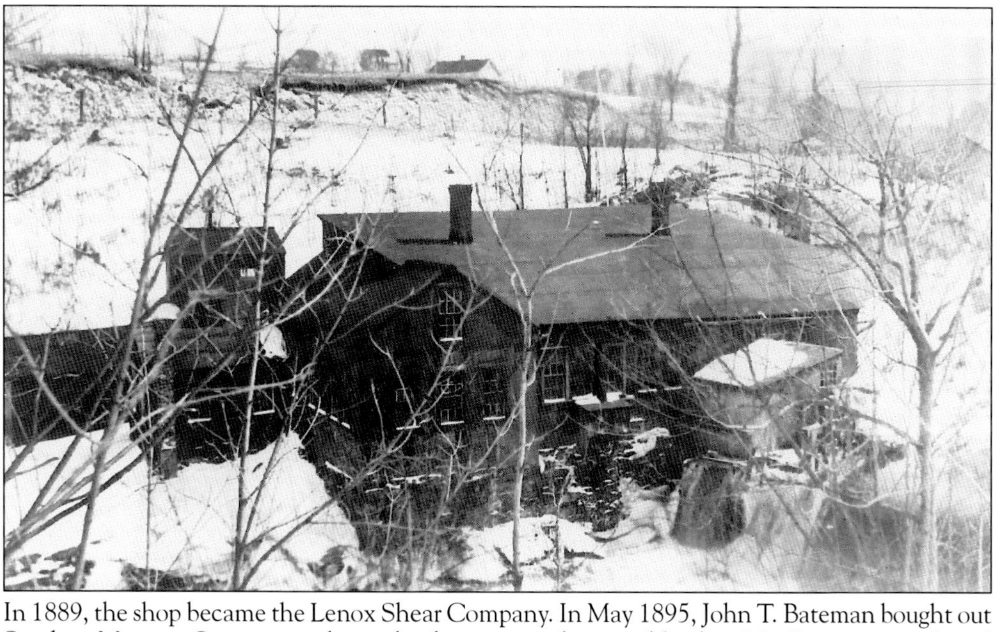

In 1889, the shop became the Lenox Shear Company. In May 1895, John T. Bateman bought out Stephen Meaney. Seven years later, the factory was destroyed by fire. Mr. Bateman purchased the former site of the Jones sawmill and built a new factory on the east side of the river. Years later, this building was sold to Alvin Tuck, who opened an Electroplate factory here.

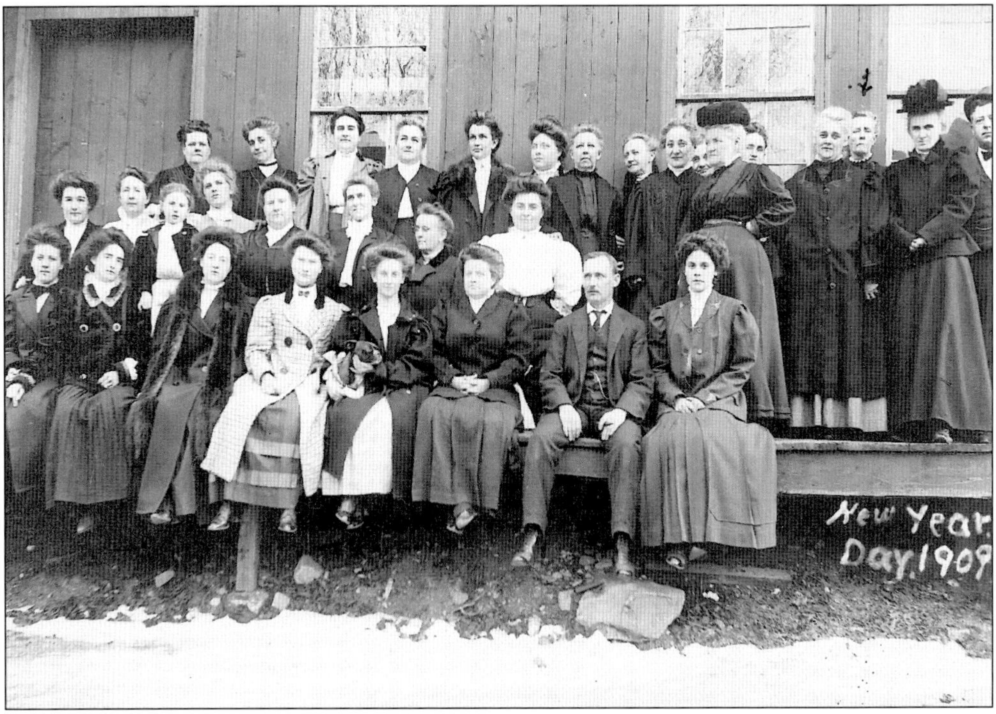

On New Years Day in 1909, these shear shop workers posed for a photograph. Included among those shown here are John T. Bateman, Cynthia Russell, Mary Baxter Street, and Fred Porter.

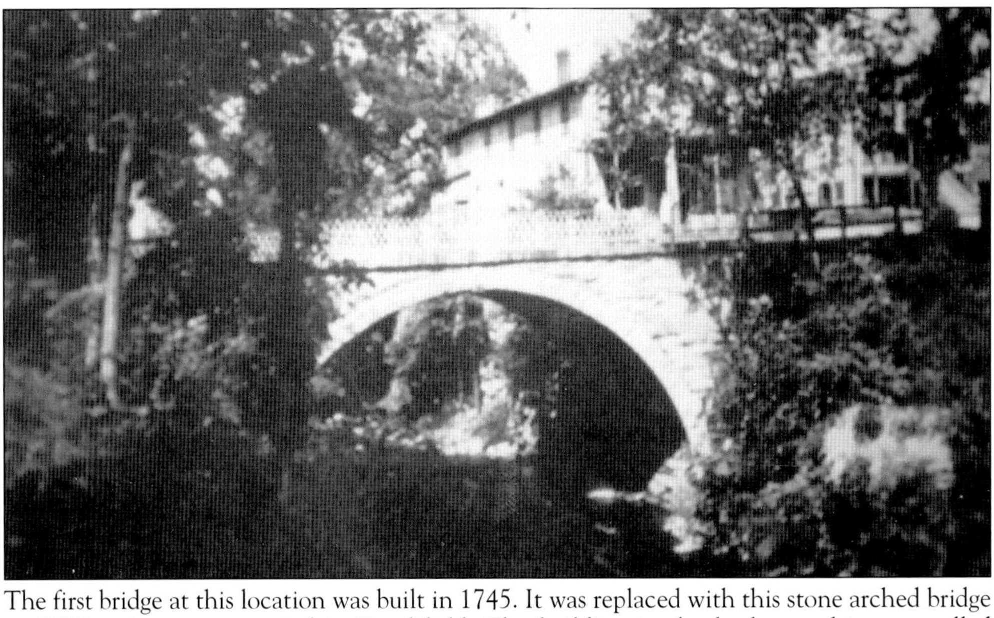

The first bridge at this location was built in 1745. It was replaced with this stone arched bridge in 1880 with stones quarried in Brookfield. The building in the background is now called the Brookfield Market.

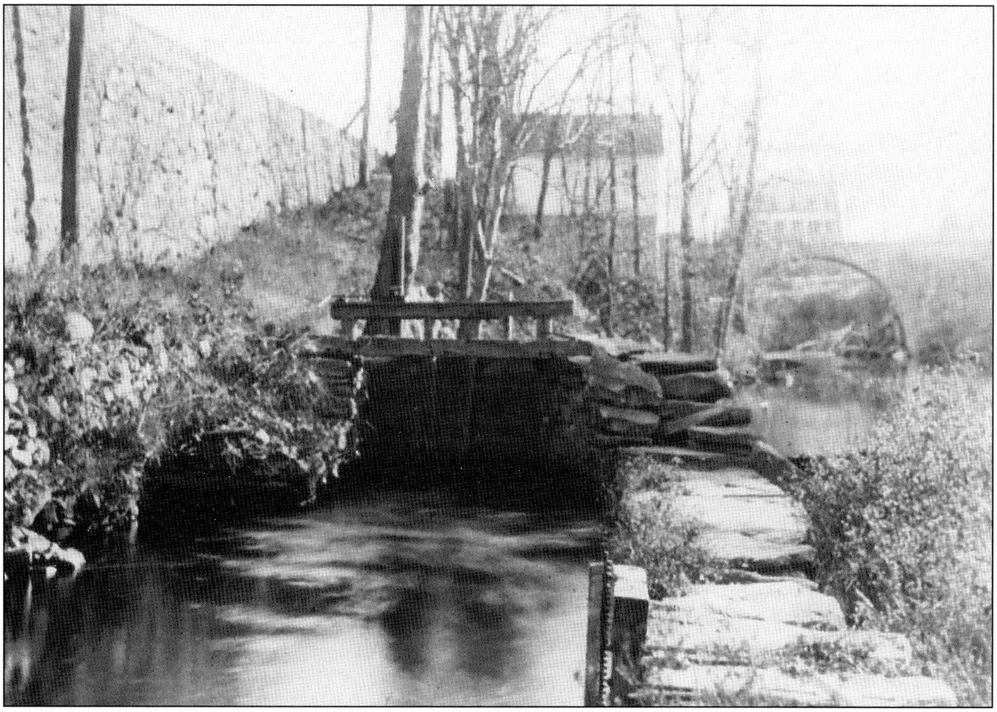

This is the sluiceway and gate that once served Henry Hawley's hat factory. Valentine Patch used it later for his shoddy factory. Shoddy is an inferior woolen yarn that is made from used fabrics that have been reprocessed. In 1907, the factory burned down. In the distance is the home called "Greystone."

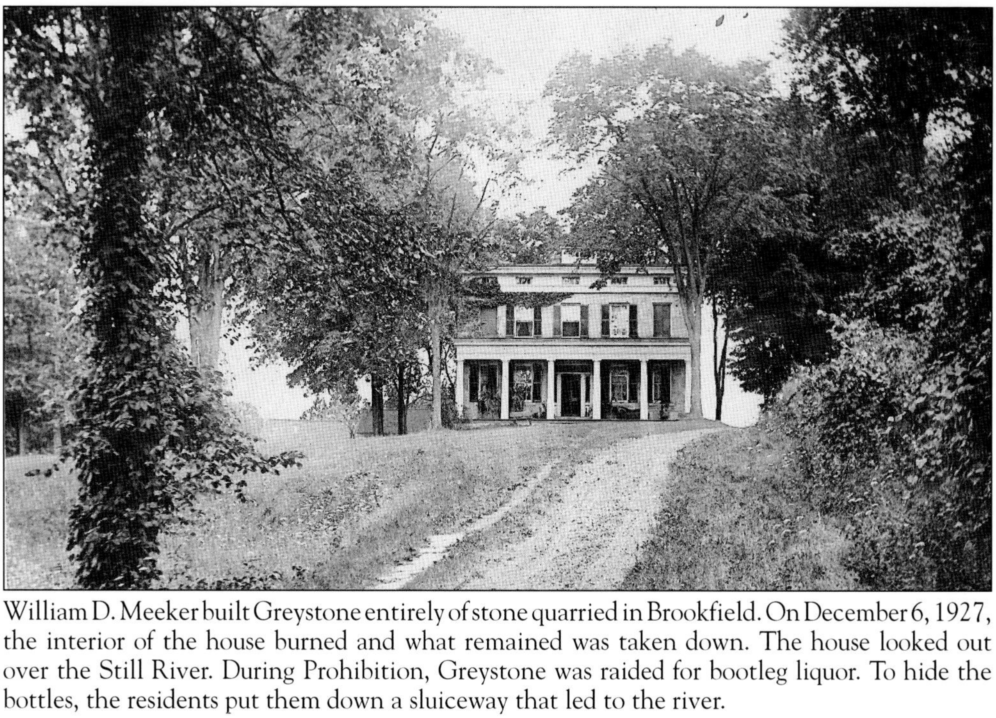

William D. Meeker built Greystone entirely of stone quarried in Brookfield. On December 6, 1927, the interior of the house burned and what remained was taken down. The house looked out over the Still River. During Prohibition, Greystone was raided for bootleg liquor. To hide the bottles, the residents put them down a sluiceway that led to the river.

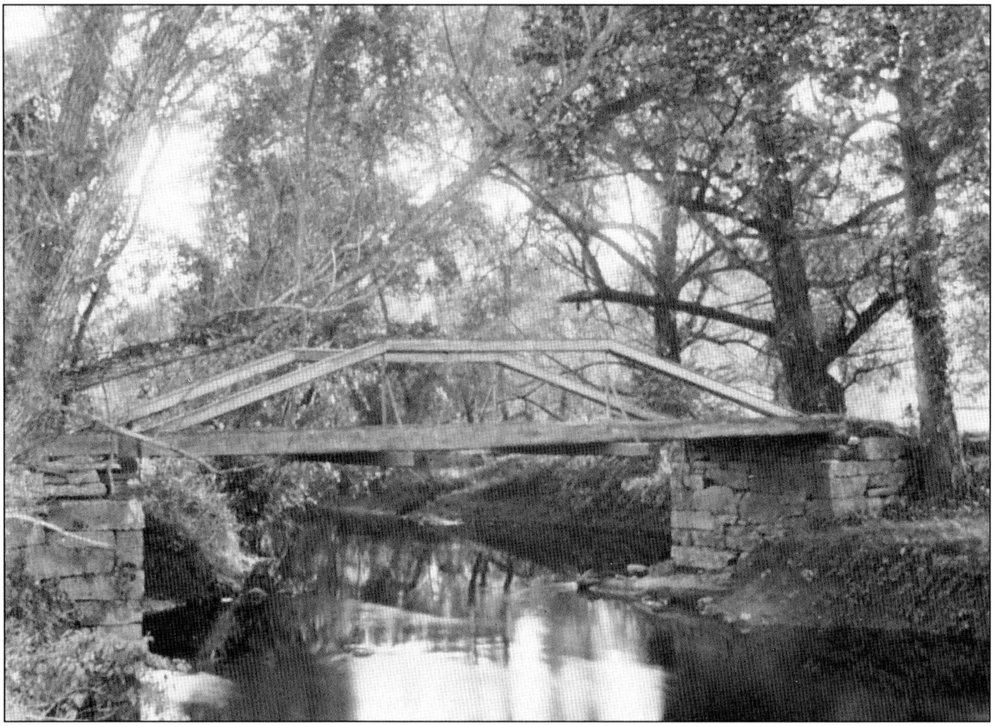

The Crosby bridge was one of many small bridges that enabled people to cross the Still River. Many of the factory owners and workers lived on the west side of the river; the factories, however, were located on the east side of the river. The bridge was located near Gallows Hill Cemetery.

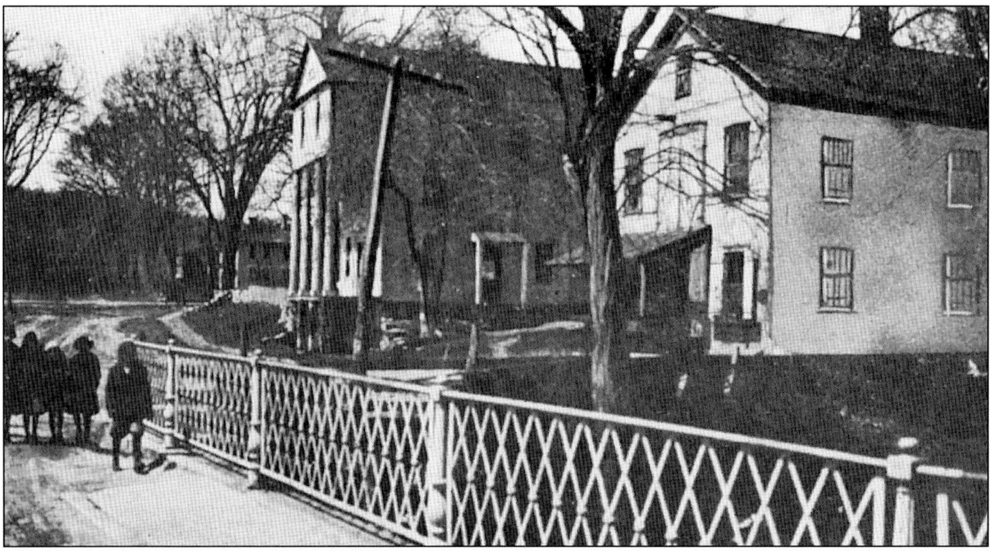

The building with the pillars contained a ballroom where dances were held. The temperance union used it as a meeting place. In 1867, a Catholic mission was organized and met here. Mary Meaney was living in the house at this time. The building next to the river was a blacksmith shop that later became a store. The railings are on the stone arched bridge that crosses the Still River.

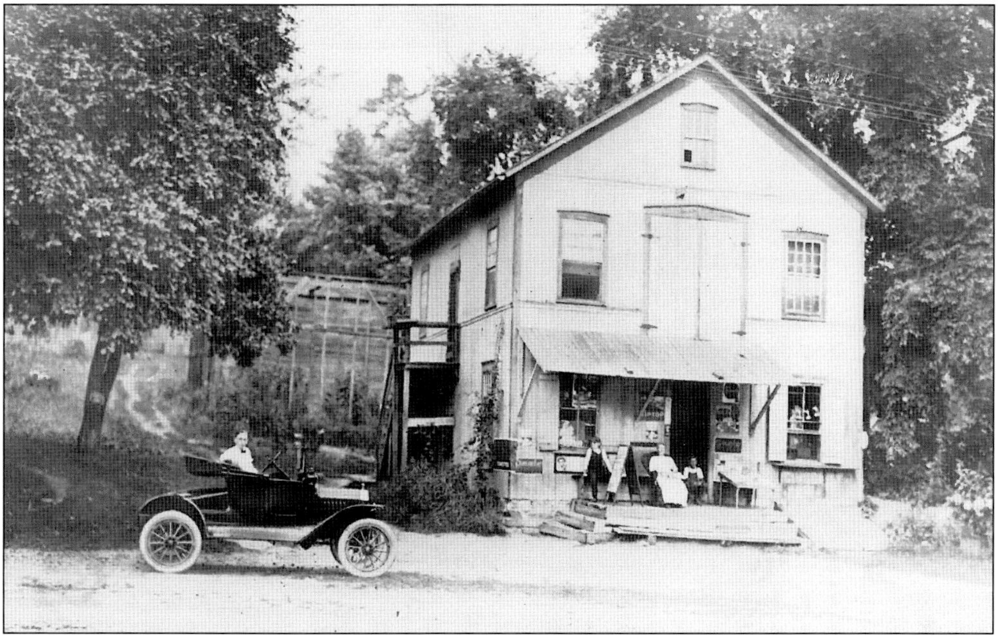

Built as a blacksmith shop, this structure, located on the west side of the Still River, has housed many businesses over the years. Shown here is the Koehler store, which was managed by Louise Koehler. One of the most popular items sold here was ice cream. Koehler was one of the suffragettes in Brookfield.

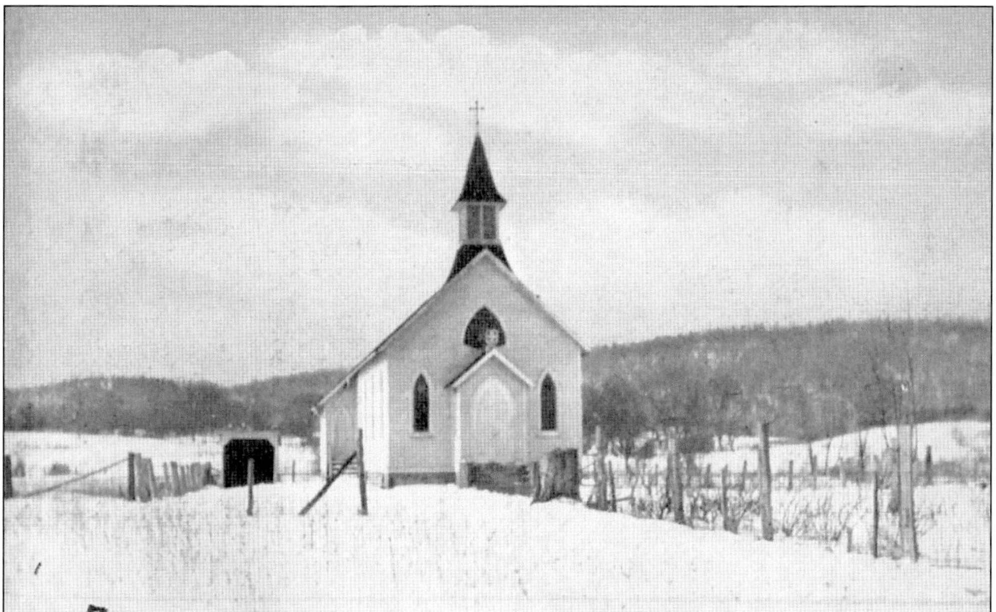

Catholic Church, Brookfield, Conn.

This building is the first Catholic church in Brookfield. It was built on Pocono Road in 1892. The O'Hare family donated the land. Each family of the parish was asked to donate $50 toward the building of the building. The windows each cost $10 and many families donated the money for the windows at the extra cost.

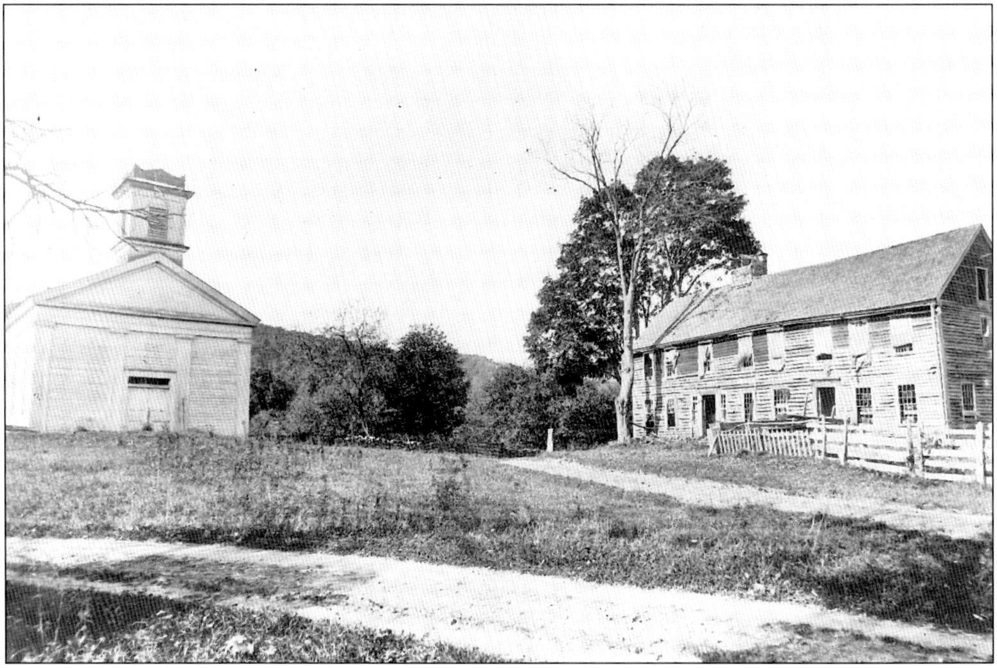

On the left is the Baptist church, built in 1846 on Old Post Road. Across the road is the Ancient Inn, which was built before the Revolutionary War. Tradition states that General Putnam, Benedict Arnold, and Jerome Bonaparte stayed here. In 1918, after the inn fell into disrepair, George Ives moved it to Danbury, Connecticut. The road marker still stands today at the corner of Laurel Hill and Station Roads.

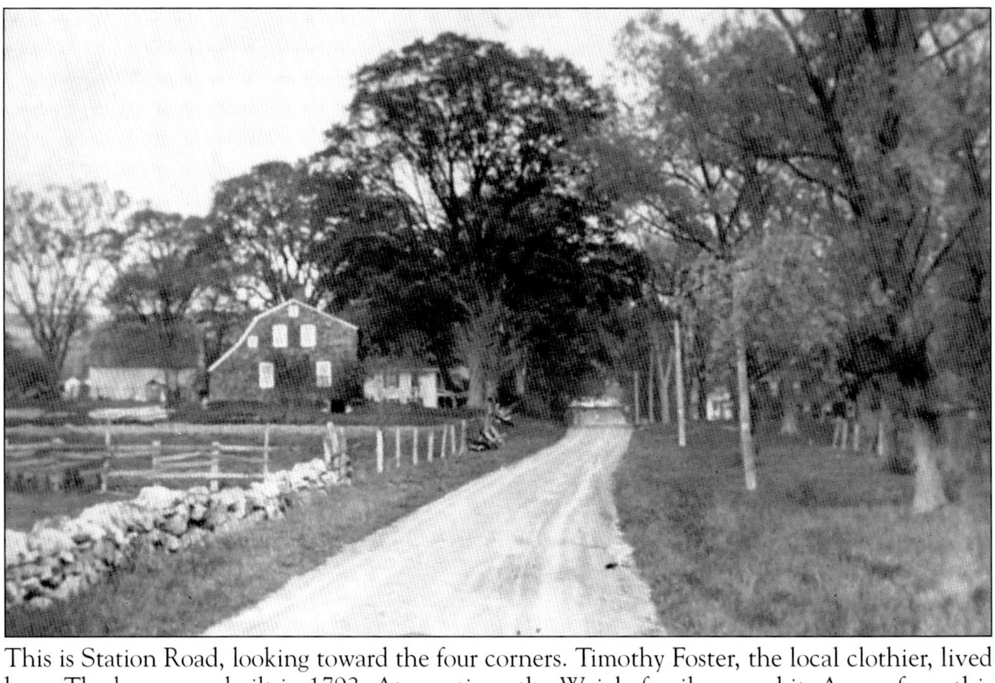

This is Station Road, looking toward the four corners. Timothy Foster, the local clothier, lived here. The house was built in 1792. At one time, the Weigle family owned it. Across from this house was the Iron Works Schoolhouse.

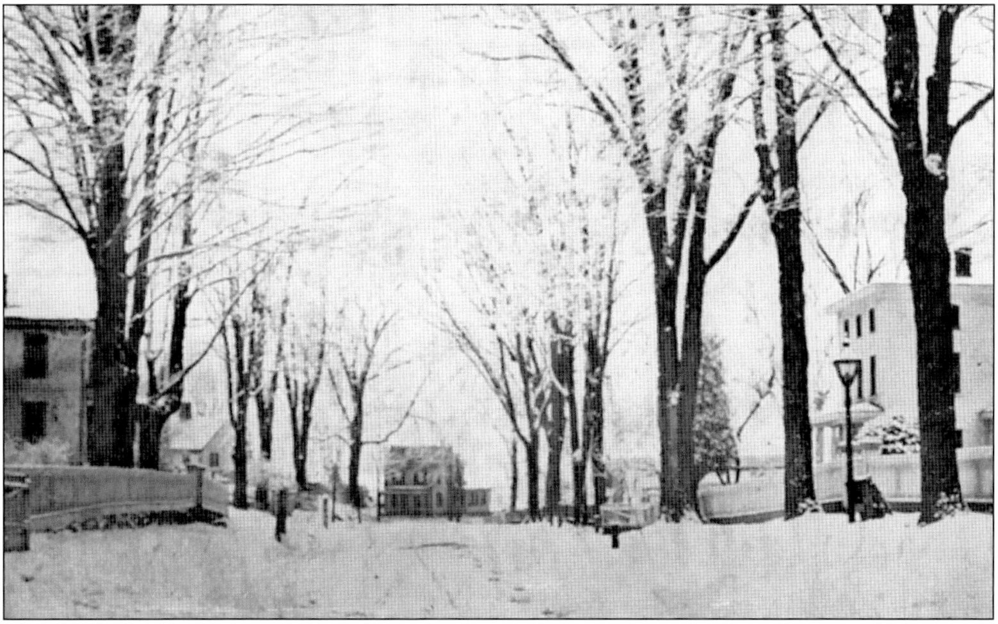

At one time, Federal Road was called Broad Way. At the top of the photograph is the Ira Keeler home, which was destroyed by fire in 1927. The road was straightened out at this point. A gas station was built on the property. The house on the right was the Greene home, which was later taken down to make way for a parking lot.

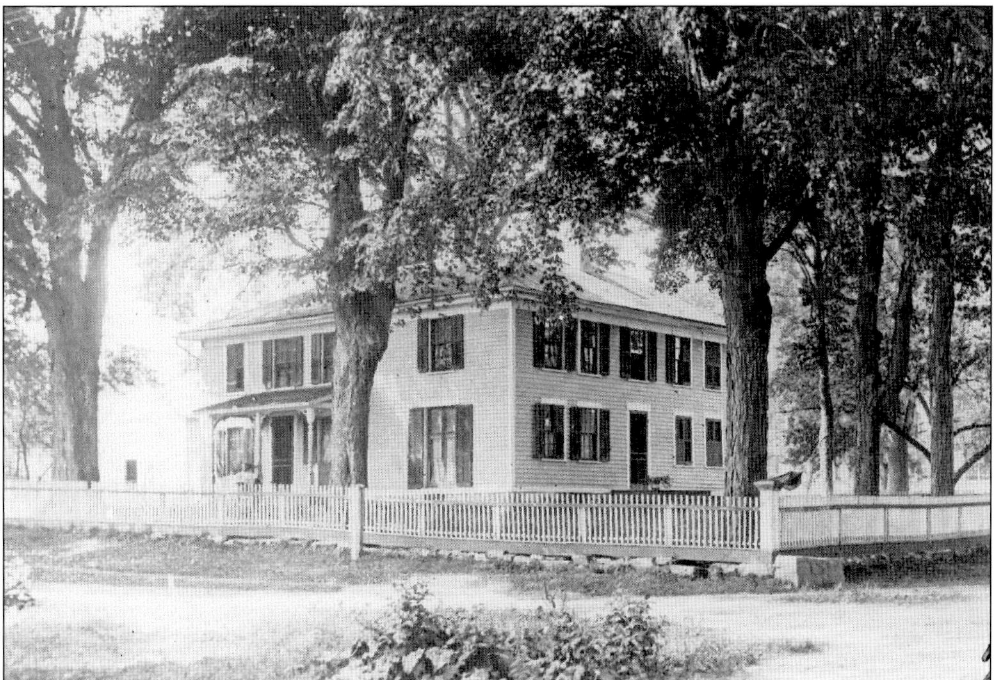

Agur Tomlinson ran a hotel here in 1793. It later became a funeral home run by Henry S. Beers. In the early 1900s, William J. Beehler replaced Mr. Beers as the funeral director. The house was taken down in the 1960s and replaced with a gas station.

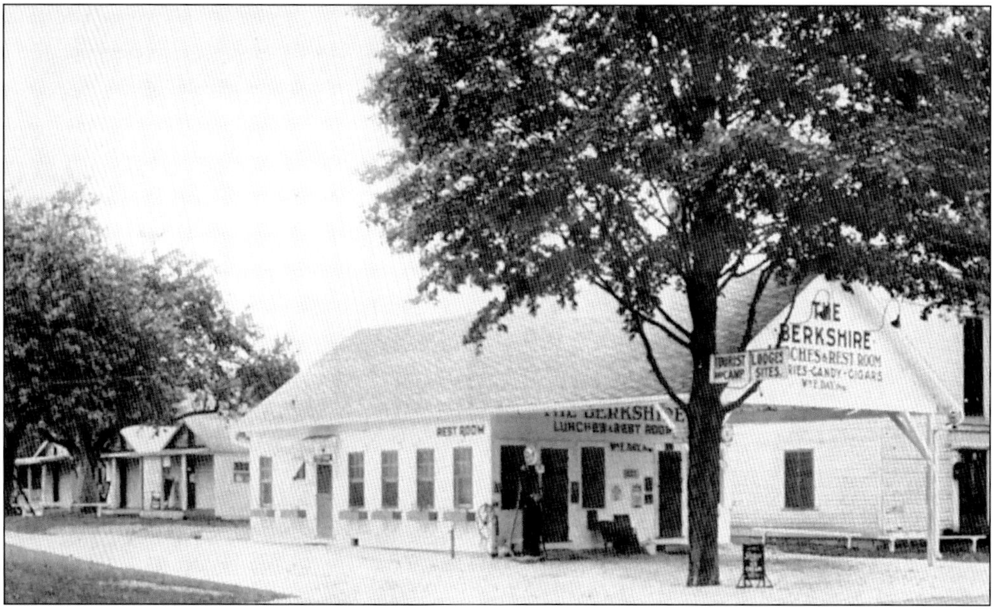

The Berkshire Tourist Cabins and Restaurant on Federal Road were built by William E. Day and S.O. Roune. The cabins were eventually put together to form a U-shaped house. The front part became a liquor store. Next to this building was "The "Chapel." The second story was removed, and what remained of the building was relocated to Federal Road. Since then, it has been home to many businesses.

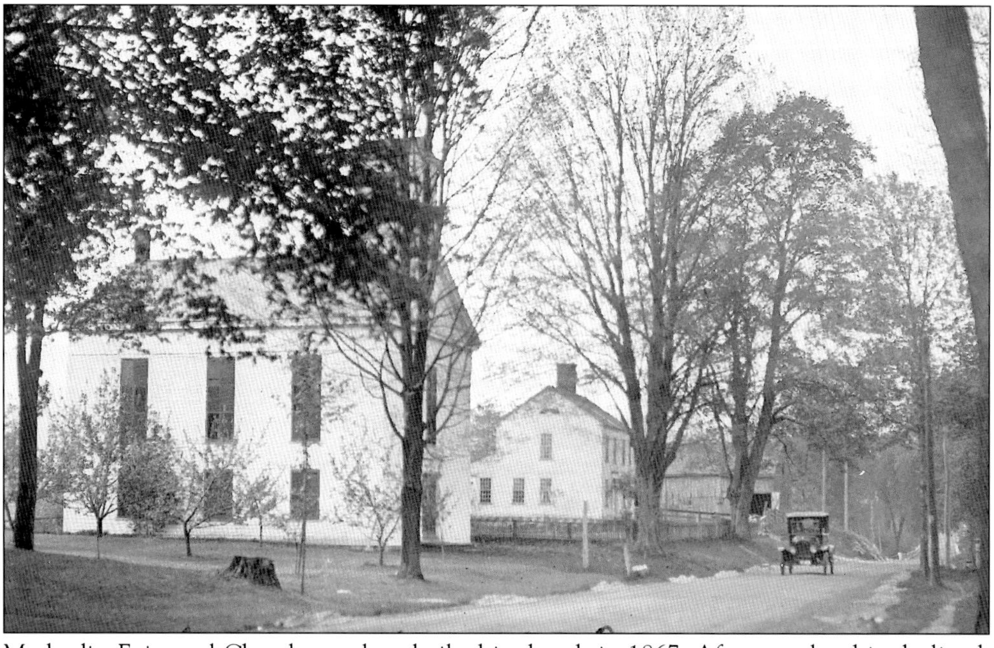

Methodist Episcopal Church members built this church in 1867. After membership declined, Henry B. Hawley purchased the church, and it became the Dutch Reformed Church in 1869. Fourteen years later, Henry Hawley moved his hat factory to Danbury, Connecticut, and the church became "The Chapel." Services were offered here for about 20 years. Eli Hamlin, a manufacturer of knives, built the house next door.

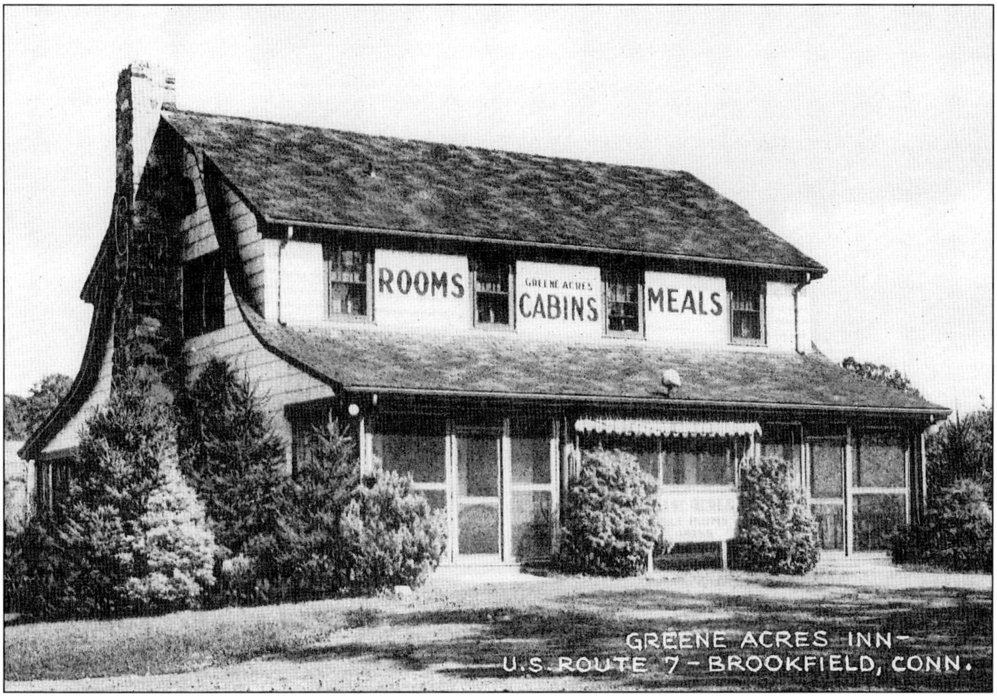

Students from the Henry Abbott Technical School in Danbury, Connecticut, built Greene Acres from 1931 to 1932. Josephine and Maud Greene, the daughters of Major Charles T. Greene, lived here. They sold Fro-Joy ice cream and Domino cigarettes, took in boarders, and served sandwiches. Cabins were built at the back of the house. The business, which was located on Federal Road, closed in the 1960s.

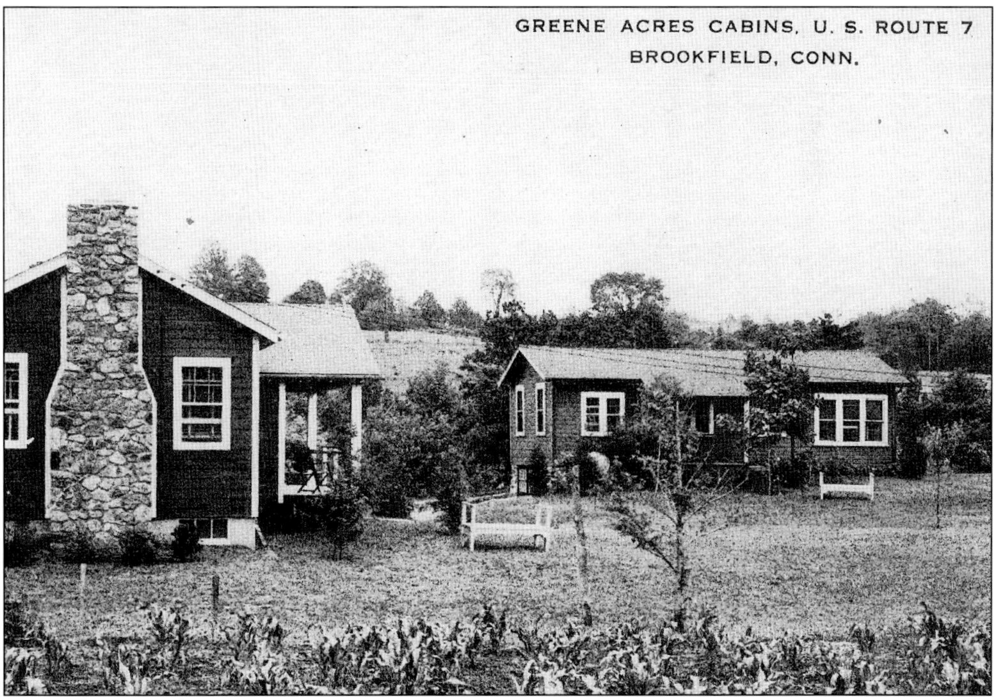

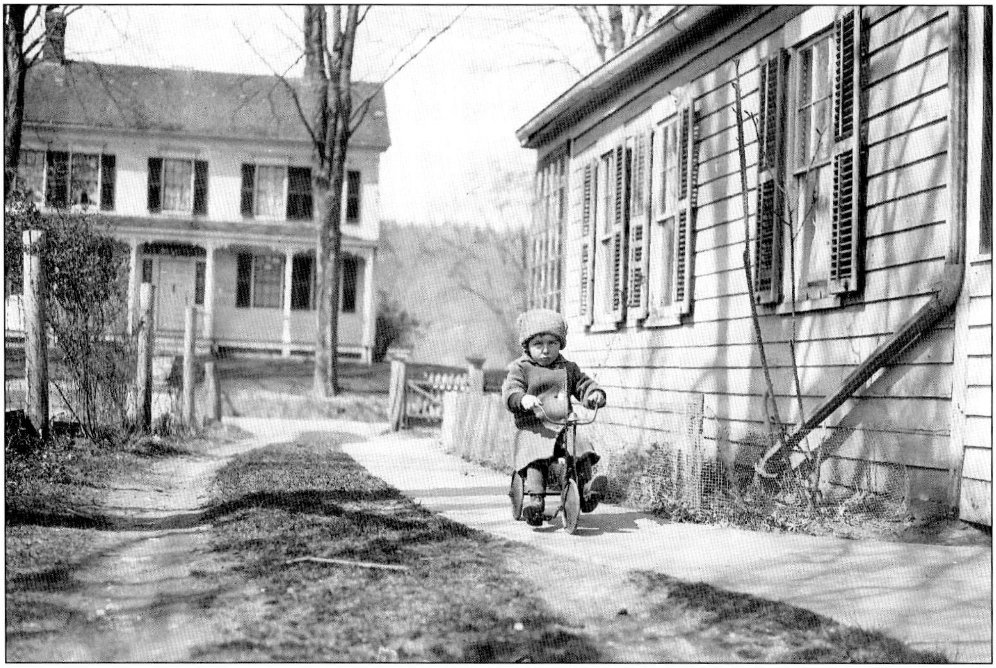

The young man riding the tricycle is Ray Waidelich. The house across Federal Road was probably built *c.* 1849. The first known owner was Elizabeth Wildman; others owners include State Senator Platt Creed and State Representative D. Clark Joyce. Eventually it was sold and became a restaurant. Over the years, the restaurant has been called the Old Stage Coach Inn, the Country Squire Inn, Olivers, and Christopher's.

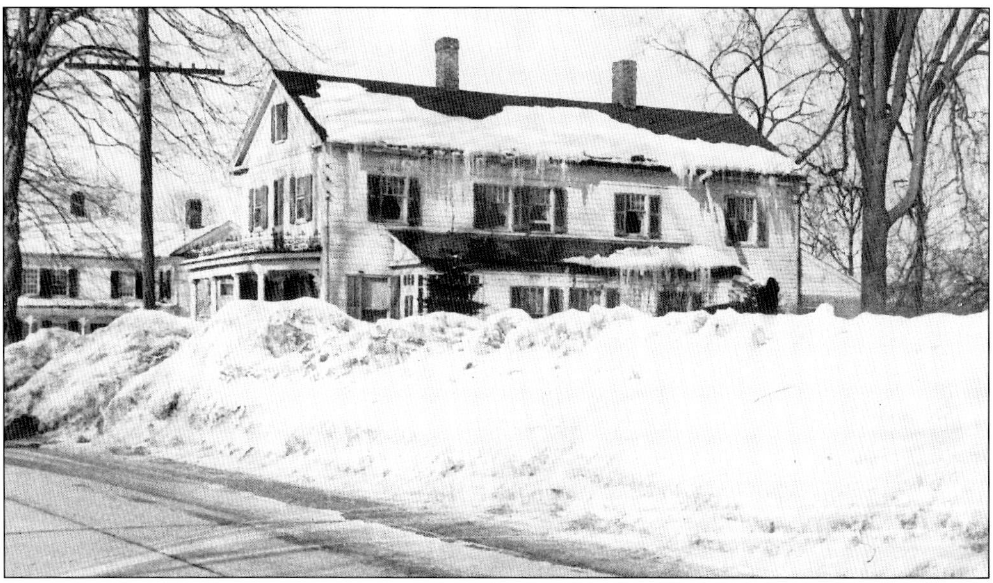

This house was built in 1840 by house painter George S. Porter. In 1926, George and Viola Waidelich purchased the house. They both served as town clerk in Brookfield. George Waidelich was the postmaster, and he used the north side of the house as the post office. Helen Matthews purchased it in 1956. She remodeled the house and it became the Donya Pottery Studio.

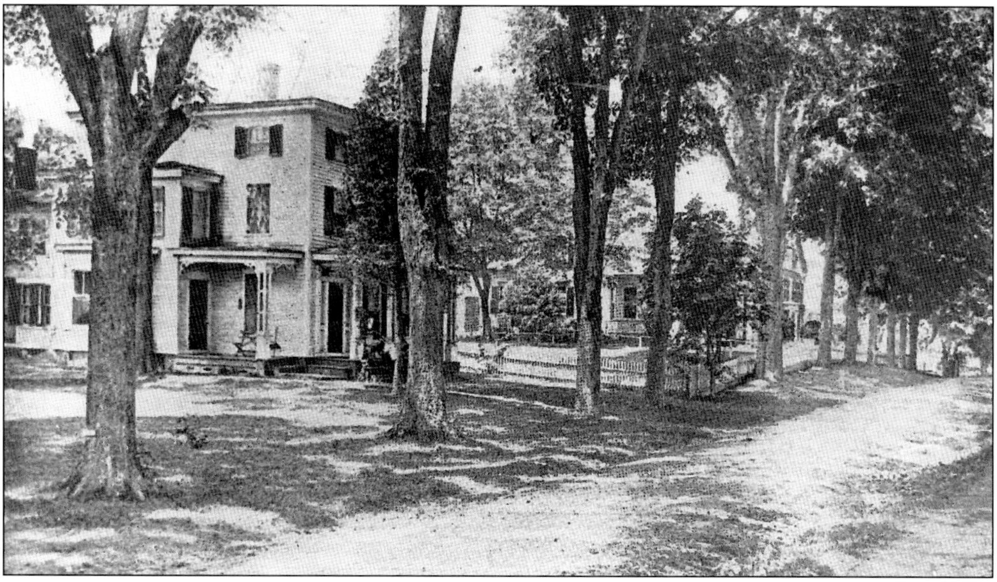

Andrew Northrop lived in this house when he was the owner of the Brookfield Lime Industry. Later it was the home of Major Charles T. Greene and his family. The house was taken down to make way for a restaurant parking lot.

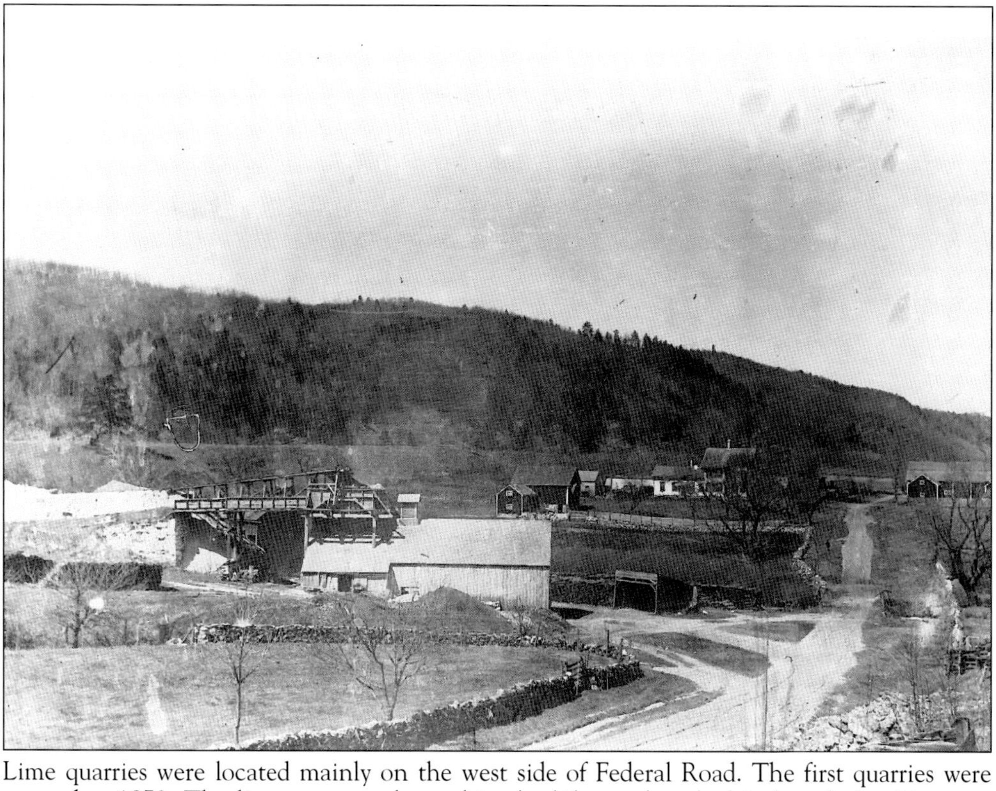

Lime quarries were located mainly on the west side of Federal Road. The first quarries were opened c. 1879. The limestone was burned in the kilns and packed in barrels for shipment. Over the years, there were many owners. In 1882, the business was sold to Pierce, Lawrence, & Vroman. The quarries stopped production c. 1909. This lime kiln was located on Federal Road.

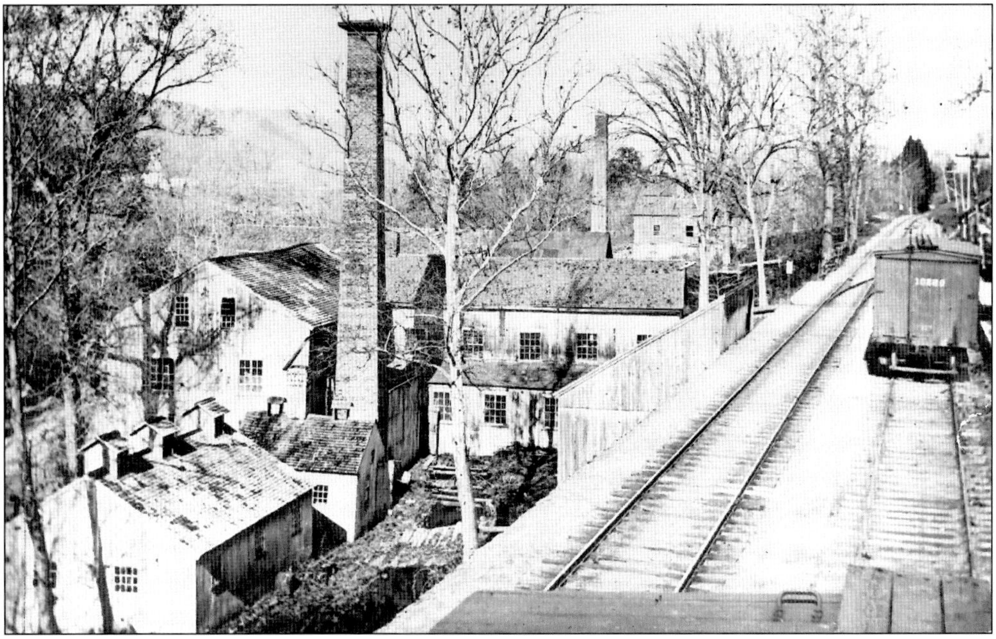

There were several small factories in the Iron Works. Shown here is the Ira Keeler cotton batting factory and Henry B. Hawley hat factory. Sidney Smith sold his hatting business to Henry B. Hawley in 1868. At that time, Mr. Hawley rebuilt the factory and employed 100 people. In 1875, he closed the business and moved to Danbury, Connecticut. Also in the photograph is the Wildman and Jones sawmill.

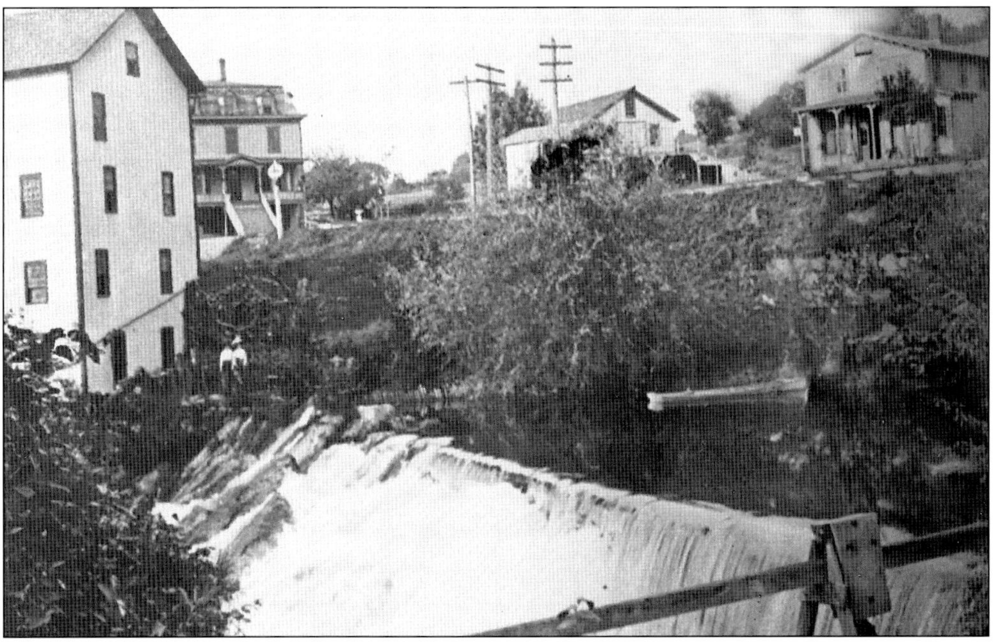

This milldam was built for the gristmill (at left). The building just behind it was a hotel. Henry S. Beers built the store at the far right. It is thought that Cornelius Dean and Levi Sturdevant moved the store down the hill, next to the Still River, in 1913. The milldam was taken down after the 1955 hurricane. Agnes May (Mrs. Arthur) Brownell took this photograph.

Two

TRAINS, PLANES, AND AUTOMOBILES

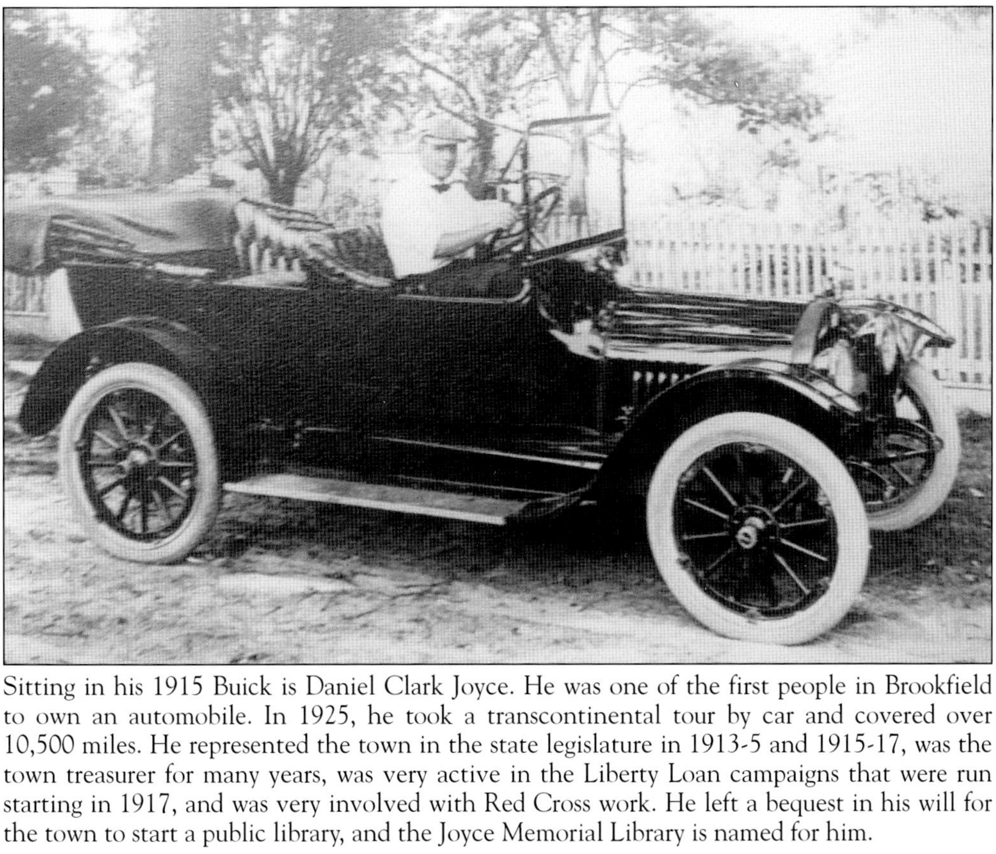

Sitting in his 1915 Buick is Daniel Clark Joyce. He was one of the first people in Brookfield to own an automobile. In 1925, he took a transcontinental tour by car and covered over 10,500 miles. He represented the town in the state legislature in 1913-5 and 1915-17, was the town treasurer for many years, was very active in the Liberty Loan campaigns that were run starting in 1917, and was very involved with Red Cross work. He left a bequest in his will for the town to start a public library, and the Joyce Memorial Library is named for him.

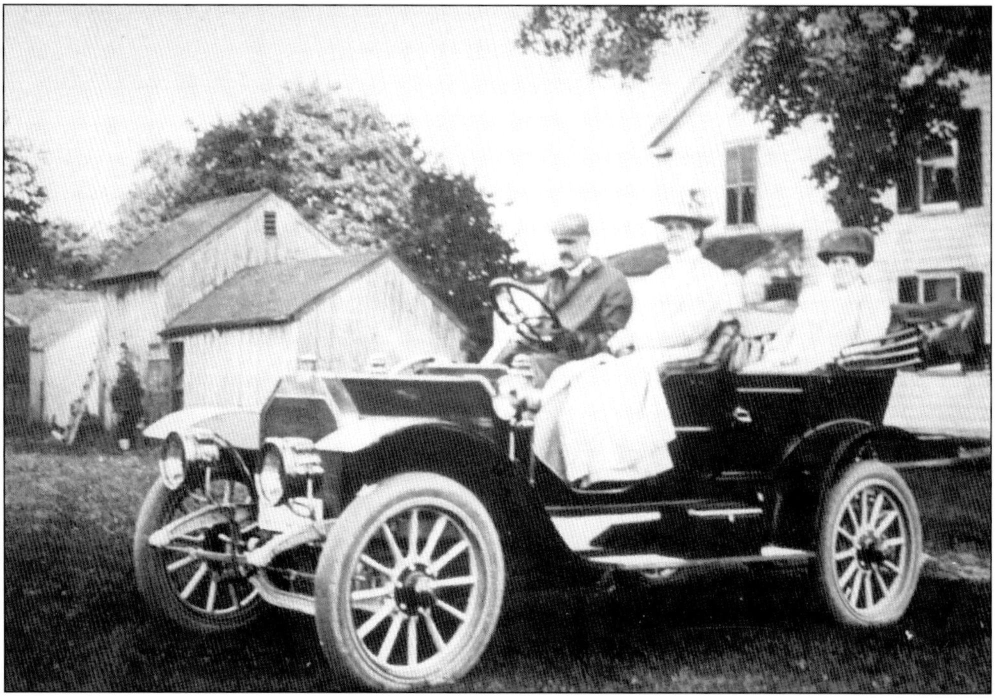

Out for a ride in his 1912 Buick is John Howard Peck and his wife, Ruamy Burr Peck. The third person is unidentified. They lived in the Obtuse district on the former Skidmore farm.

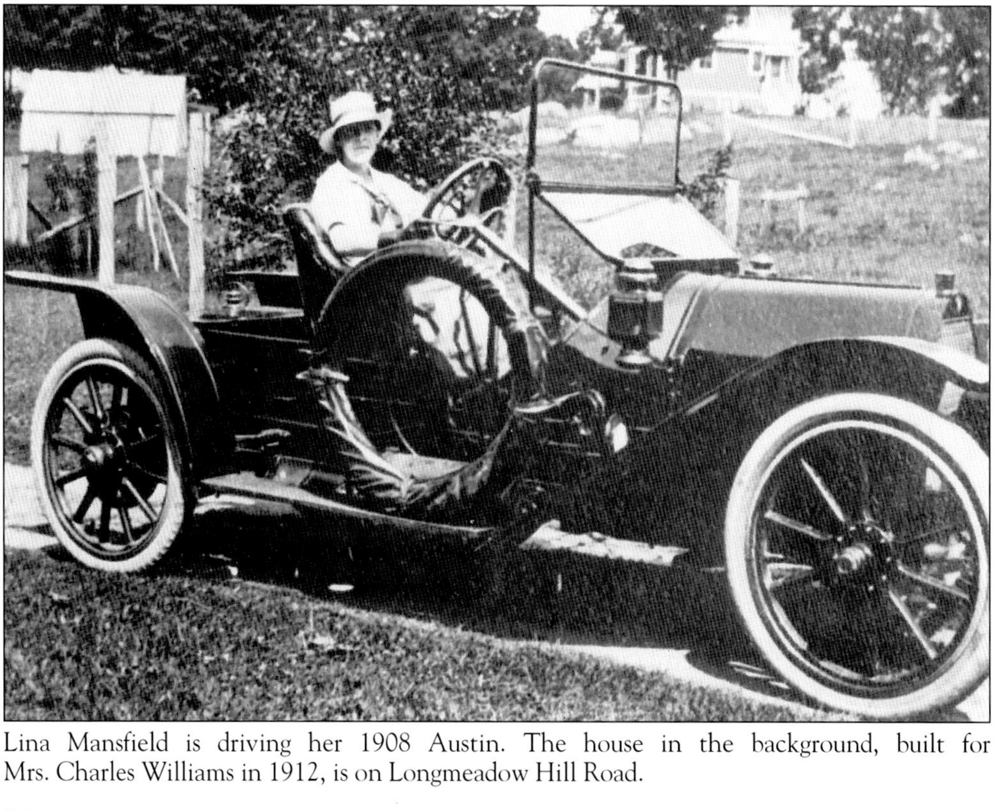

Lina Mansfield is driving her 1908 Austin. The house in the background, built for Mrs. Charles Williams in 1912, is on Longmeadow Hill Road.

Mildred Martini Bowers is shown standing beside her 1929 DeSoto.

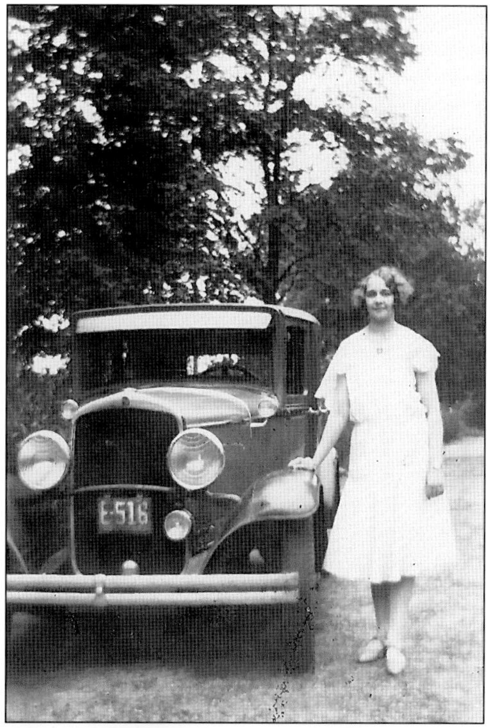

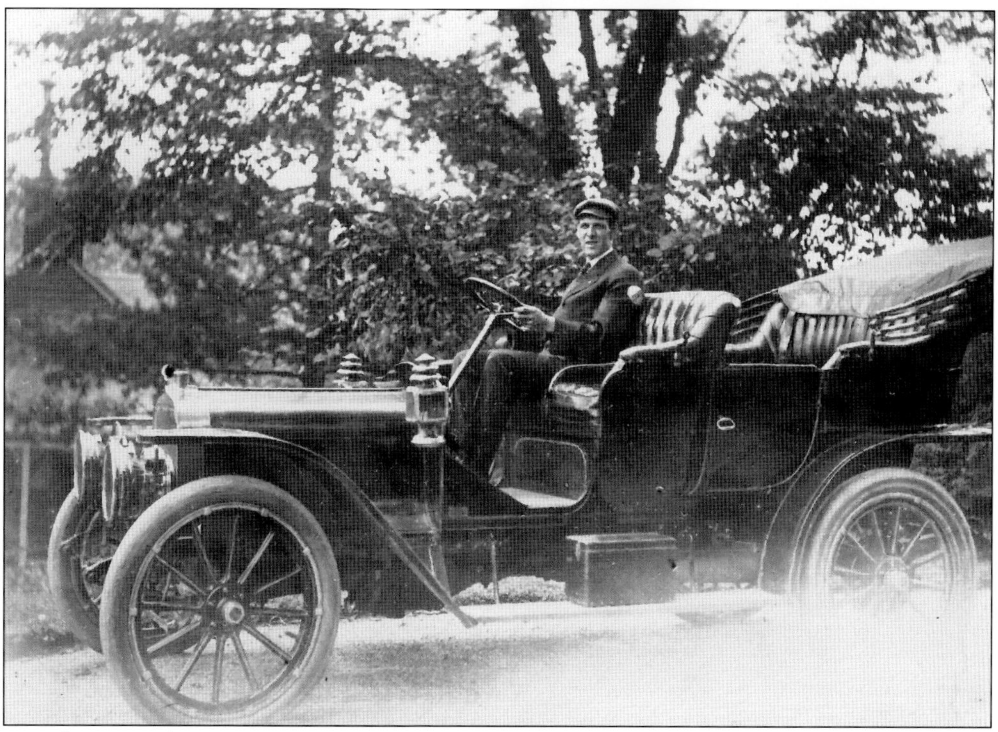

Seen here in July 1908, Paul Fletcher Weld proudly shows off his Corbin automobile. Born in Brookfield in 1880 to Edmund and Hannah Meeker Weld, he was a schoolteacher and local photographer. The Corbin automobile was built in New Britain, Connecticut.

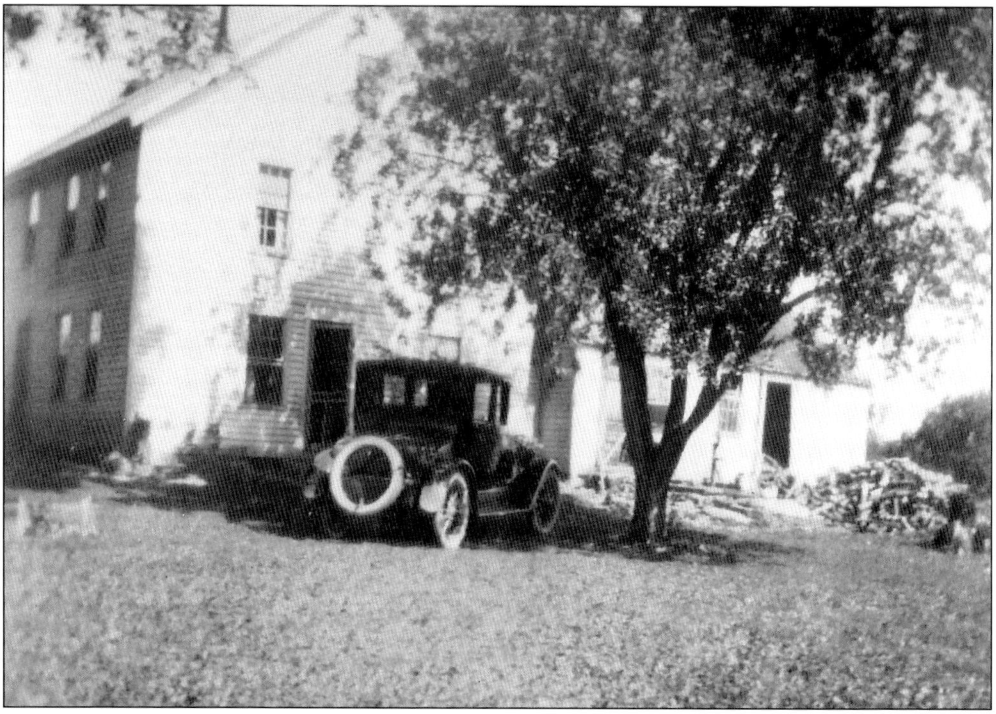

The horse and wagon soon gave way to the automobile. At the side door of the Thornhill farmhouse is their 1921 Hudson. The house is located on Obtuse Road, North.

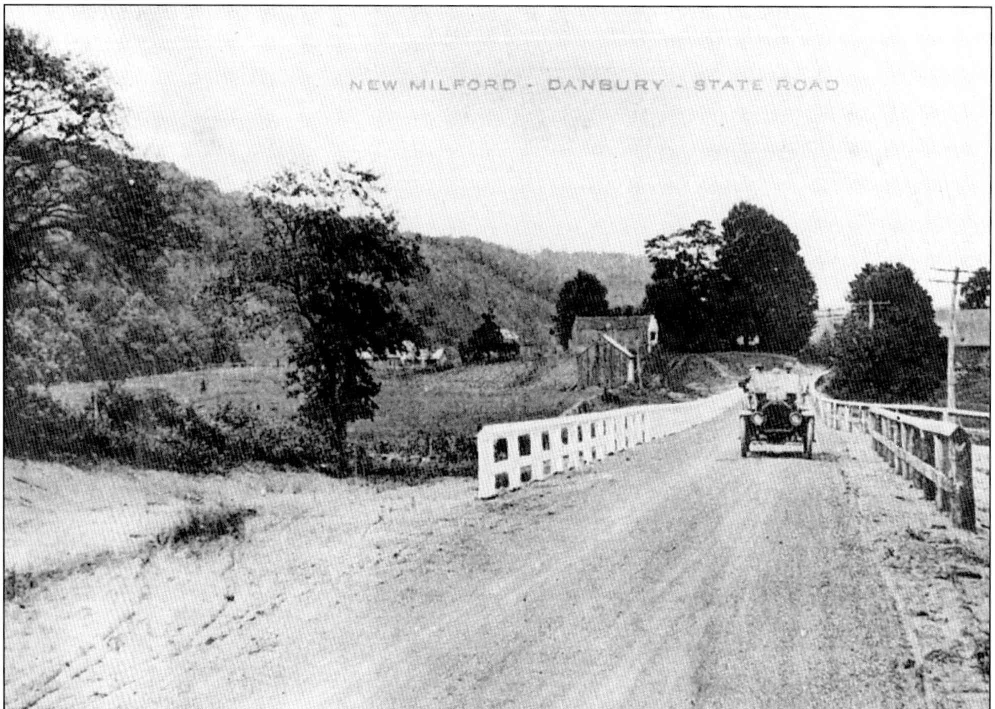

Federal Road to New Milford was once unpaved and free from traffic.

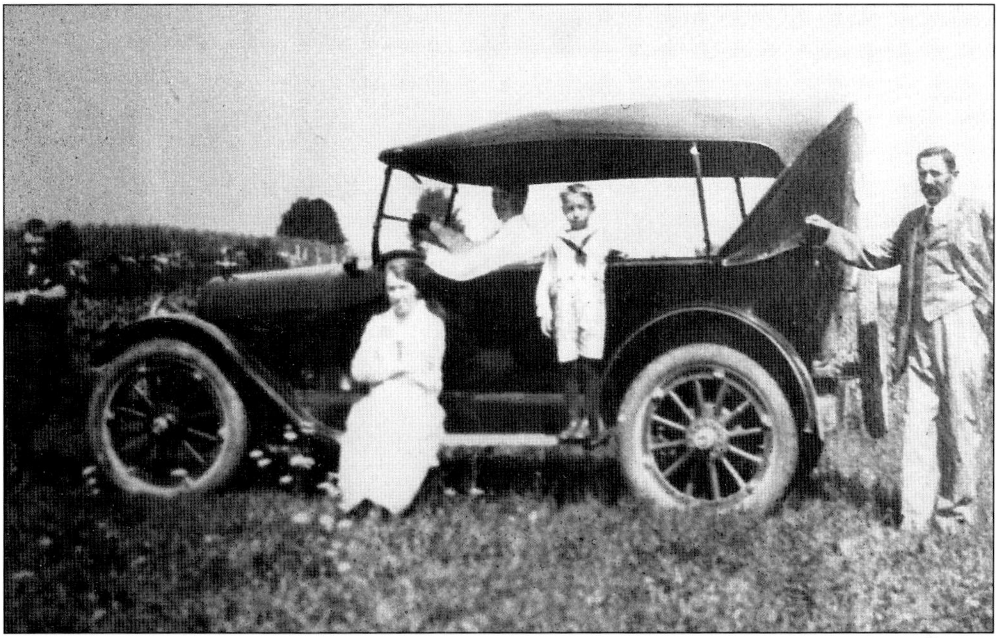

The Gurski family shows off their 1922 Oldsmobile in 1923. Standing in front of the car is Frank Jr. On the running board are Eva and Stanley, and Harry is at the wheel. Frank Sr. is standing at the back of the car.

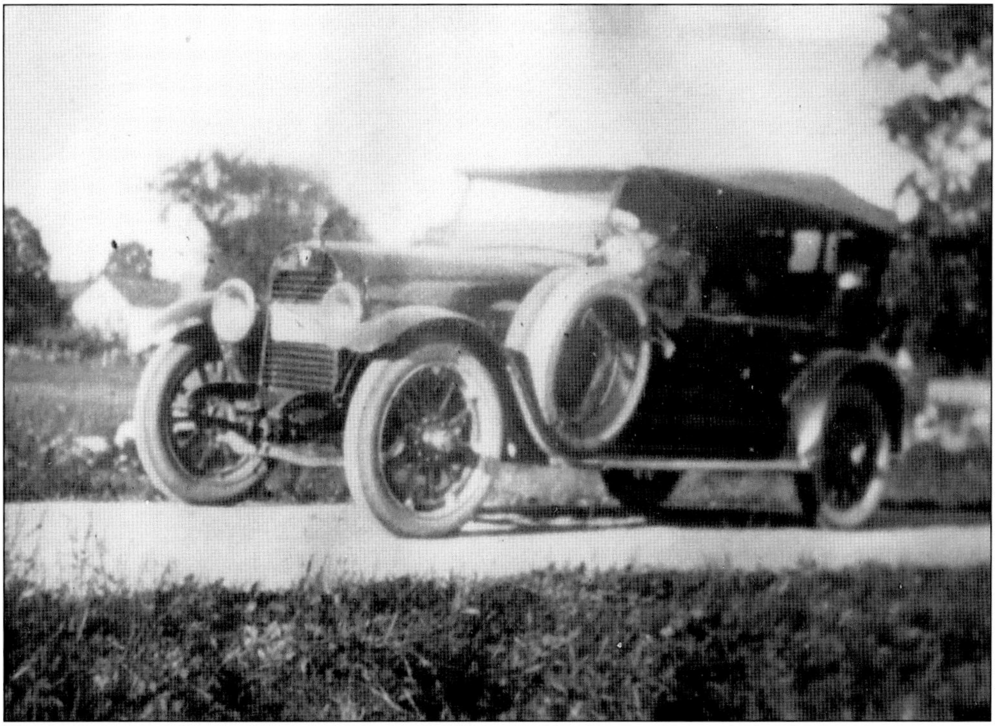

The Gruet family owned this 1929 Chevrolet.

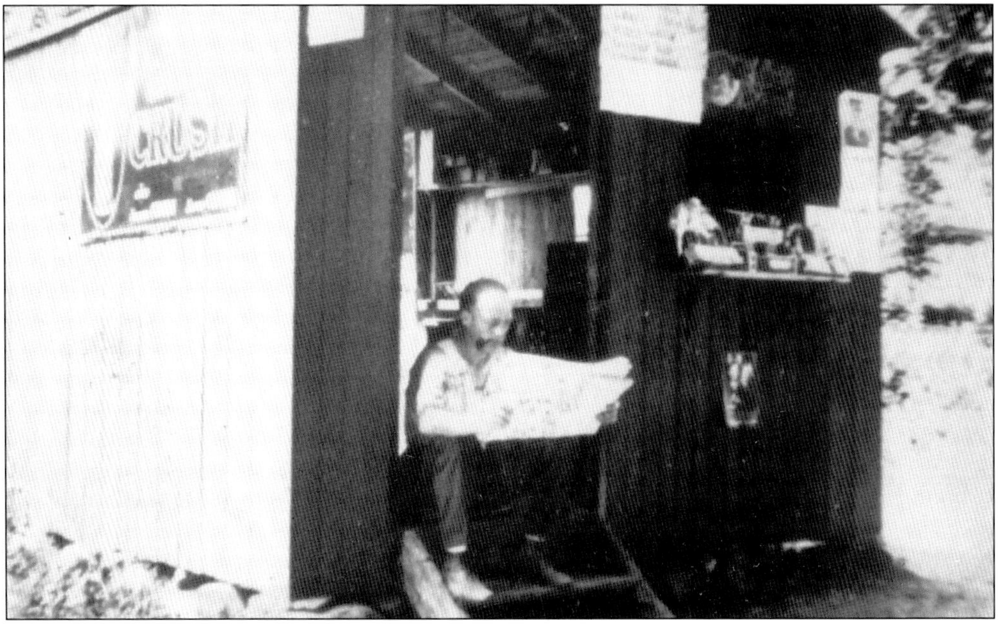

In 1919, Angie Gruet opened one of the first gas stations in Brookfield, selling gas for 10¢ a gallon. Sitting on the steps is her husband, Amadee Gruet, affectionately known as "Baldy." There was one gas pump and a refreshment stand. It was located on the corner of Federal Road and Station Road.

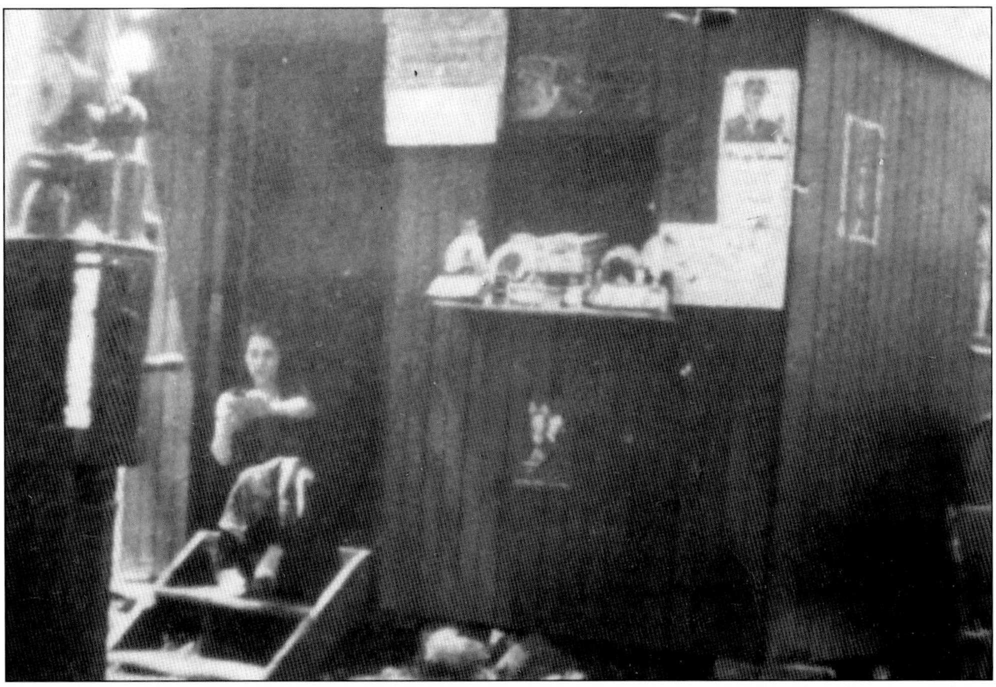

In this photograph you can see the one gas pump that Angie Gruet started with. She pumped gas by hand in the early years. After running the station for 25 years, the Gruets sold the business. They purchased the old Iron Works Schoolhouse, which was in back of the business, and turned it into a house.

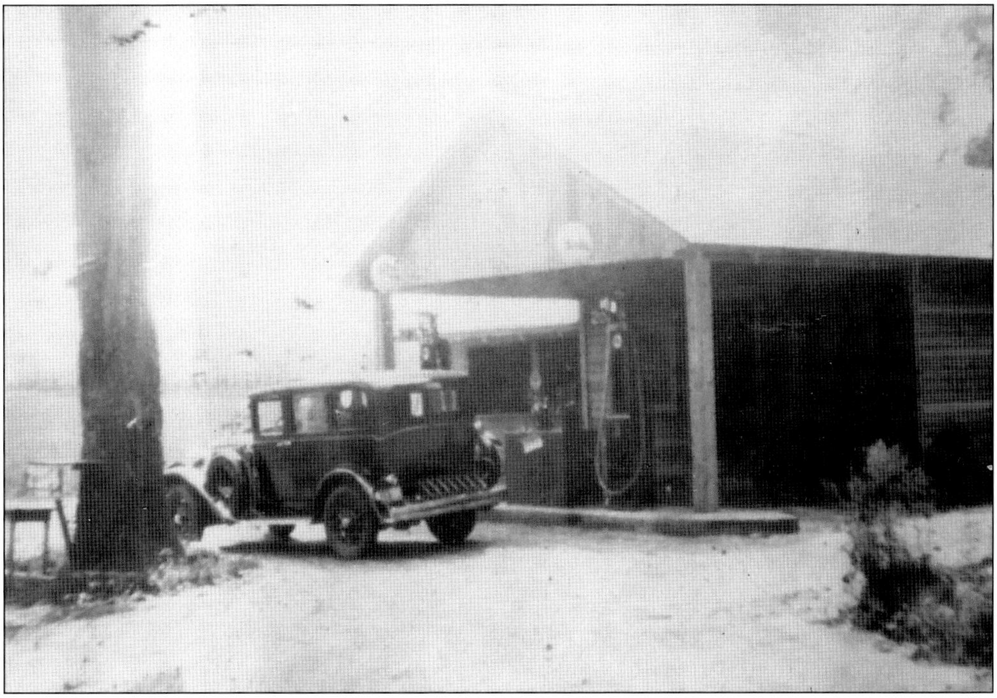

As business grew, so did the gas station. Angie eventually added two gas pumps, a canopy, and a small restaurant, where she served sandwiches and sold ice cream. On rainy days, the children in the neighborhood were allowed to play under the canopy. It was now called "Cozy Corner."

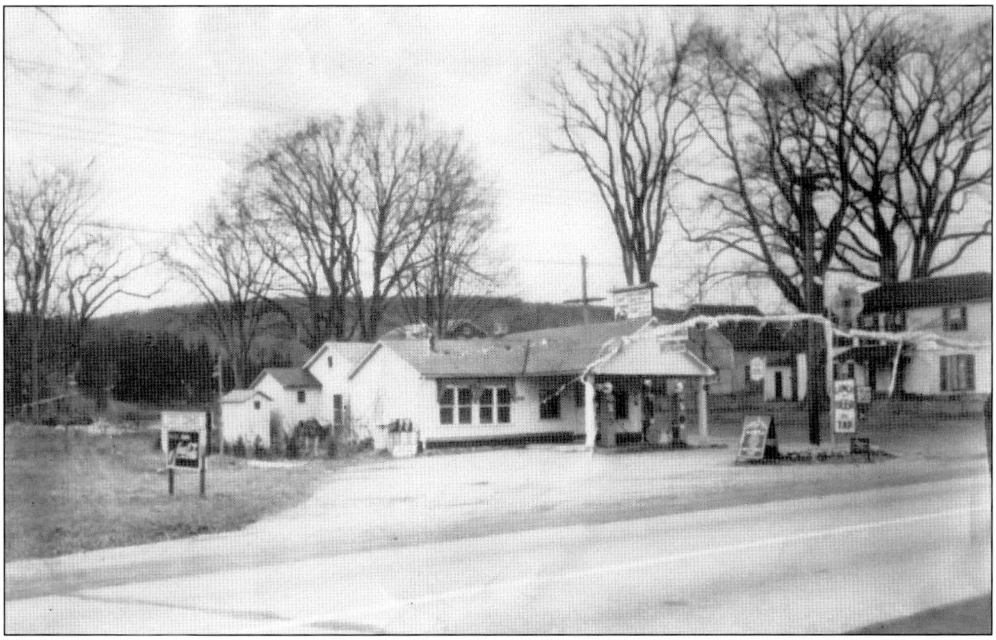

The station, which started out with just one pump, eventually grew to have three. The restaurant grew and a taproom was added. During Prohibition it was against the law to serve beer without food. It is said that "Angie became the best pie maker in town." The original station was taken down and today it is the Mobil gas station at the Four Corners.

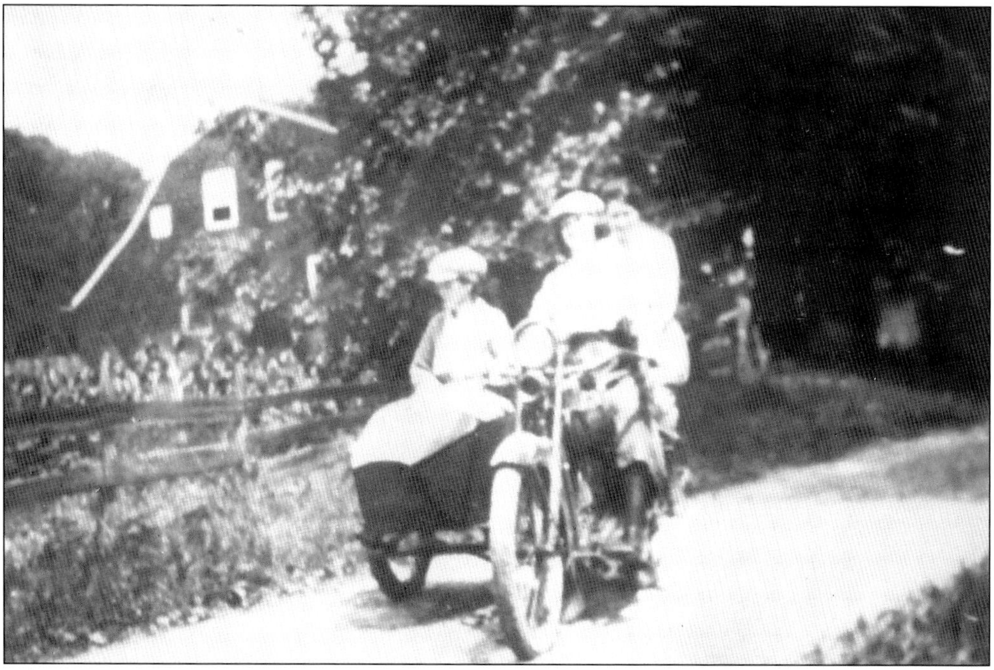

Taking a ride on this motorcycle are Julie Weigle, Angeline Weigle Gruet, and Clemetine Weigle. The house in the background is the Weigle house on Station Road.

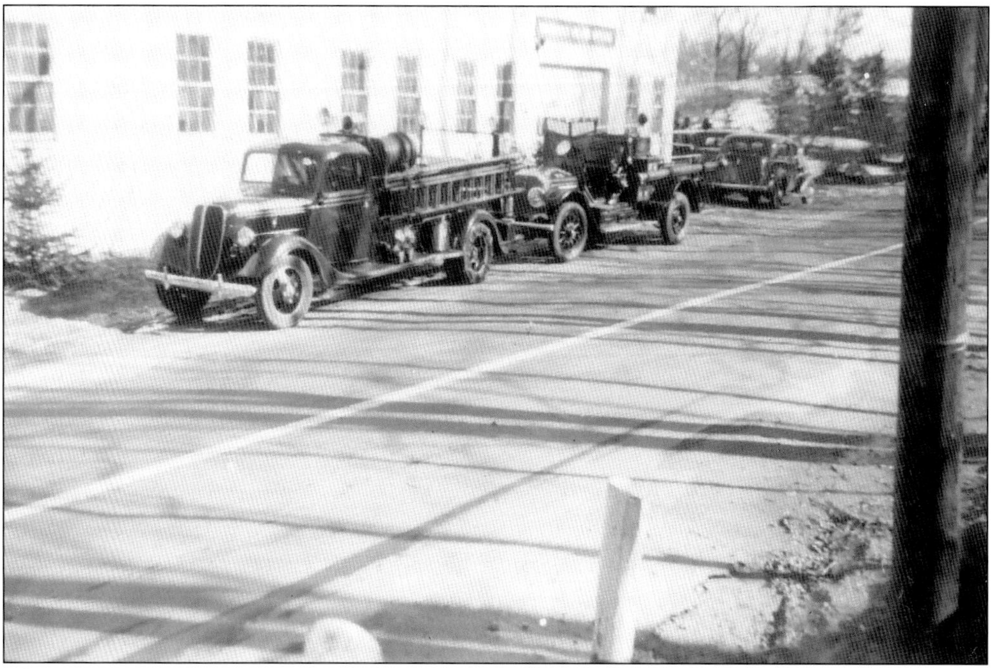

The Brookfield Volunteer Fire Company was formally established on May 7, 1934, with 20 members. The first piece of equipment that was purchased was a 1911 hand-drawn chemical extinguisher. The first station house was located in the old Grange Hall on Whisconier Road, which had also been used as the second opera house for the Greene School of Music. A new firehouse was built in 1953 on Route 133.

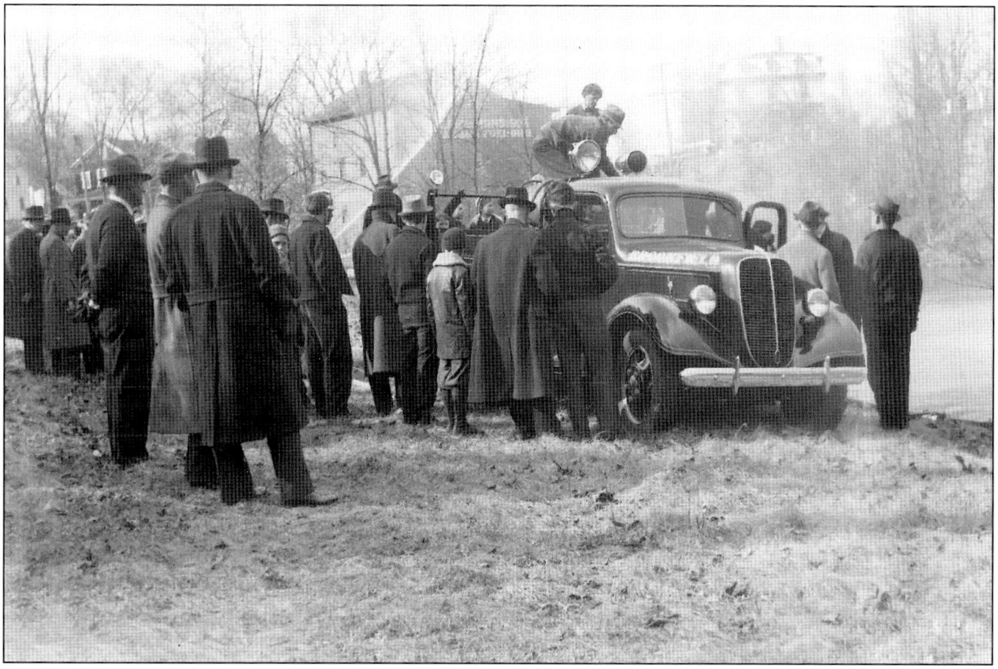

The first truck was a 1937 V-8 pumper. In 1944, a Diamond-T pumper was purchased. The next piece of equipment, an American LaFrance pumper, was purchased during World War II. A demonstration of the new truck was held on the grounds next to the gristmill and the Still River.

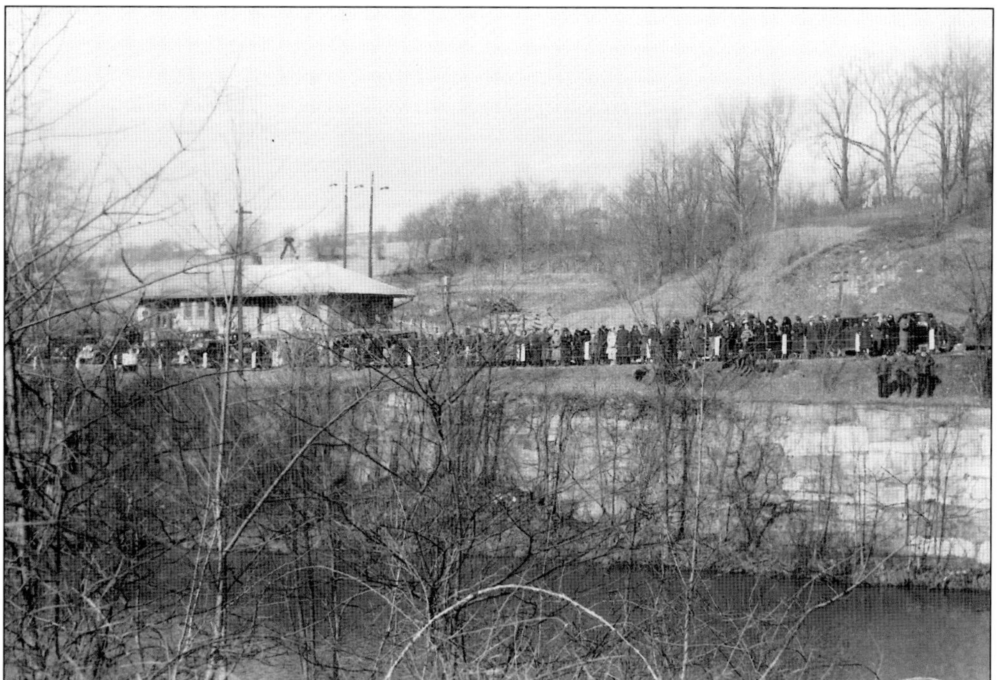

Crowds came out to see the demonstration of the first fire truck. In the background is the Iron Works train station. Notice the men standing on the retaining wall along the Still River.

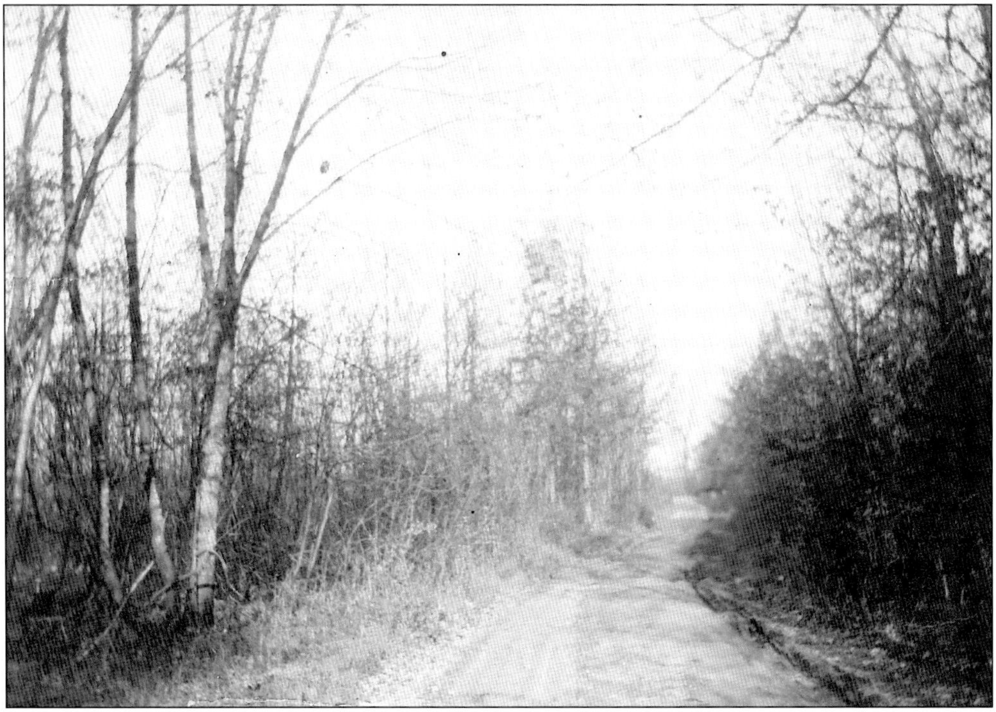

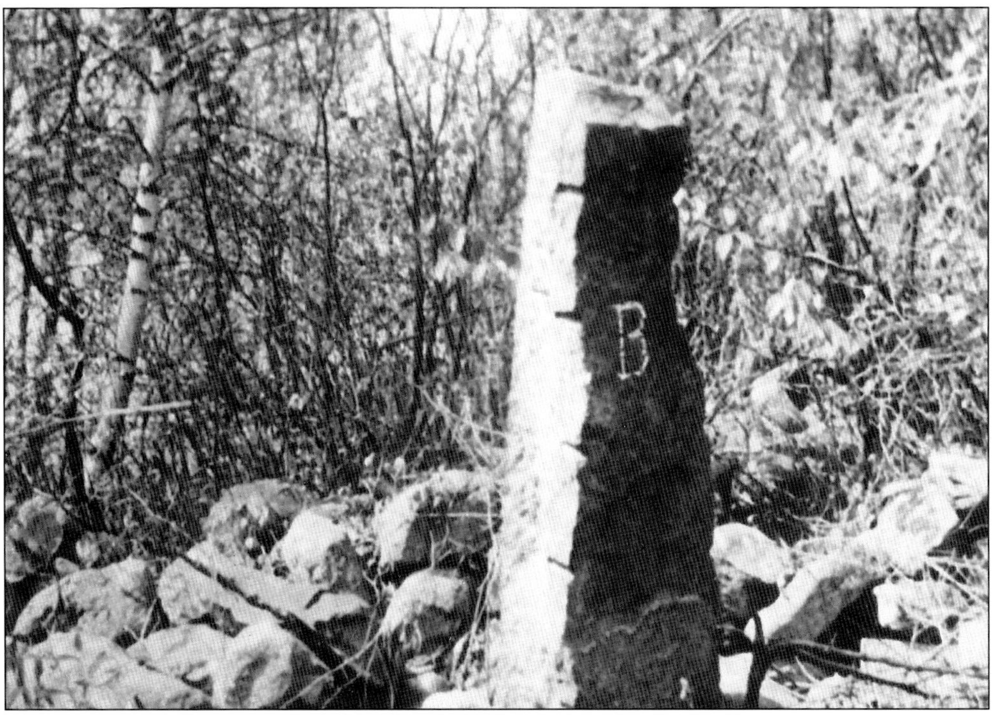

This marker, located at Hennings Grove, is the boundary of Danbury, New Fairfield, and Brookfield. The grove was used for many activities, including picnics. The stone is still standing, but the "B" has been washed away.

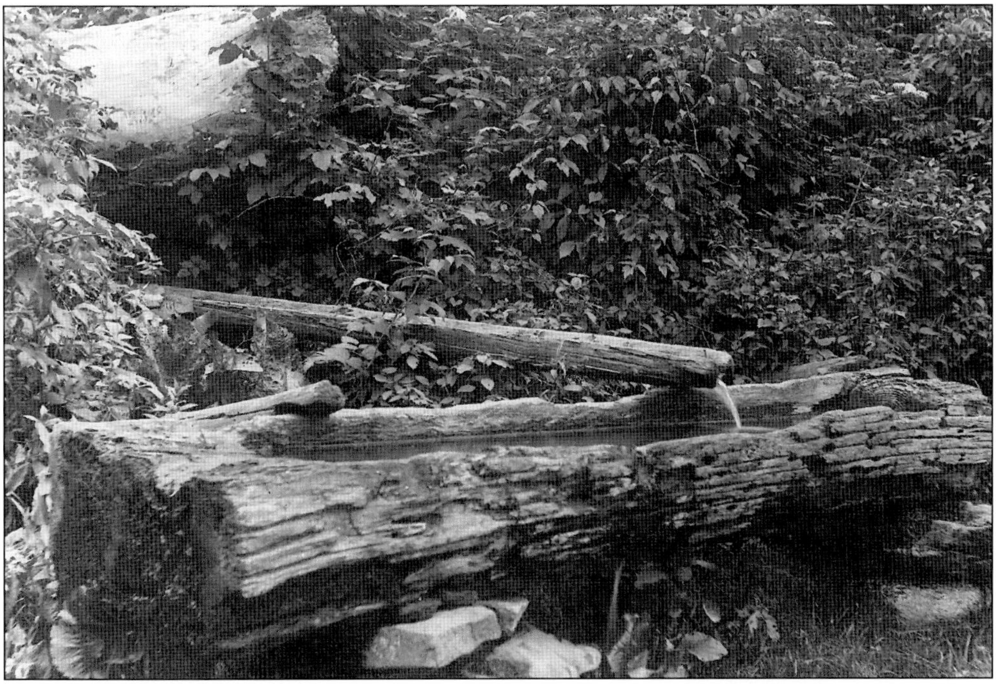

In 1915, this watering trough was located on the White Turkey Road (now Candlewood Lake Road). It was opposite the George Rockwell Place. Paul Fletcher Weld took the photograph.

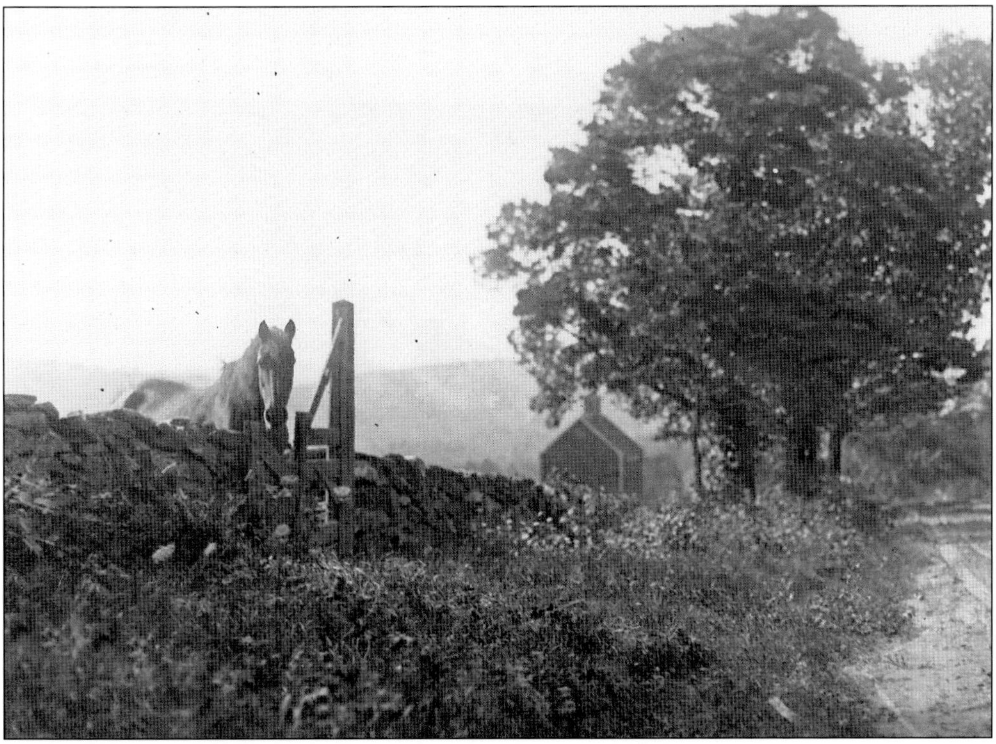

"Don" stands in the field, watching the traffic go by on Whisconier Road (Route 25). This tranquil scene was taken in 1912. The Curtis family owned the horse.

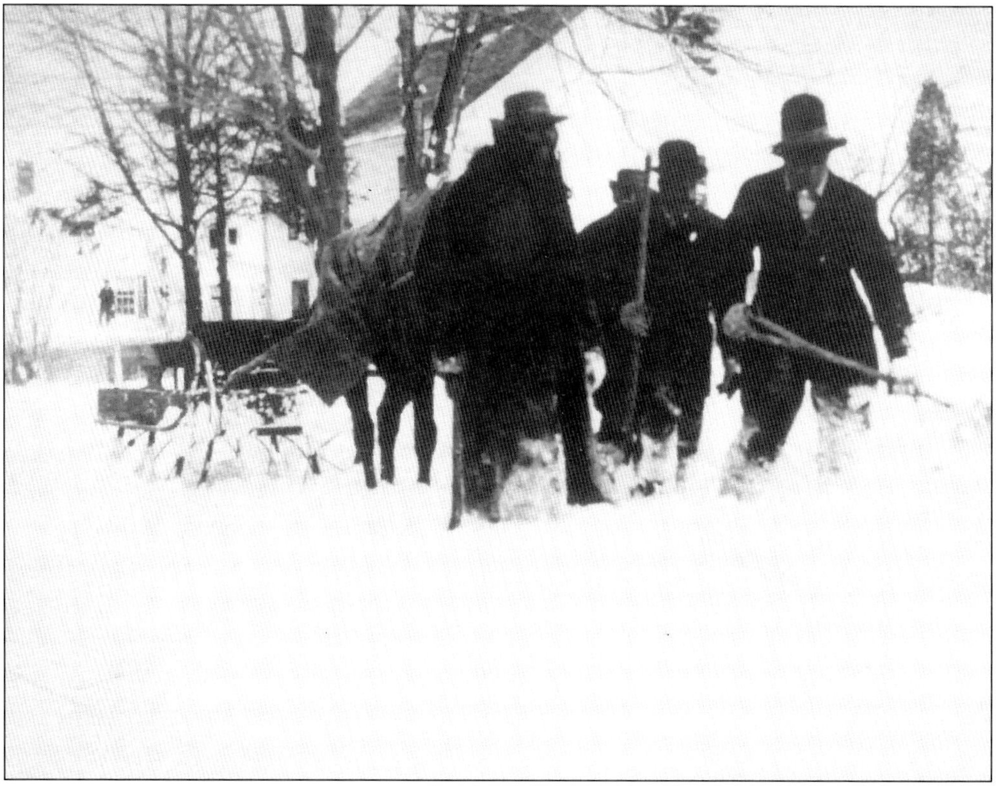

In the winter, roads were seldom plowed. Instead, they were packed down and the holes were filled in. This allowed the runners on sleighs to glide smoothly over the snow.

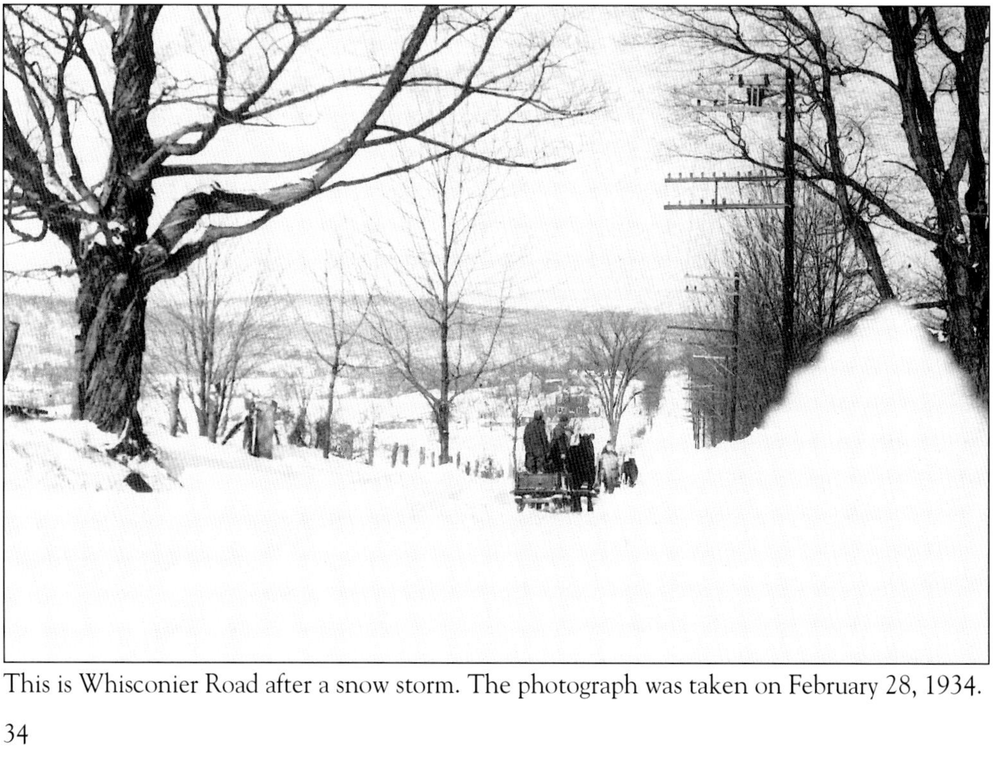

This is Whisconier Road after a snow storm. The photograph was taken on February 28, 1934.

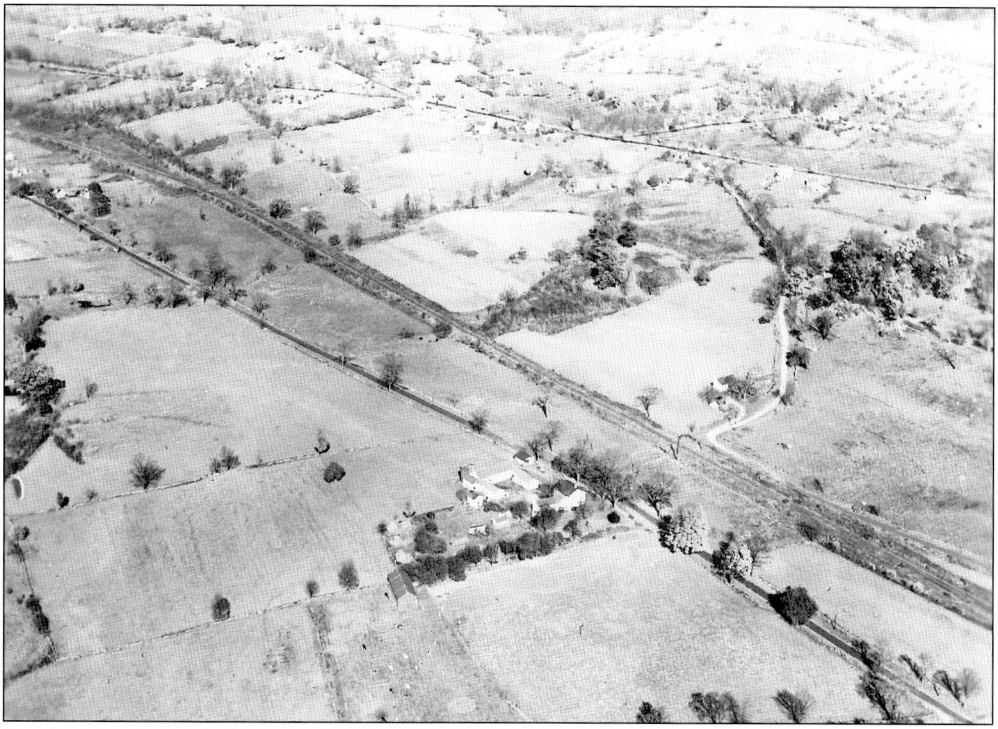

Stanley Gurski took this aerial view of Pocono Road in the 1930s. The farm (center) was the Peck farm. Across from the house was Oak Grove Road. At one time, it connected with Pocono Road. The Peck farmhouse and buildings burned to the ground in 1972; it was a spectacular fire that raced up and down Pocono Road.

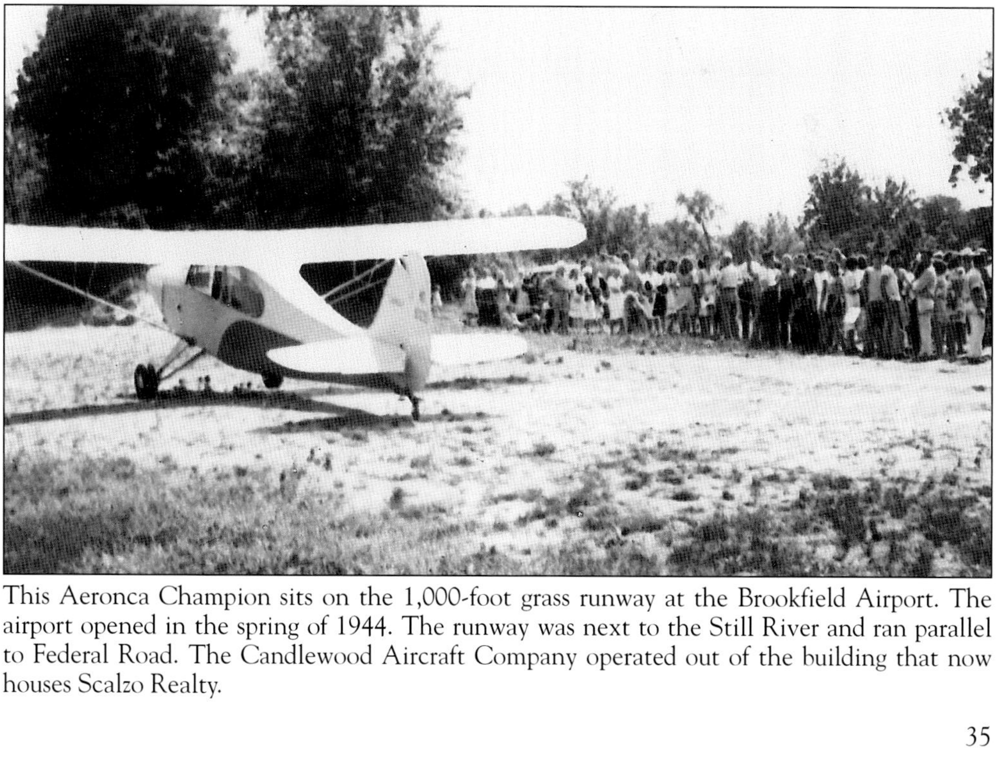

This Aeronca Champion sits on the 1,000-foot grass runway at the Brookfield Airport. The airport opened in the spring of 1944. The runway was next to the Still River and ran parallel to Federal Road. The Candlewood Aircraft Company operated out of the building that now houses Scalzo Realty.

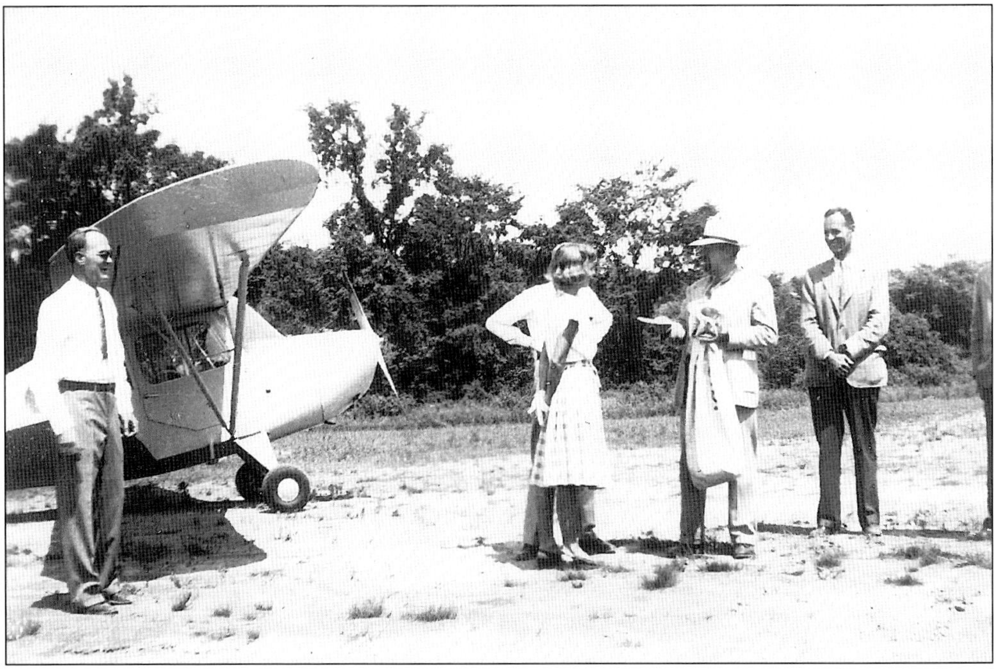

To mark the 20th anniversary of airmail service out of New England, the post office asked local postmasters to form a committee and plan a celebration of the event. Postmaster Virgil Geddes decided to have letters airmailed out of Brookfield. Those participating in the ceremony were actress Margaret Sullivan (a Brookfield resident), postmaster Virgil Geddes, first selectman Royal Alcox (left), and Wendell Davis.

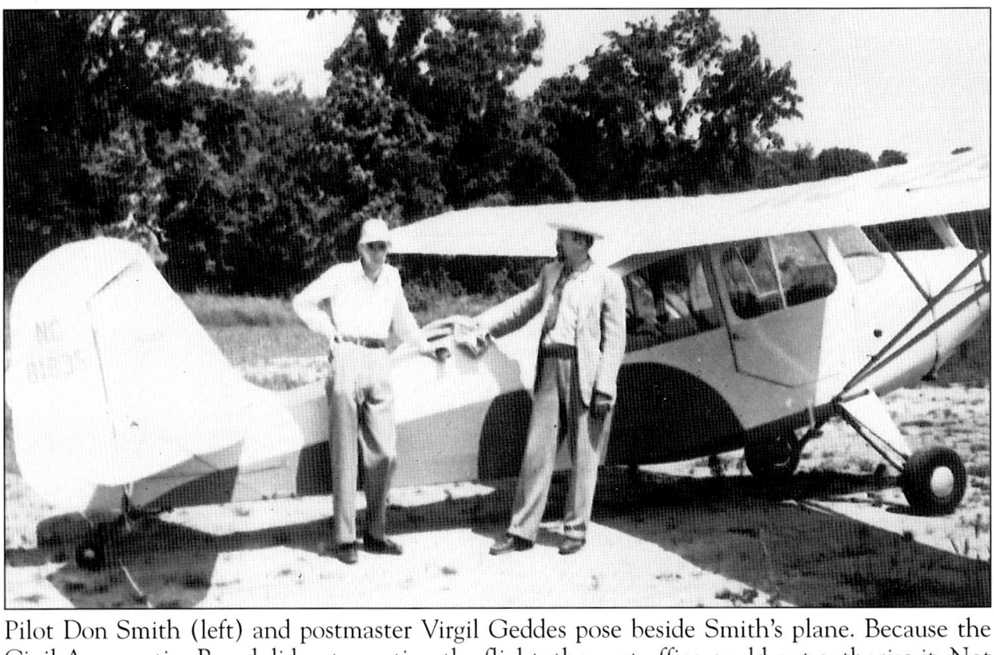

Pilot Don Smith (left) and postmaster Virgil Geddes pose beside Smith's plane. Because the Civil Aeronautics Board did not sanction the flight, the post office could not authorize it. Not one to let anyone down, Mr. Geddes had the mail flown out of Brookfield. He told the pilot not to come back until nightfall. That night, he mailed the letters by regular mail.

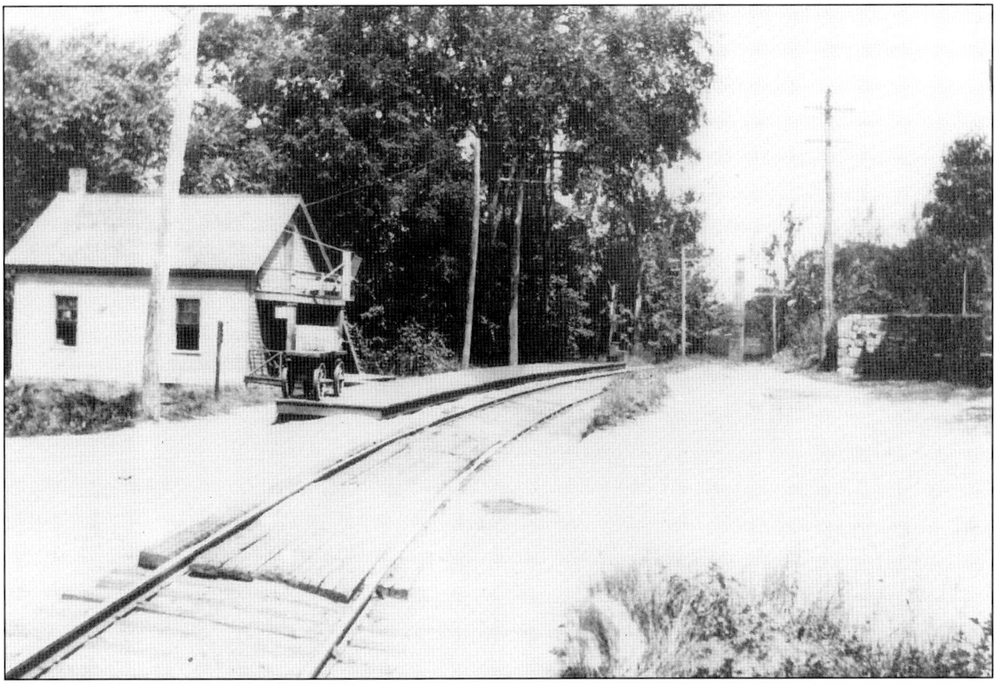

In 1840, the Housatonic Railroad built the first station in the Iron Works District. It was located between the railroad tracks and the Still River, and served mainly as a freight depot. The building shown here eventually burned to the ground.

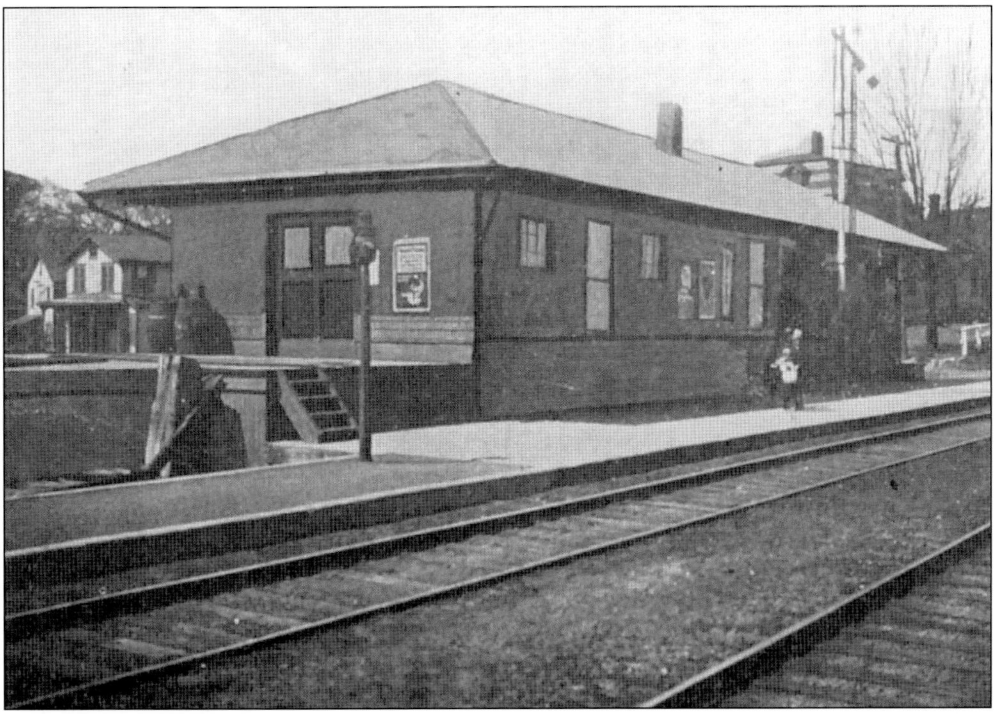

The new train station was built *c.* 1913. At the same time, the tracks were relocated to their present position.

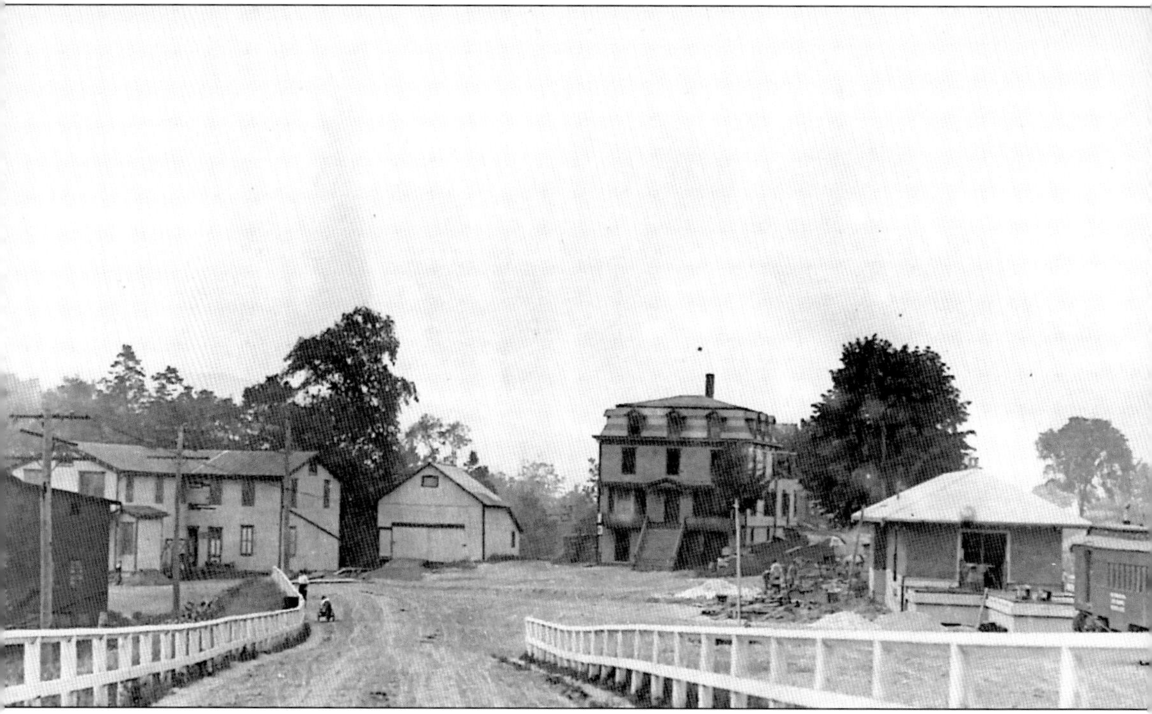

This photograph of the train station in the process of being completed was taken *c.* 1913. The building next to it is the hotel that replaced the American Hotel, which burned down. The next building is Dean Store (now Brookfield Market). Before the present tracks were laid, the store was moved from the hill behind the train station. Notice that the market still has the windows boarded up and there is no porch.

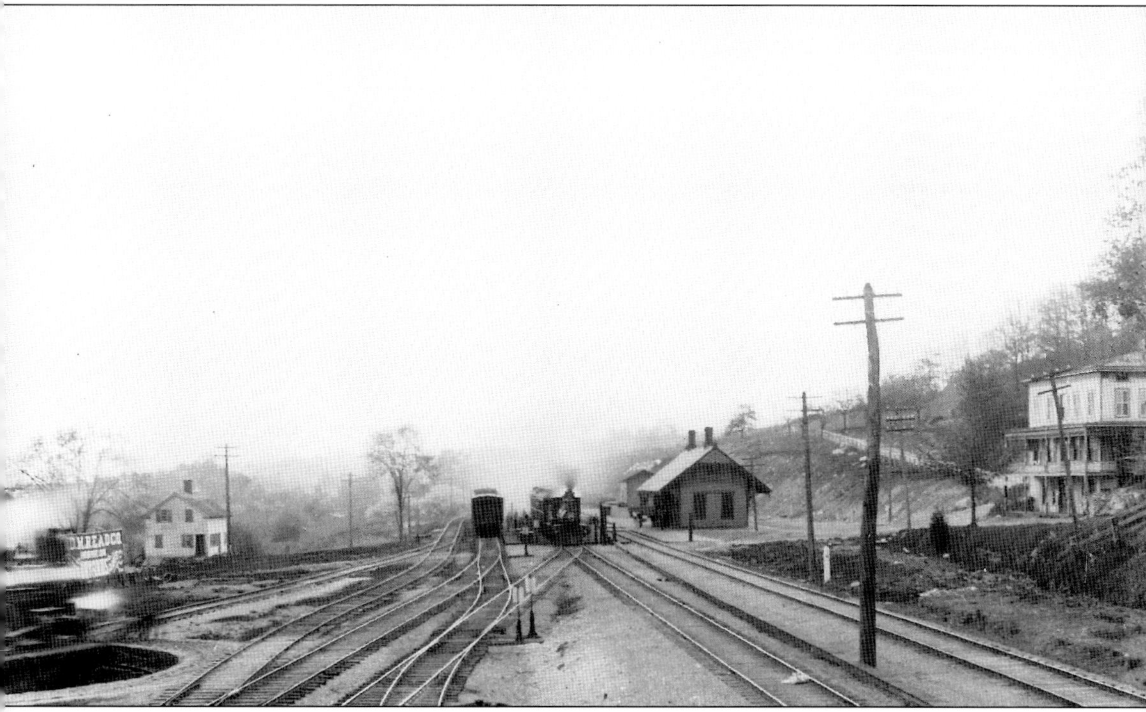

In 1840, the Housatonic Railroad connected New Milford and Bridgeport. At this time, the Junction Station was built on Stony Hill Road. On the left is the turntable; the station is shown in the center, and on the right is the hotel. In the early 1900s, as many as 40 trains a day passed through this station. Just after World War II, the station was taken down.

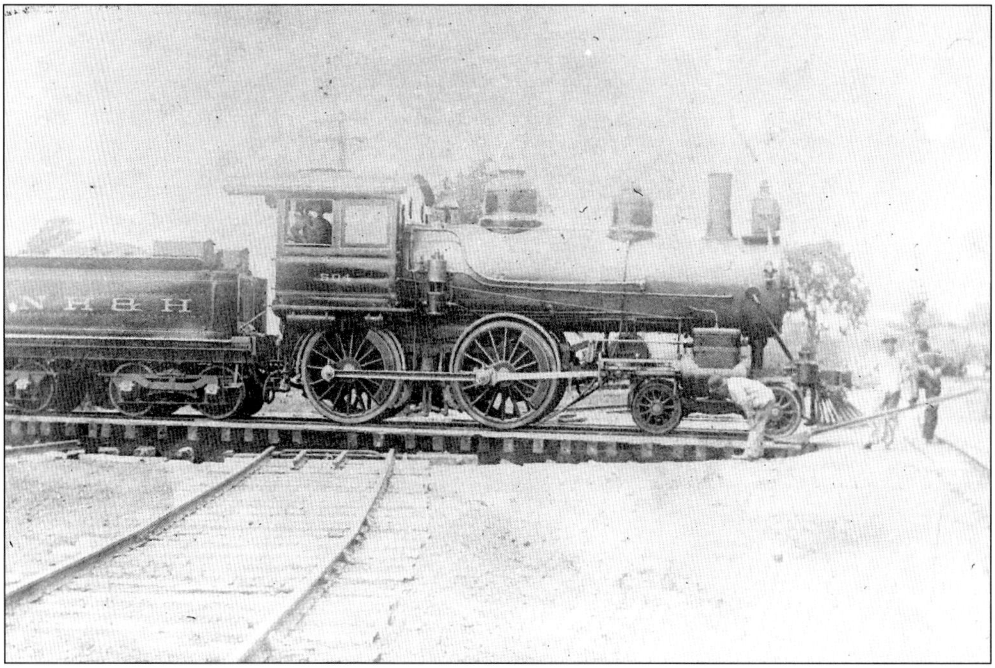

In 1898, the Housatonic Railroad merged with the New York, New Haven, and Hartford Railroad. Shown here is one of their engines being turned on the turntable at the Junction Station. Before Brookfield had its own high school, many of the students commuted to Danbury by train to attend school.

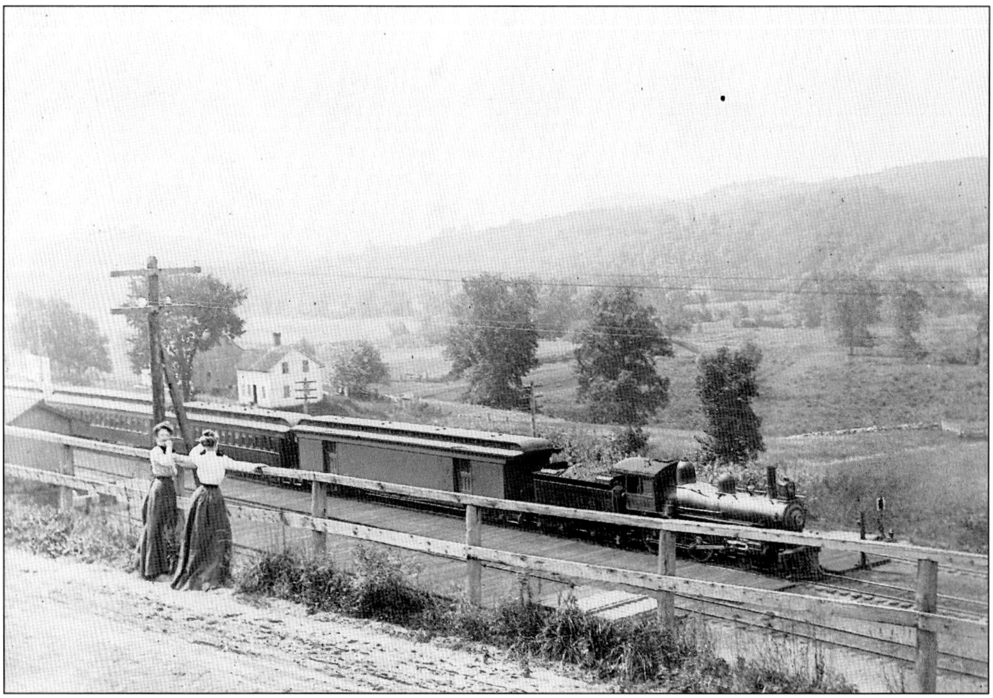

These women are watching the train at the Junction Station. Agnes May Brownell (Mrs. Arthur) took the photograph.

Three

Brookfield Center

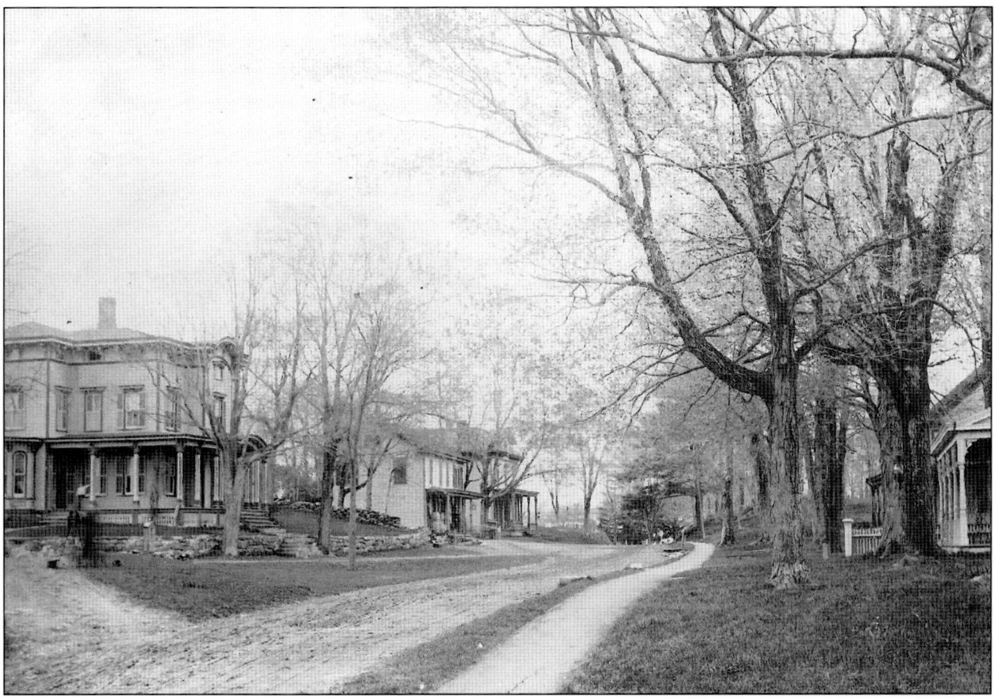

This area is where the first church was built. It was an early center of social activities. Barzillai Kellogg built the house on the left as a wedding present for his daughter Angline in 1887. She married Benjamin Griffin. The Village Store is the next building. The home beside the store was built about the same time as the store, on the site of the old Preserve Smith Tavern. The porch on the right was on the house built in 1829 by Henry L. Peck. The view is looking north on Whisconier Road.

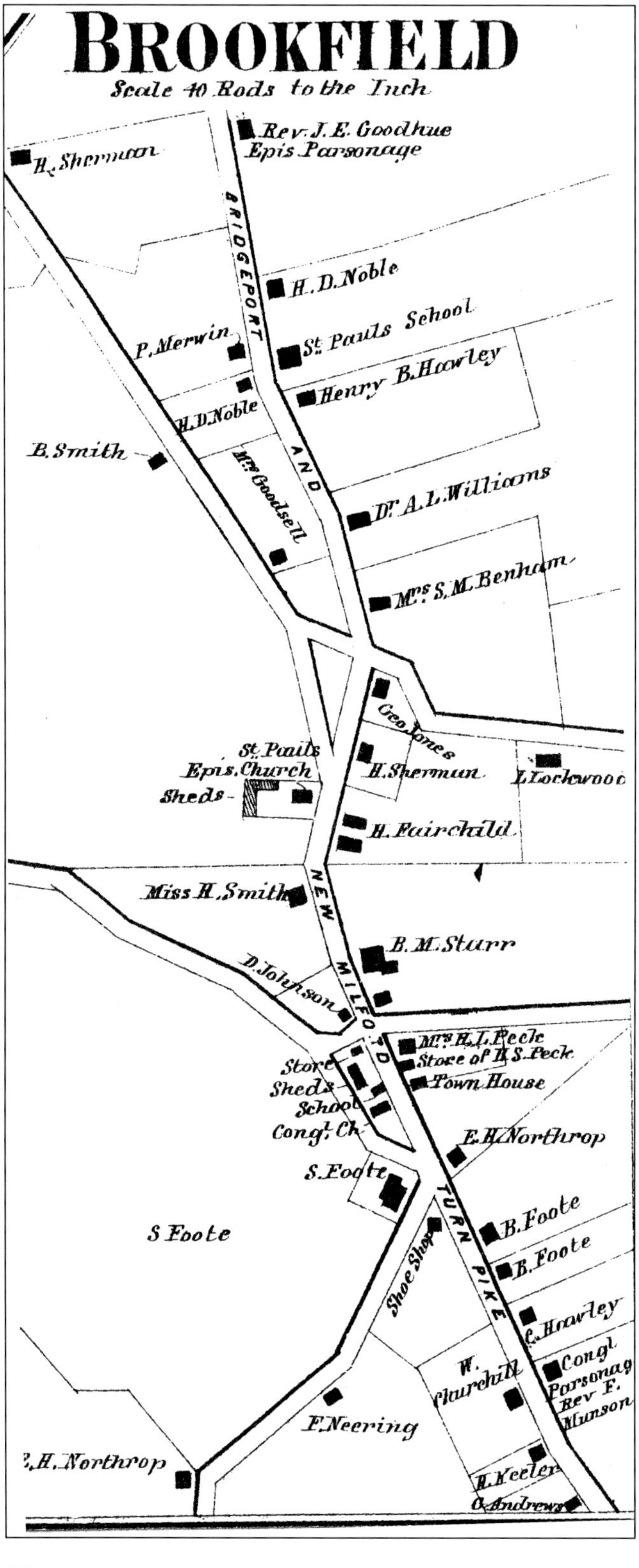

This *c.* 1867 map of Brookfield Center shows churches, homes, and businesses. Listed on the map are S. Foote, manufacturer of boots and shoes; H.D. Noble, rector of St. Paul's School; Henry Peck, dealer in dry goods and groceries; A.L. Williams, physician and surgeon; F. Munson, minister of the Congregational church; and the Town House. The word "shed" appears on the map next to the Congregational church and the Episcopal church. The sheds that are referred to are horse sheds.

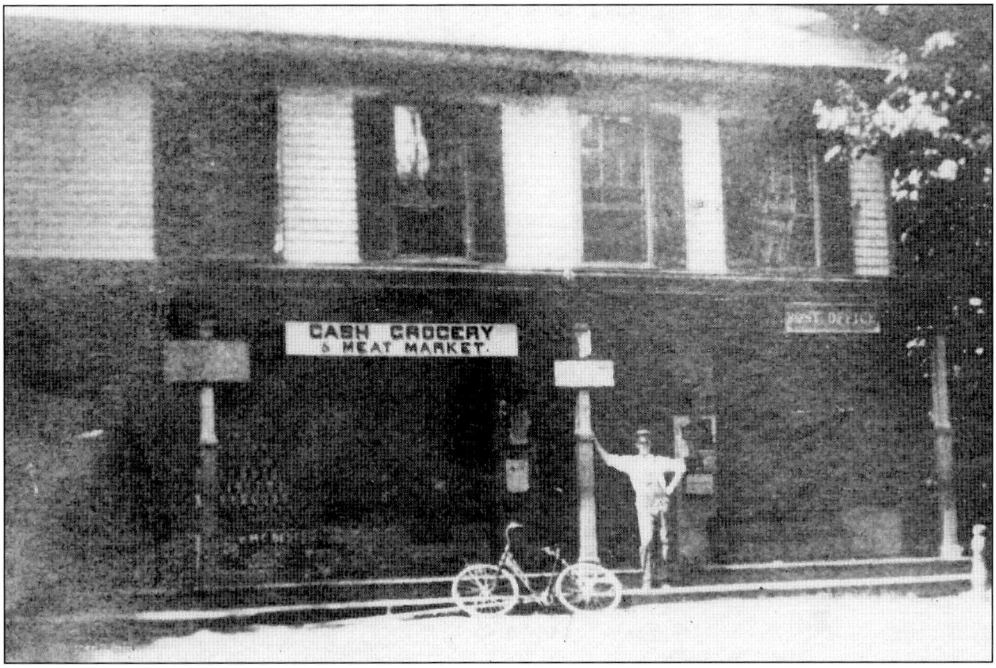

Henry Smith Peck built a store in 1867 on Whisconier Road. For 30 years, he and Alfred Somers ran the Peck & Somers Store. From 1907 until 1924, William Pickney ran the store. The post office was located in the store. A room over the store was used for meetings. Tradition states that the first telephone in Brookfield was installed here. Today it is the Village Store.

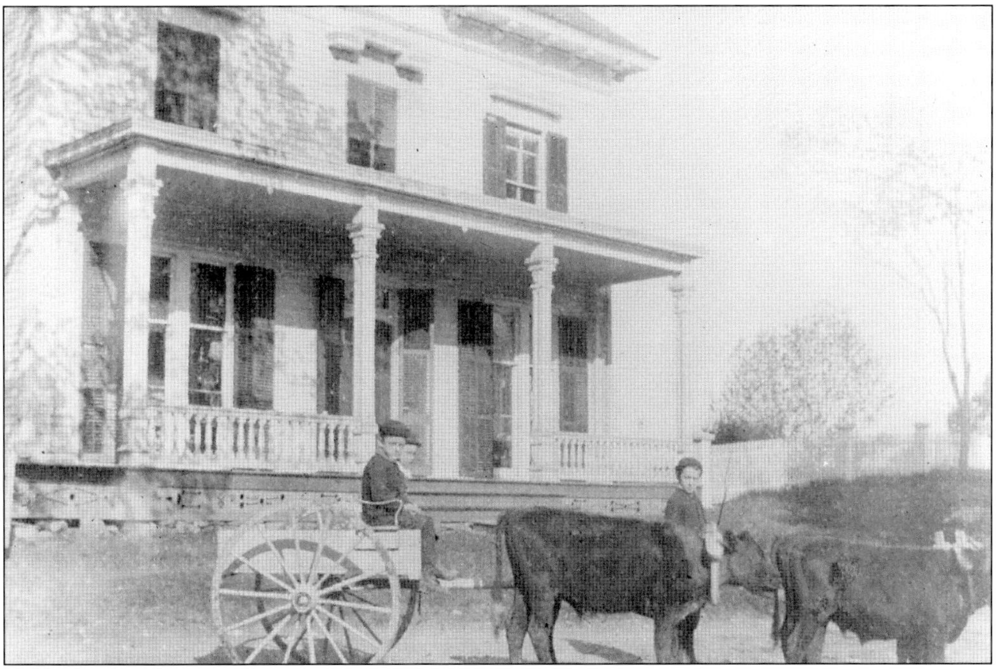

At the same time that Henry S. Peck built the store, he married Eliza A. Fairchild, the daughter of Hiram and Betsey (Gelston) Fairchild, and built this house next door. Over the years, the house has changed. The porch was removed and the roof has been lowered.

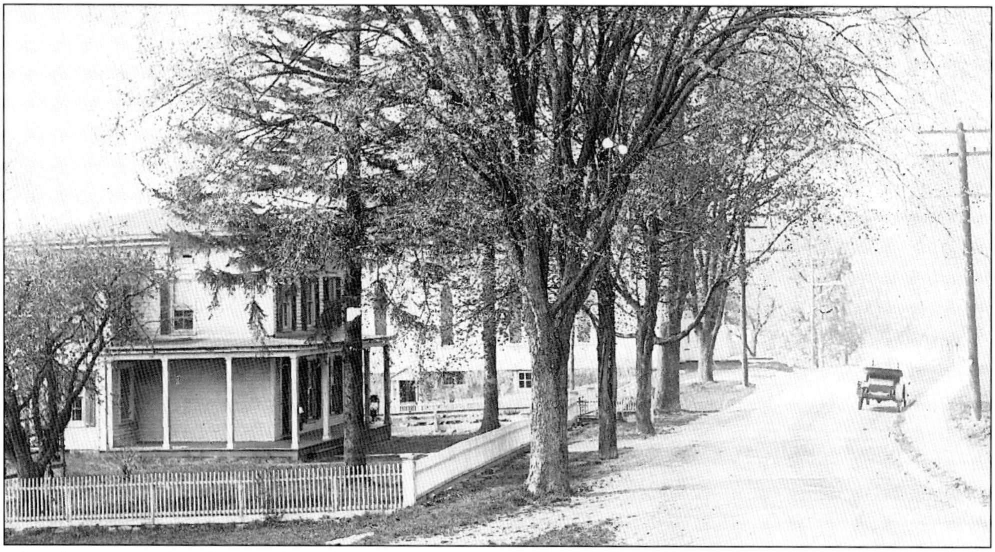

The house with the picket fence was built in 1870 as the second parsonage for the Congregational Church of Brookfield. The picket fence was removed in 1931. The first minister to live in the house was Rev. Asa C. Pierce. The house was sold in 1955. The building in the background is the second church building of the Episcopal Church. The view is looking north on Whisconier Road.

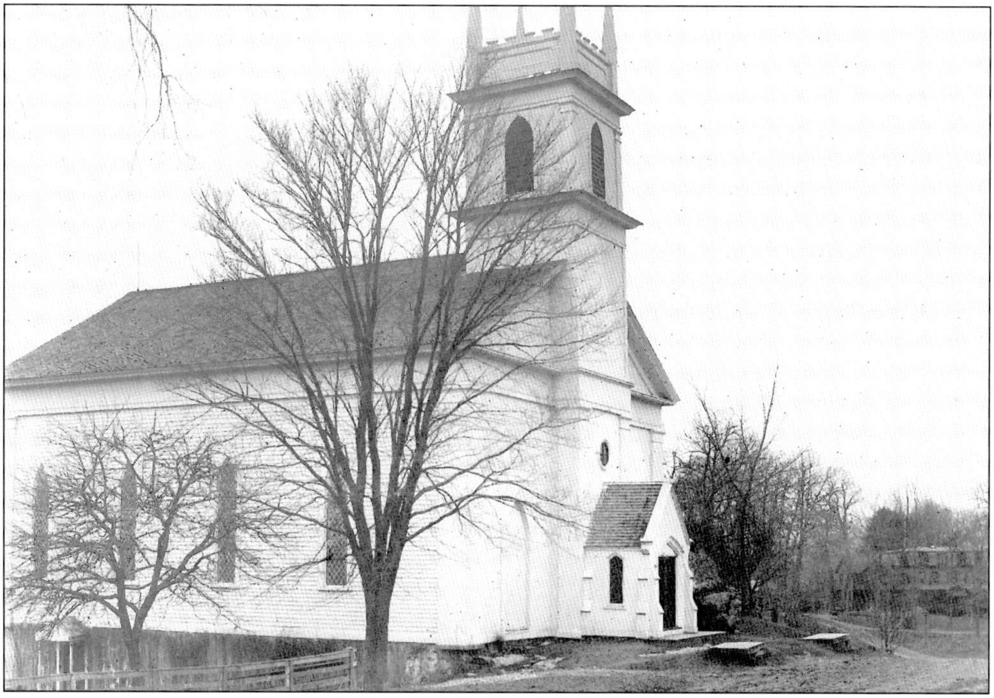

The Episcopal Society of Brookfield built its first church on a plot of land near the Congregational Church of Brookfield. The building was eventually sold to the Methodist Episcopal Society, and in 1838 a new wooden building (shown here) was built on the site of the present church. Ninety-nine years later, on Valentine's Day, the building burned to the ground and a new stone church was built.

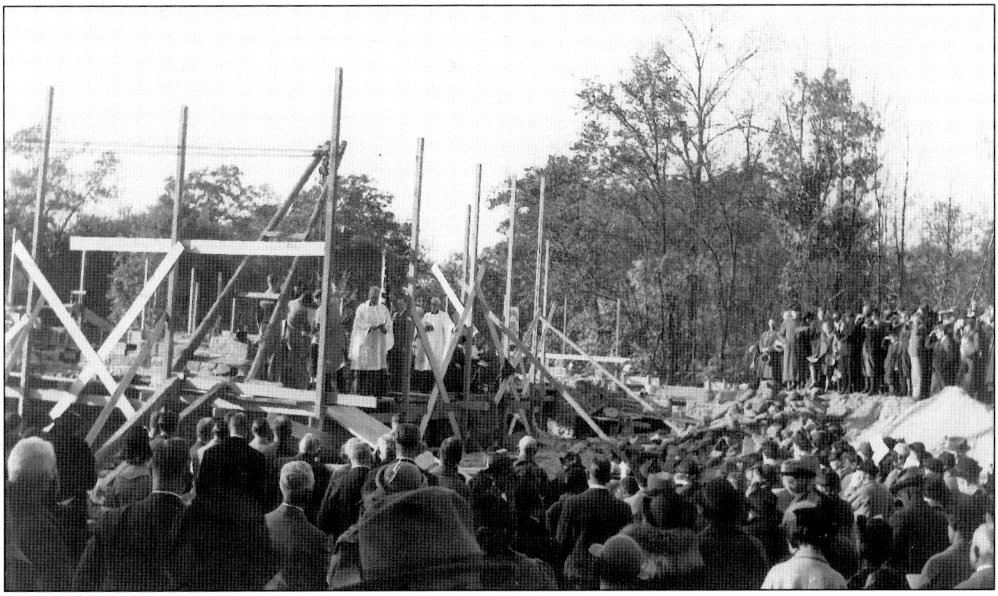

Following the Valentine's Day fire, a new stone church building was built on the site of the old building. The laying of the cornerstone of the new building is shown in this photograph. Much of the stone was quarried in Barkwood Falls, in Brookfield, and from old stone walls. Frederick H. Beckwith of Bridgeport was the architect.

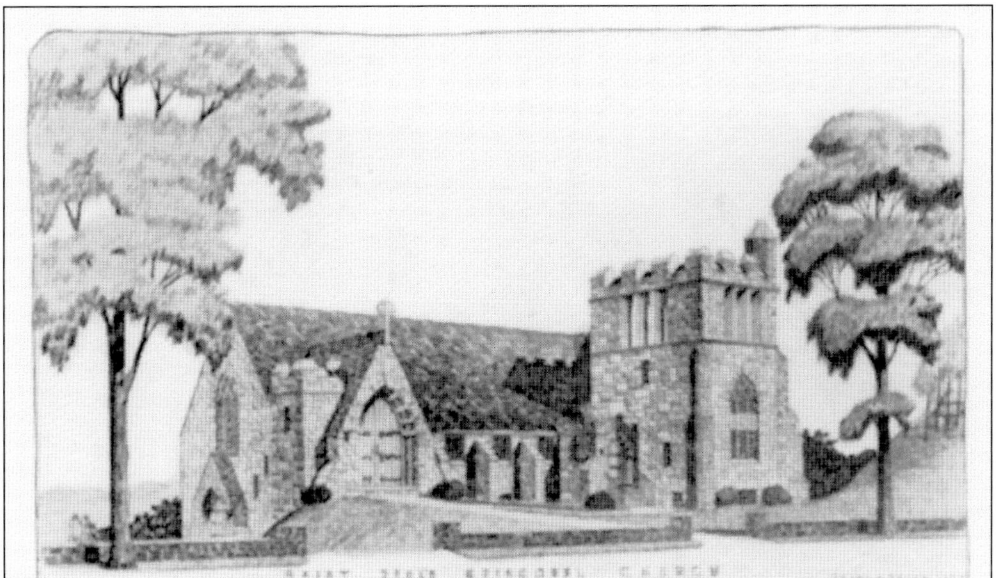

The building of the Third Episcopal Church in Brookfield was done under the supervision of Fred Beers. He didn't want this church to burn down as the previous church had done. The new building was built in the English Gothic style. It was modeled after a church in Dorset, England. Leonard Howard designed the stained-glass windows.

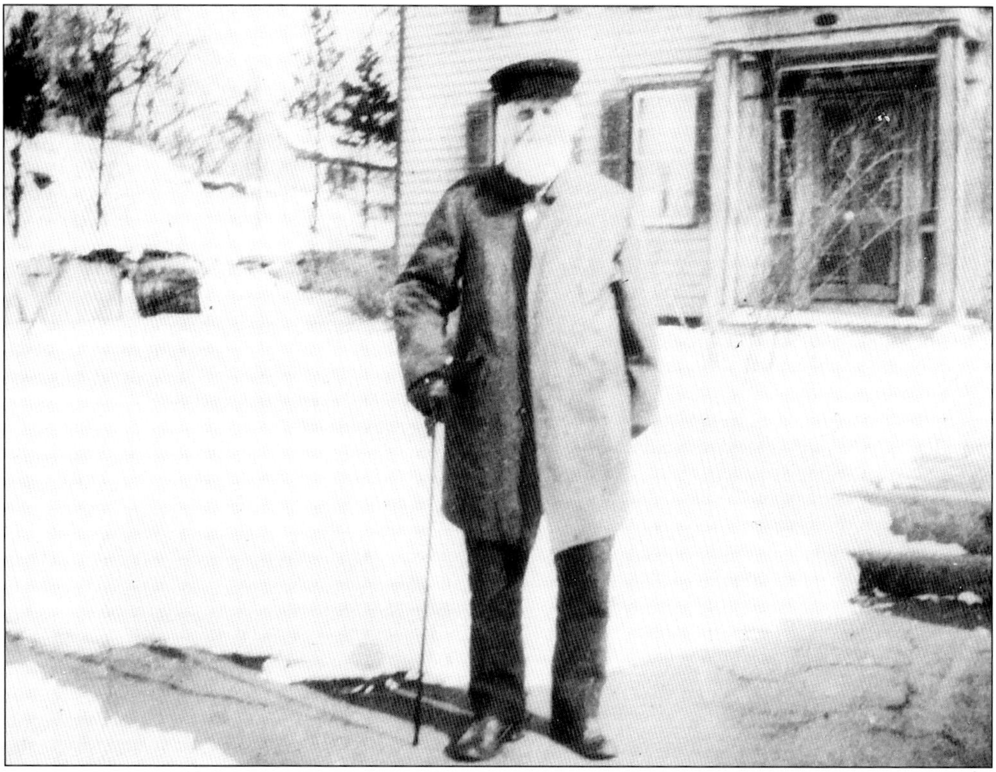

Doctor Amos Williams came to Brookfield in 1833 and practiced medicine here for 63 years. Not only was he the town's physician, he was also the medical examiner, postmaster, registrar, and Brookfield representative in the 1883 legislature. In 1896, he was out on a call and was killed by a train in the Iron Works District. He is buried in Central Cemetery.

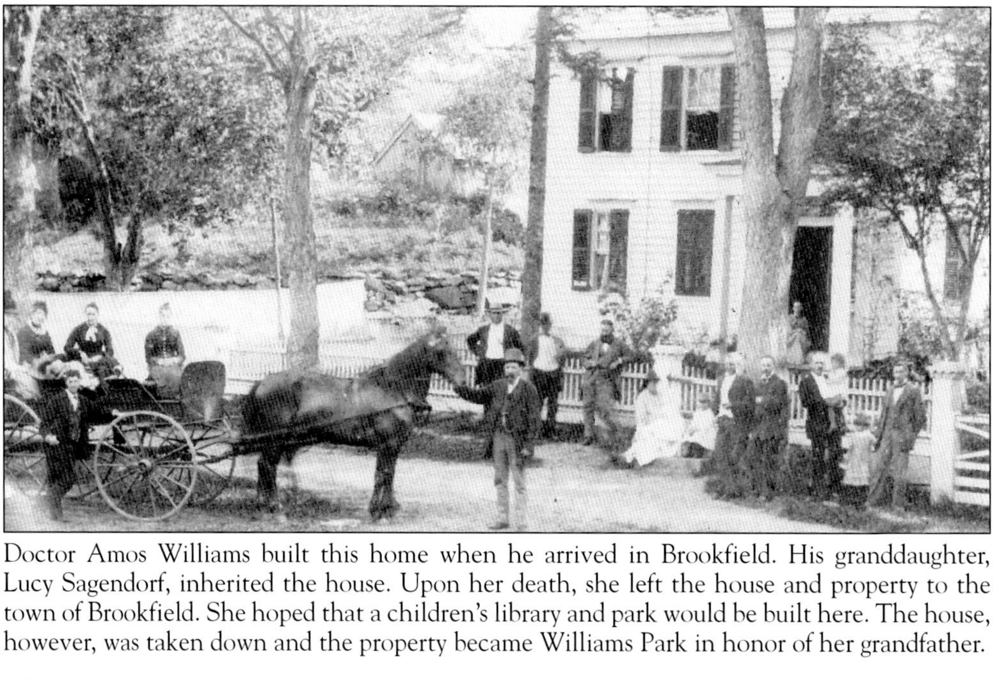

Doctor Amos Williams built this home when he arrived in Brookfield. His granddaughter, Lucy Sagendorf, inherited the house. Upon her death, she left the house and property to the town of Brookfield. She hoped that a children's library and park would be built here. The house, however, was taken down and the property became Williams Park in honor of her grandfather.

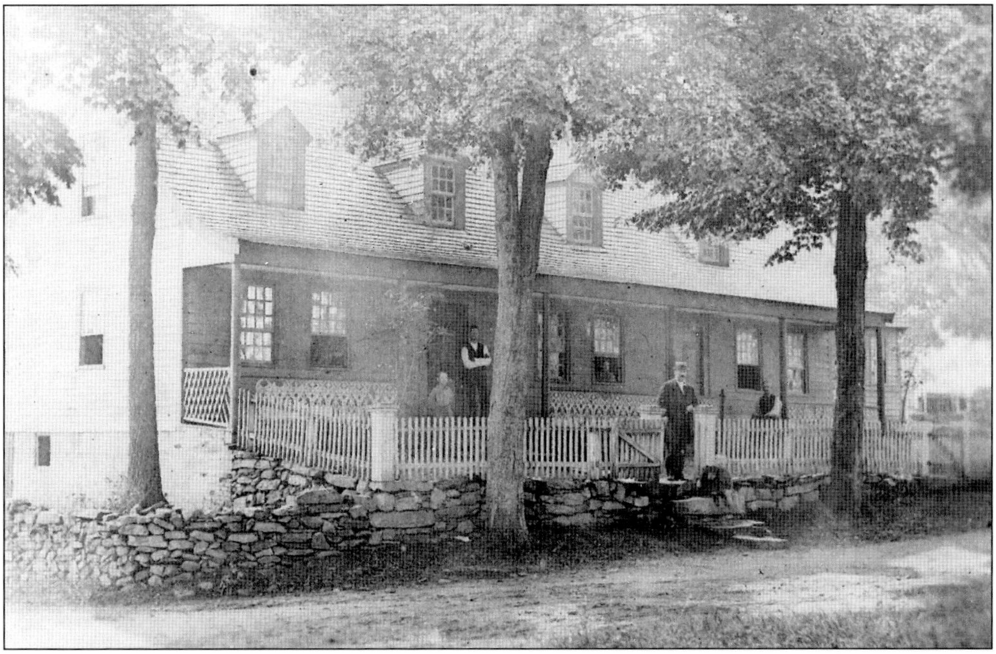

The Bungalow, originally a tavern, has had many stories attached to it. One story claims that James Fennimore Cooper's book *The Spy* was based on the house. The second tradition was that the Masonic Lodge held meetings here. Before the Masonic Hall was built, the members met in local homes. Daniel Holley, an owner of this house, was the Worshipful Master of the lodge.

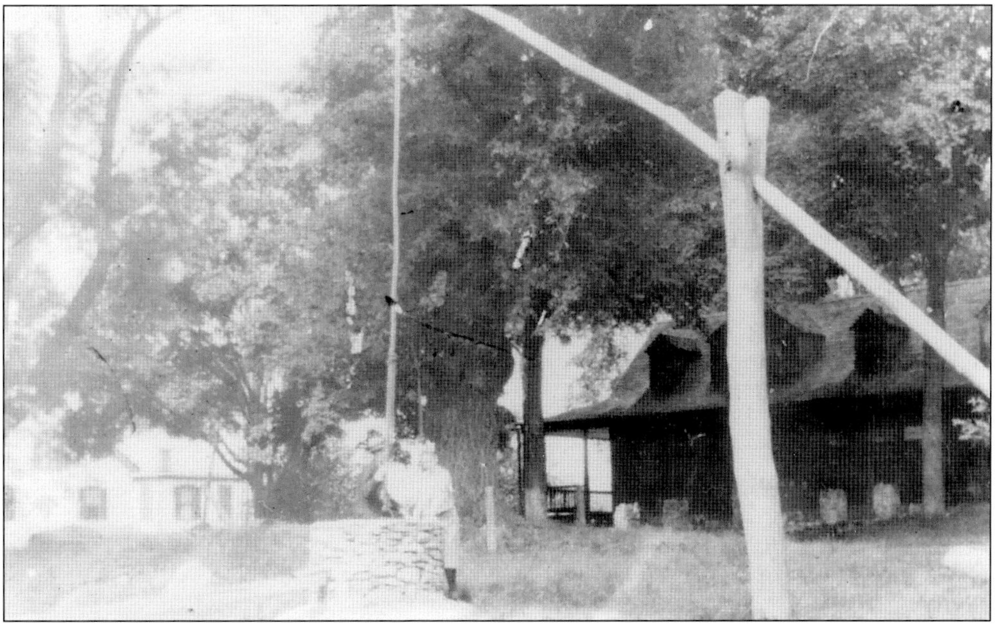

Daniel Holley ran a hat shop across the street from the Bungalow, on land near the well shown in this photograph. The date of this home has always been questioned, but the following has been researched about the date: Shadrack Hubbell brought land from Isaac Northop in 1773, and no building was mentioned. When he sold the same property to Amos Wheeler in 1777, a house is mentioned.

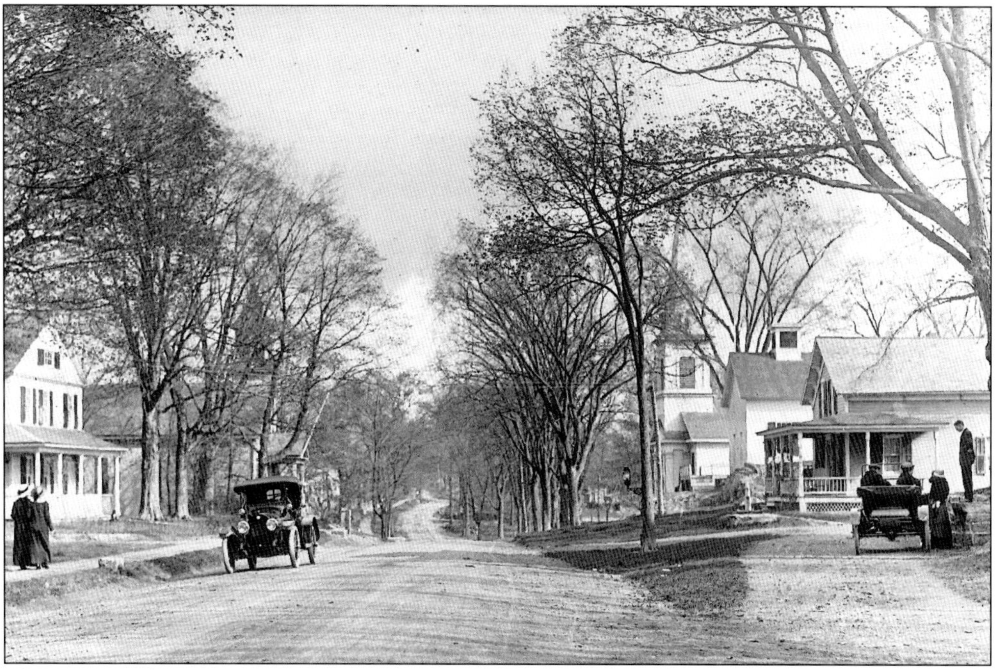

This view is looking south on Whisconier Road. On the left is the Henry L. Peck house and the old town hall. On the right are the Congregational Church of Brookfield (in the distance), Center School, and a home. This house was built as a store on the site of the former Daniel Johnson tailor shop.

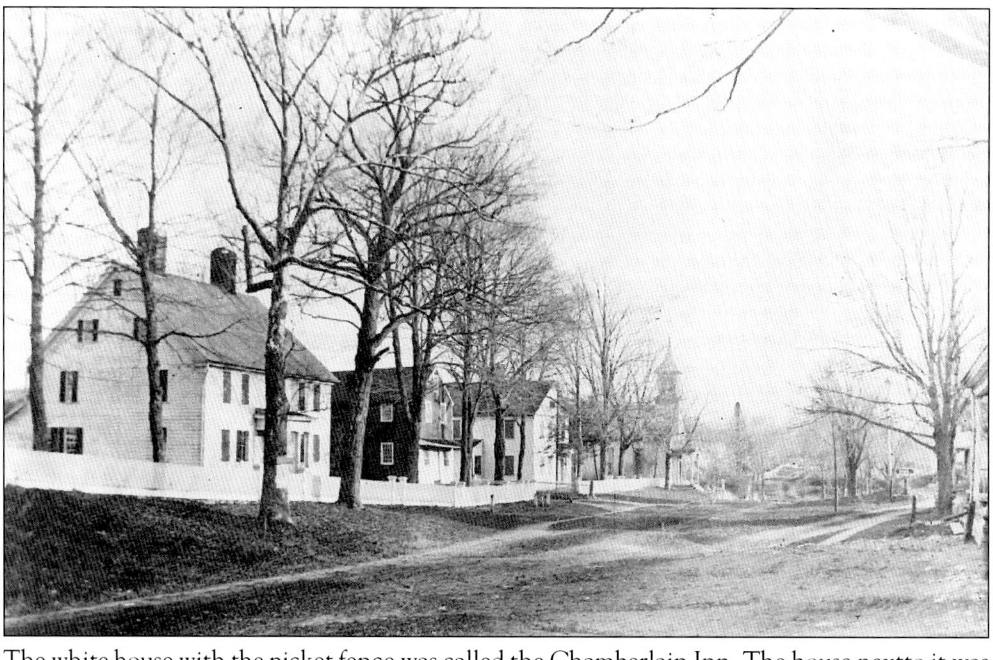

The white house with the picket fence was called the Chamberlain Inn. The house nextto it was a store; the next building is the Peck house, followed by the old town hall. The store has since been removed, along with the picket fence. The view is looking south on Whisconier Road.

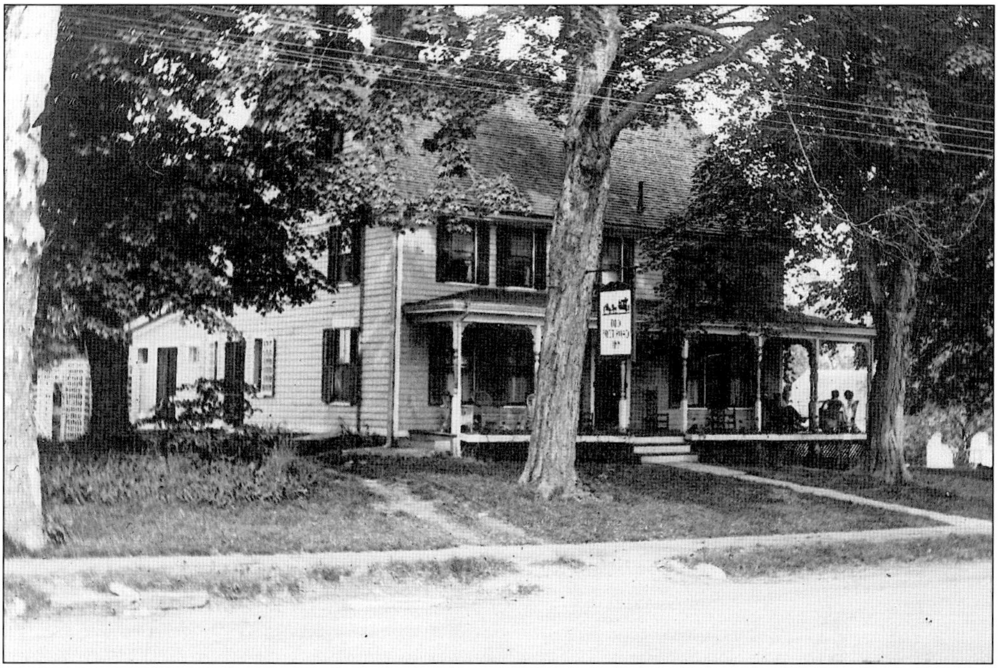

Daniel Jackson built this home *c.* 1770. One owner was Colbe Chamberlain, who ran an inn called the Chamberlain Inn here. From 1801 to 1807, Colbe Chamberlain was also the postmaster. In 1917, Mary T. Haight purchased the old inn and opened the Old Post Road Inn. The inn closed in 1928.

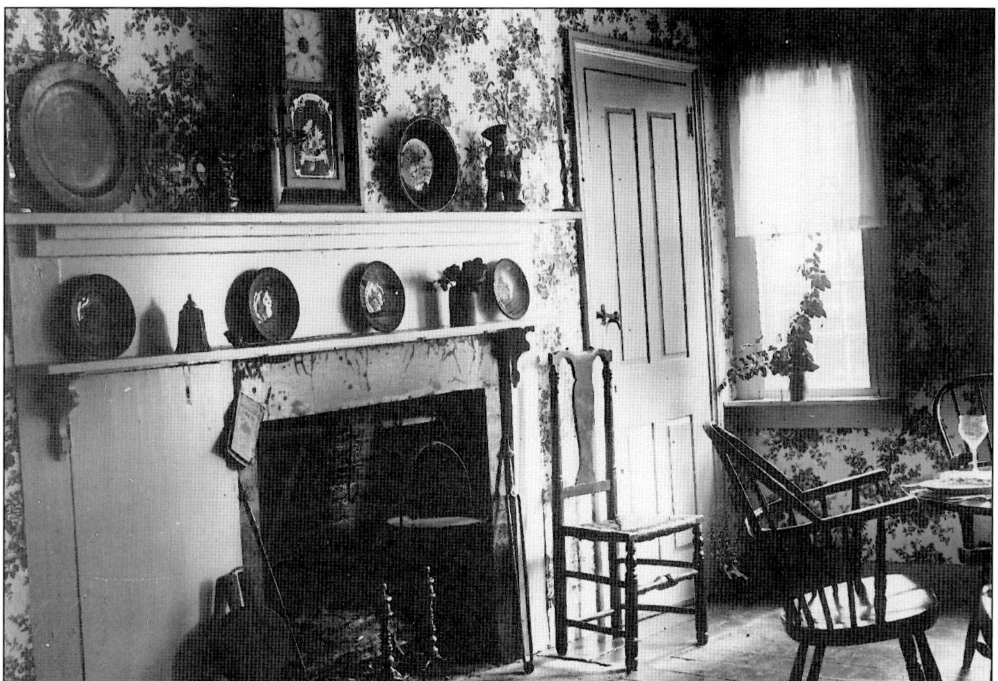

This was the dining room in the Old Post Road Inn. Tradition has it that President Howard Taft and John D. Rockefeller were guests here.

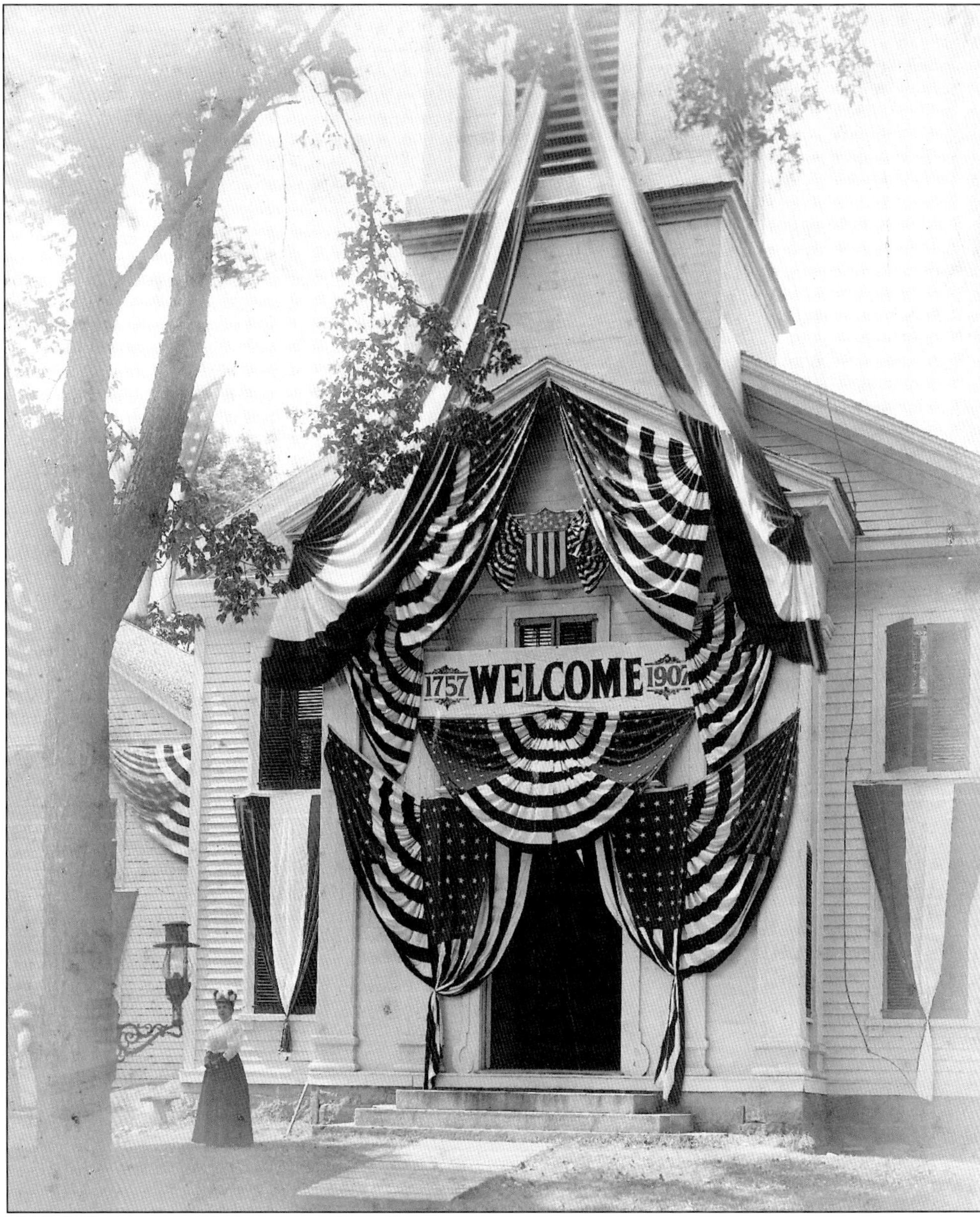

The Congregational Church of Brookfield was established on September 28, 1757. At that time, the first building was dedicated and Rev. Thomas Brooks was ordained. Brooks was the first pastor; in 1788, the town was named for him (previously, it had been called the Parish of Newbury). The first meetinghouse was barn-shaped and had box pews. The pulpit was raised and had a sounding board. Eventually, galleries were added, and in 1820, a steeple was added. No bell was ever placed in the steeple. Instead, the two churches (the Congregational and Episcopal churches) used the bell in the Town House to call parishioners to worship. In 1854, the present building was erected on the site of the first church building. In 1907, the church celebrated its 150th anniversary with much pomp and circumstance, as seen in this photograph. The first addition was built at that time. There have since been three more additions made to the building.

This view of the rear of the Congregational Church of Brookfield was taken between 1907 and 1939. Silvermine Road, at one time, went in back of the church. In 1954, the church needed to build another addition, but the road went through the church's property. The church and the town exchanged parcels of land, and Silvermine Road was moved to its present location.

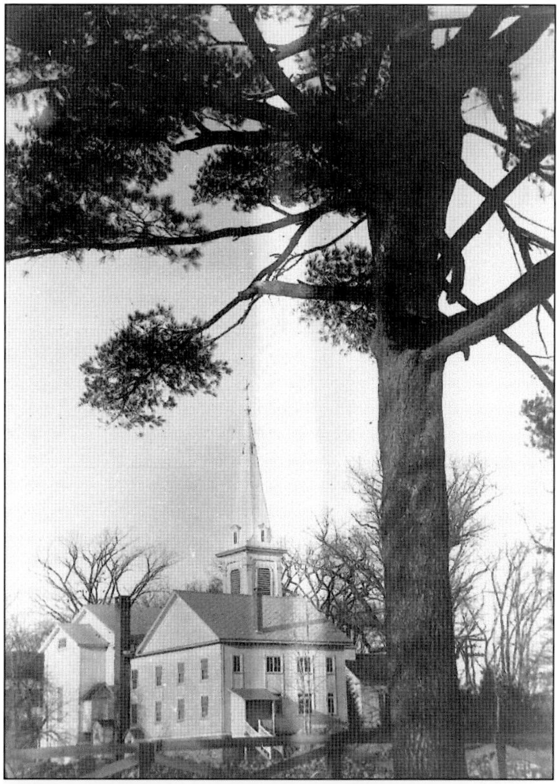

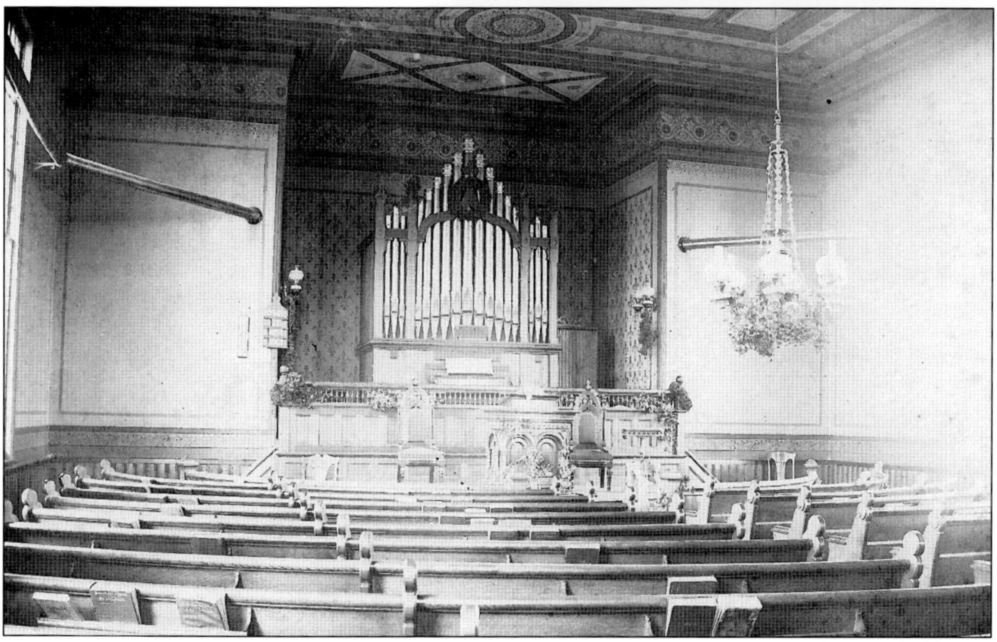

In 1888, the interior of the Congregational church was remodeled. Center and side aisles were put in with semi-circular pews. The walls were frescoed and an ornate ceiling was added. The pulpit was replaced with an oak desk. The pipes came from the two stoves (one on each side) in the back of the room.

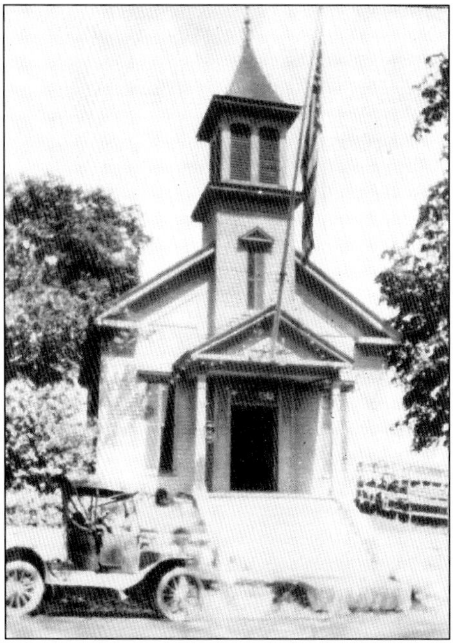

This is the second town hall built on this site. The first was built in 1797 and was taken down and replaced in 1876. The lower level contained the Judge of Probate office and vault. The first Judge of Probate was Ebenezer Blackman, who was appointed in 1850. In 1951, the building became the Joyce Memorial Library. When a new library was built in 1975, the Brookfield Historical Society began using this building as a town museum and research center.

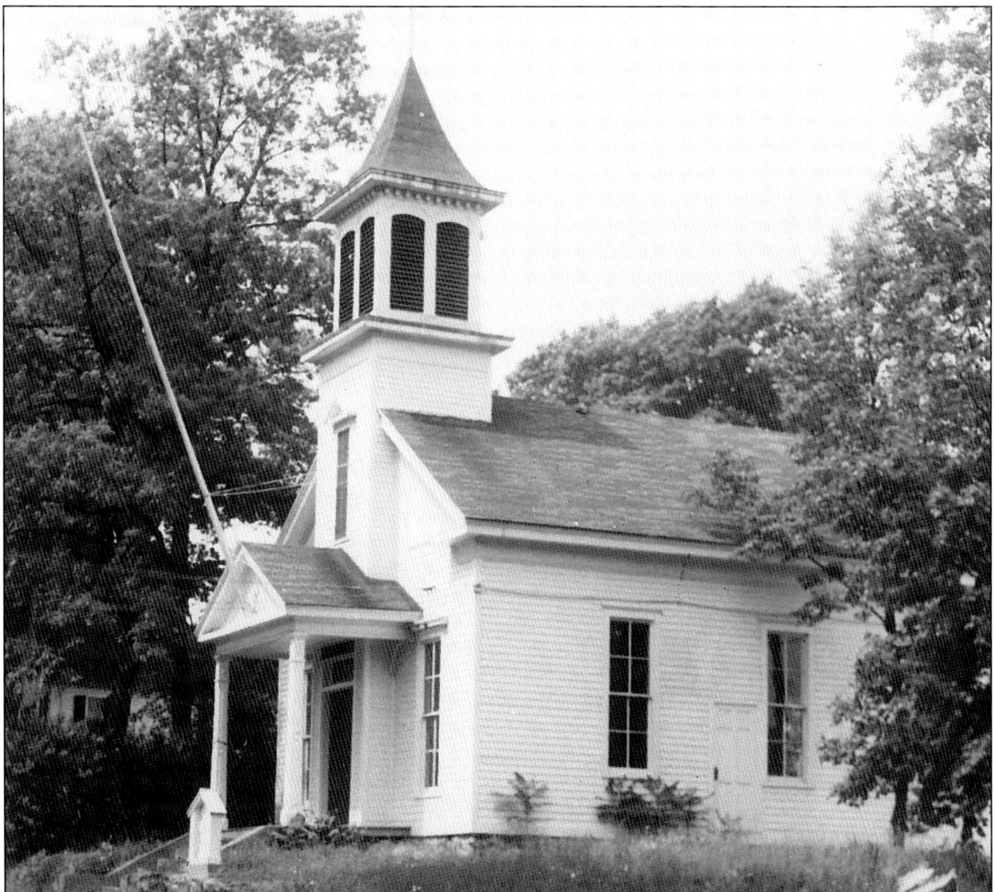

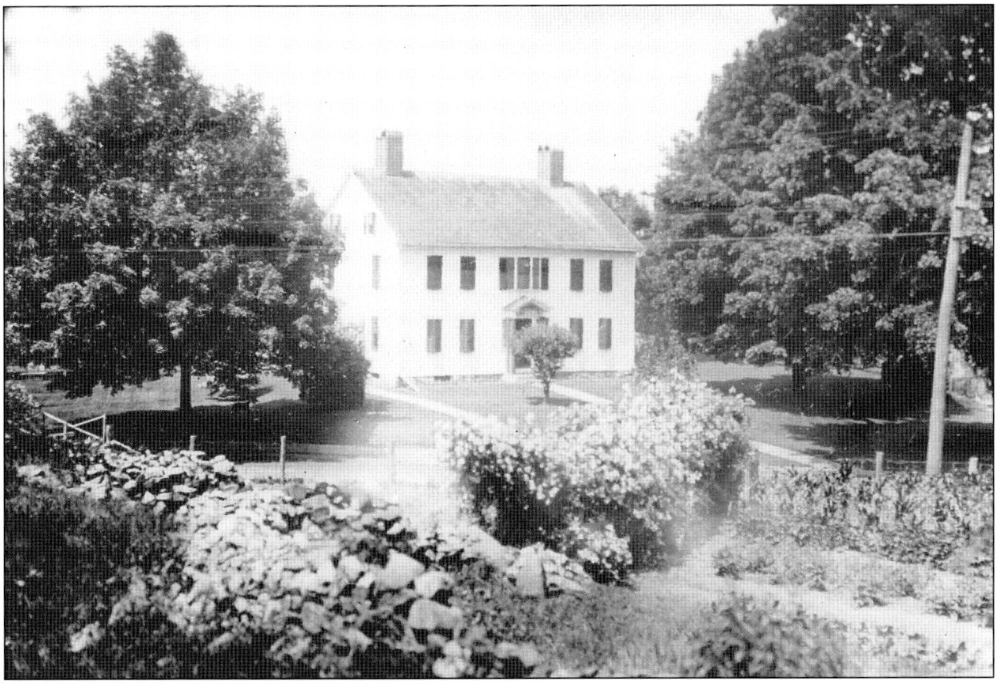

Built by John A. Peck in 1812, this house is now the third parsonage of the Congregational Church of Brookfield. Clarena Peck inherited the house. She married Sherman B. Foote, who was a farmer and a shoemaker. The home stayed in the family for many years. Frank Flahive eventually purchased it, and upon his death in 1958, it was sold to the Congregational Church.

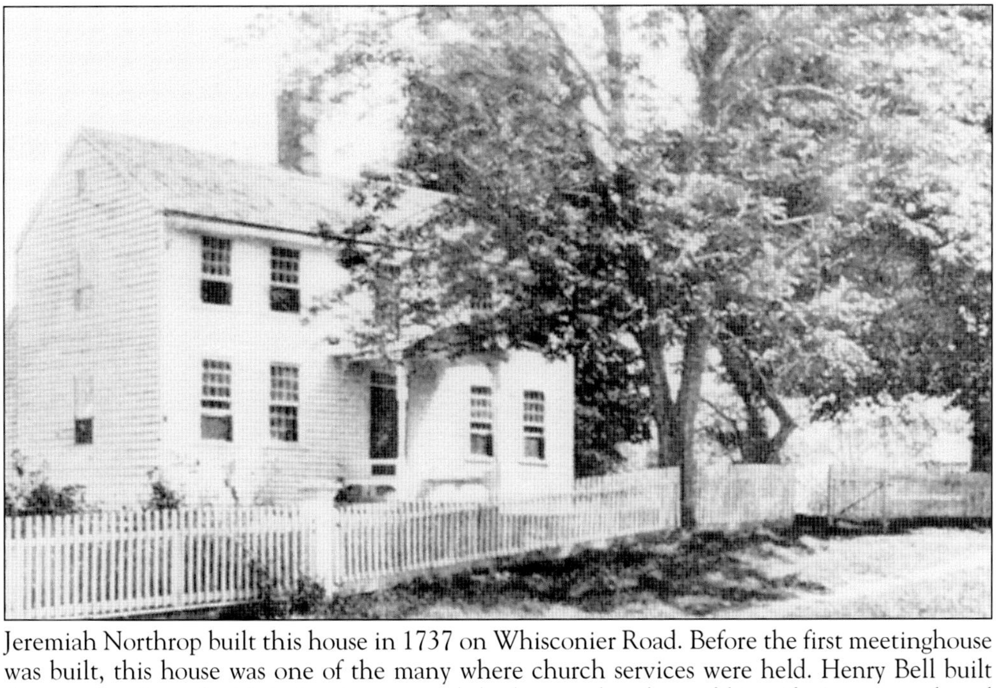

Jeremiah Northrop built this house in 1737 on Whisconier Road. Before the first meetinghouse was built, this house was one of the many where church services were held. Henry Bell built the stone walls and added plantings around the house when he and his wife, Irene, purchased it in the 1940s.

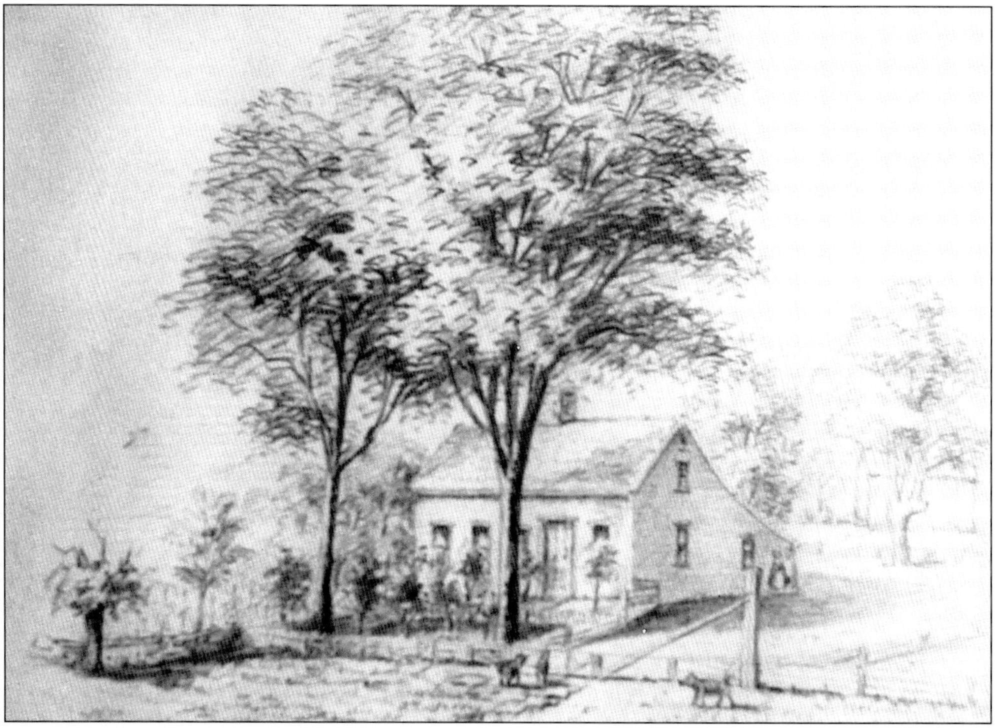

This drawing is of the home of Revolutionary War soldier Isaac Lockwood. He served in Colonel Swift's company, Second Regiment, Continental Line. The house was located on Winding Road. It has since been taken down.

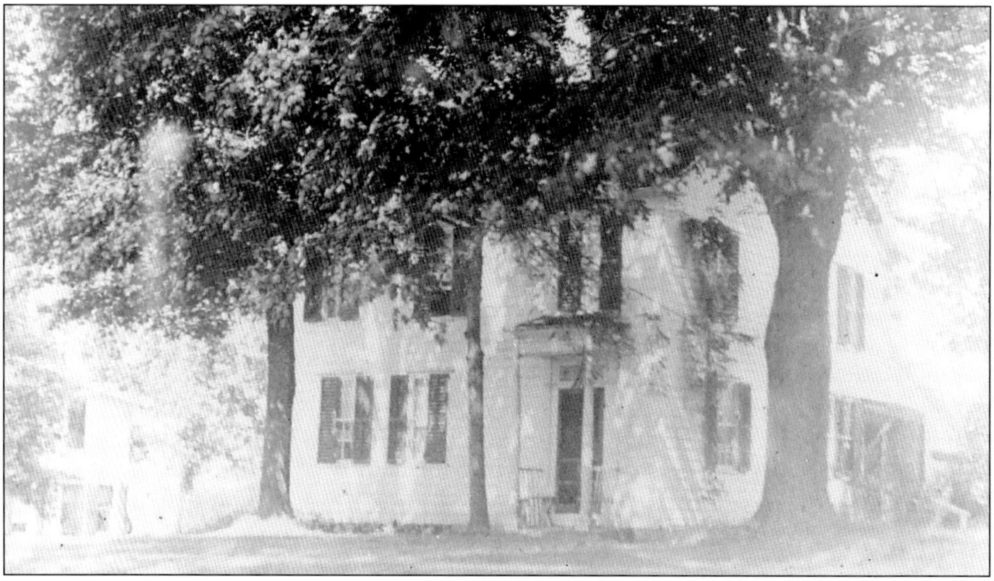

Heman Burch built this house *c.* 1815 on Whisconier Road. In 1927, the owners added the shutters with a cut-out candle design, and the house has been called Candleglow ever since. In 1827, a building was erected in the southwest corner of the yard. Federal Lodge #41 used the second floor as a Masonic Hall. The lower floor was a store run by Booth Peck. The store was eventually taken down.

Four

Growing up in Brookfield

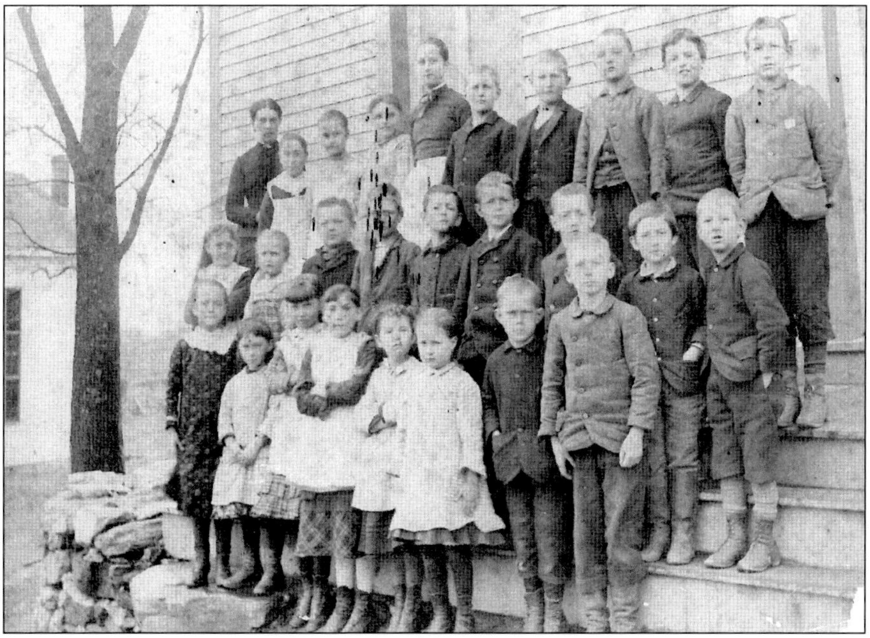

The Center School pupils and their teacher shown in this 1883 photo are, from left to right, as follows: (front row) Matty Griffen, Lucy Sagendorf, unidentified, Eva Stitzel, Emma Frisbie, Susie Pinckney, Henry Griffen, and ? Giddings; (middle row) Edith Griffen, Hattie Pinckney, Howard Keeler, William Leach, Henry B. Hawley, Ernest Griffen, Lucius Hawley, John Sagendorf, and Clarence Jones; (back row) Florida Merwin (teacher), Florence Sagendorf, Ida Pinckney, Amelia Hawley, May Bishop, Charles Pinckney, William Pinckney, James Leach, Fred Hawley, and Paul Jones. Center School was opened by 1762 as the fourth school in the Parish of Newbury. On the left is the Congregational Church of Brookfield.

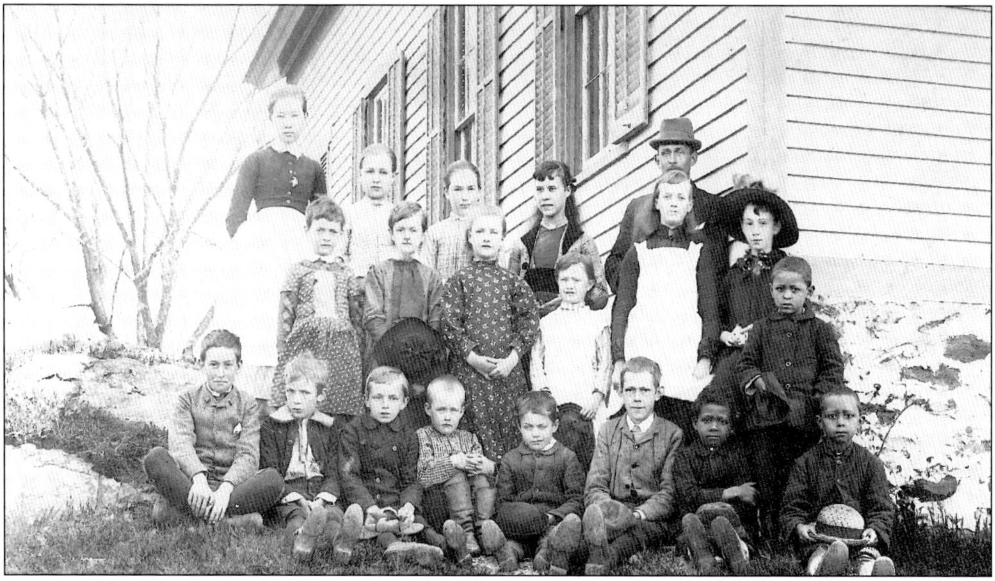

Center School was one of eight one-room schools in Brookfield. In 1938, the Consolidated School was built; Center School later became the town hall. This photograph was taken in 1890.

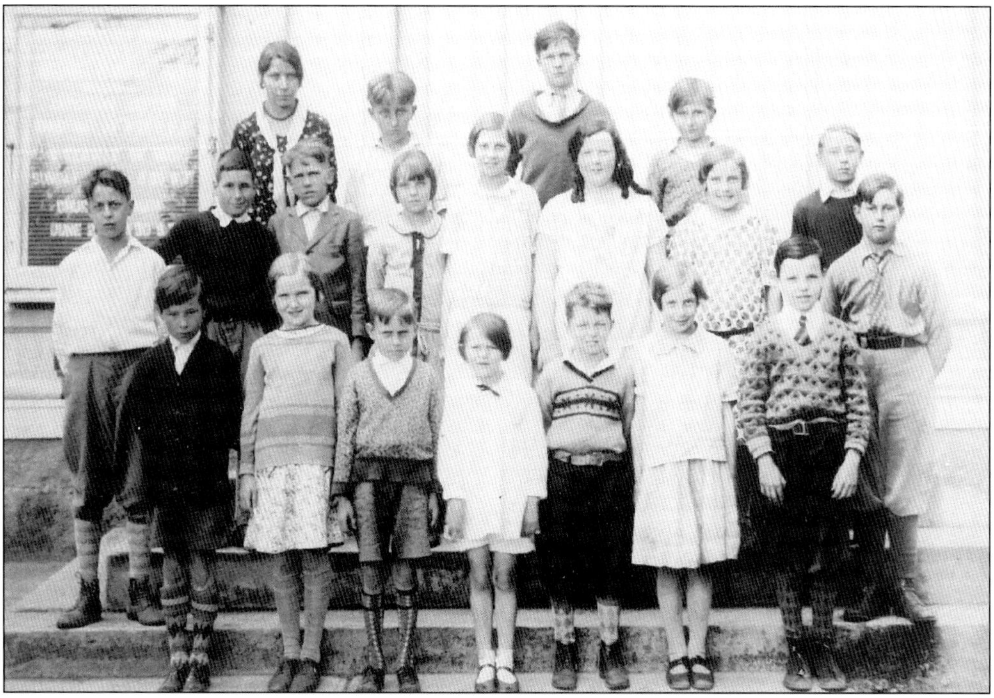

In 1930, Center School students posed on the steps of the Congregational church. They are, from left to right, as follows: (first step) Richard Mann; (front row) Clarence Bristol, Jean Durgy, Howard Bluge, Margaret Carpenter, Sammy Smith, Anastasia Tybursze, and Edward Townsend; (middle row) Kenneth Hooper, Daniel Morehouse, Natalie Fabian, Louise Johnson, Pauline Collins, Valeria Tyburszec, and Stanley Gurski; (back row) Helen Tucker (substitute teacher), Donald Lane, John Cahill, and Stephen Obeda.

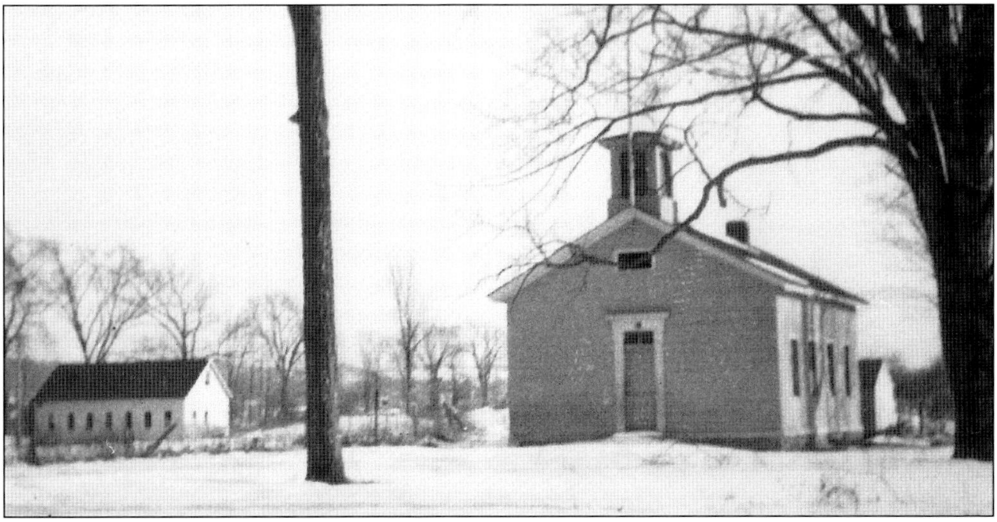

The first school in Brookfield was the East Iron Works School, located at the junction of Farview Road and Whisconier Road. Eventually, there was also a West Iron Works School, located on Station Road. When East Iron Works closed, the two schools merged and all of the students attended the West Iron Works School (shown above). The building in the background is where Nick Hultman built wooden mobile homes in the 1940s.

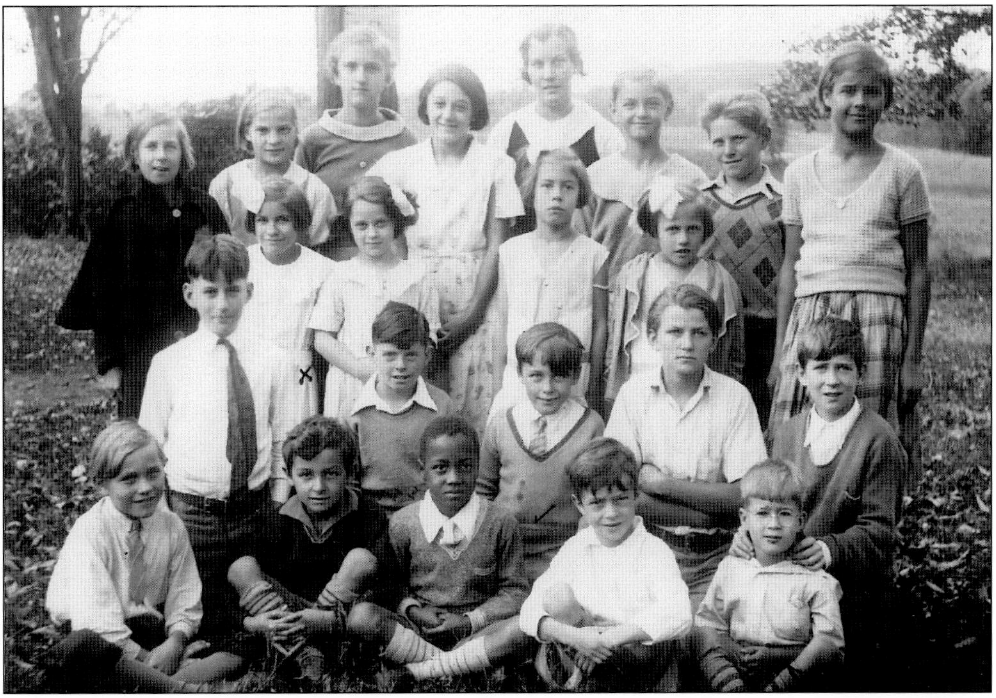

These students attended the Iron Works School in 1933. They are, from left to right, as follows: (front row) John Babon, Harold Koehler, James Smith, Peter Tyburszec, and Edward Silsby; (second row) Herbert Norman, Ronald Pinckney, Raymond Waidelich, Chester Knapp, and Leroy Pitcher; (third row) Isabelle Pitcher, Mildred Waidelich, Marie Alaby, Frances Alaby, and Sophia Babon; (fourth and fifth row) Mary Babon, Margaret Konecko, Louise Gruet, Helen Pendergast (teacher), Estelle Konecko, and Kenneth Pinckney.

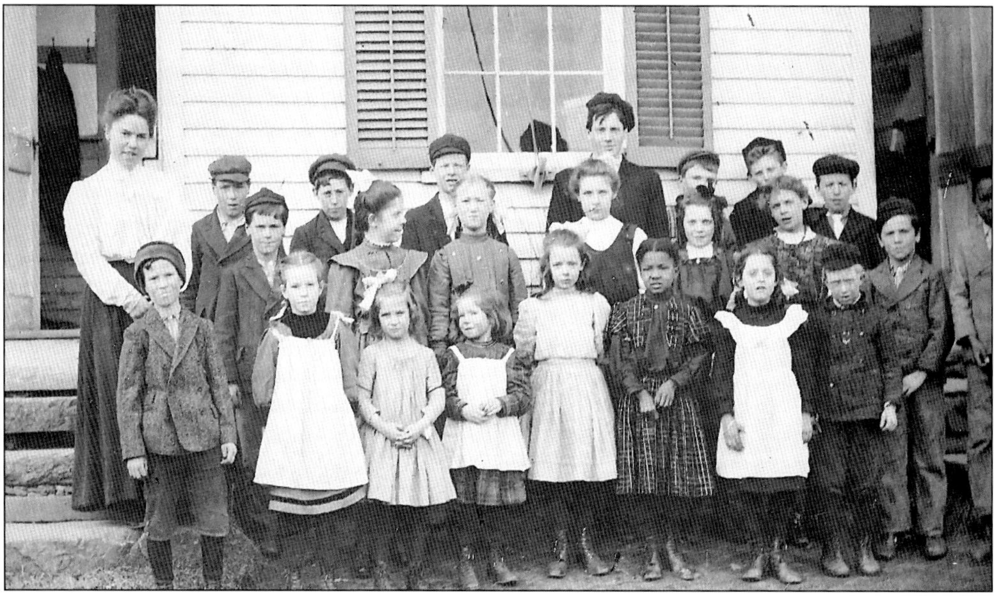

By 1761, there were four school districts in the Parish of Newbury—the Iron Works, Whisconier, Pocono, and Obtuse Districts. This photograph was taken c. 1907 of the students in the Obtuse District. The two young men in the back row (in front of the windows) are William and Jay Thornhill. The young man on the right in the middle row is James H. Smith.

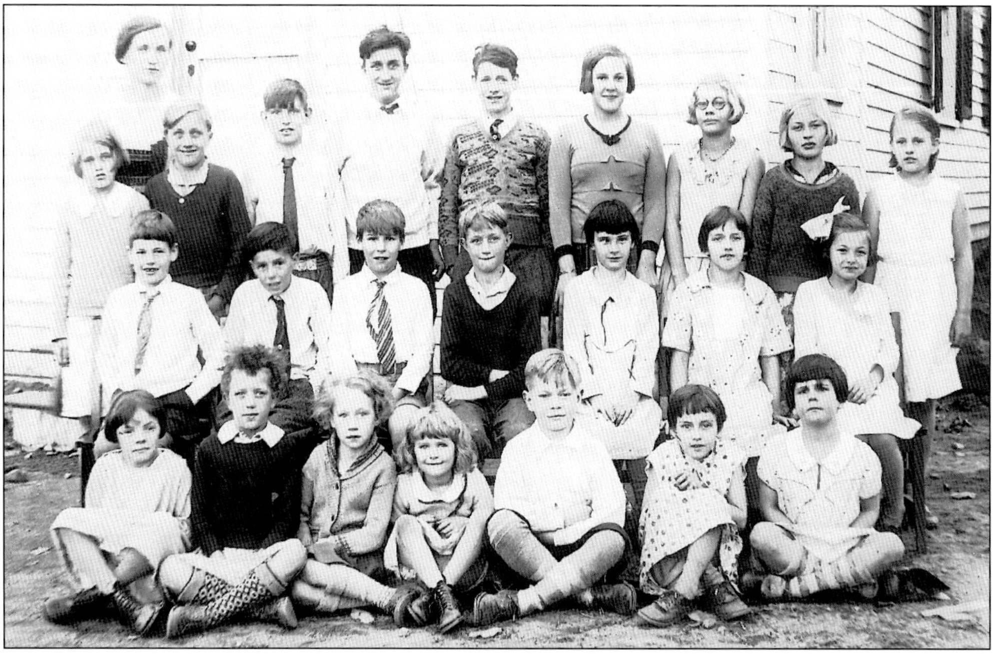

These Obtuse School students, shown here in 1932, are, from left to right, as follows: (front row) Ethel Wilson, Virginia Pettit, Harriet Pettit, Viola Wilson, Paul Piskura, Lois Leach, and Barbara Anderson; (middle row) Thomas Murphy, Walter Wilson, Russell Anderson, Stuart Pettit, Alberta Maynard, Carrie Leach, and Mary Murphy; (back row) Mrs. Boddie (teacher), Virginia Taylor, Florence Pettit, Russell Wilson, Burton Leach, Martin Lynch, Helen Anderson, Clara Piskura, Katharine Piskura, and Ruth Taylor.

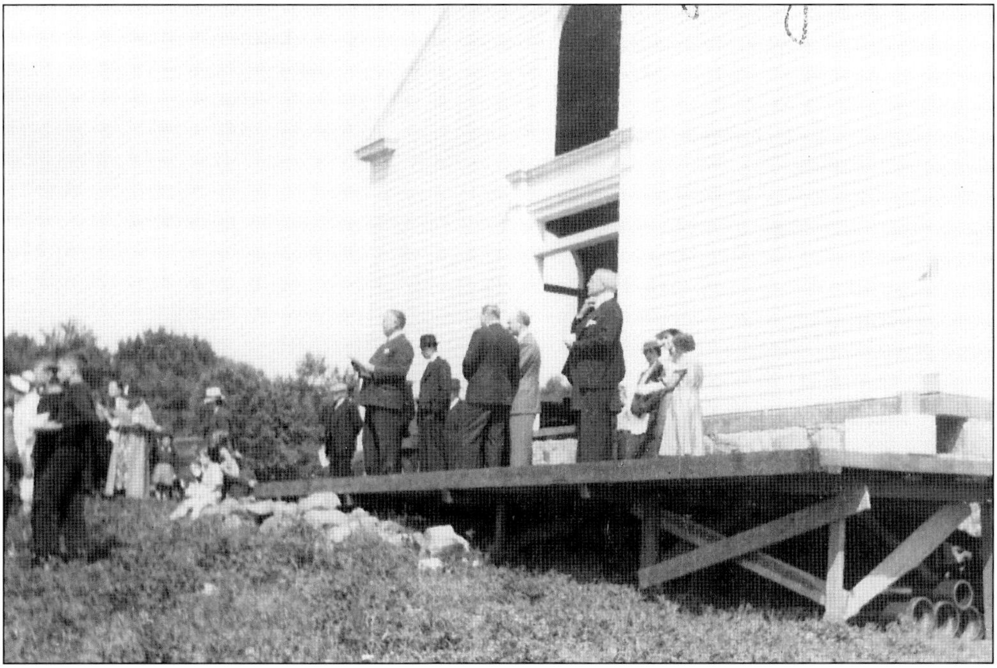

In May 1938, there was a ceremony of the laying of the cornerstone of the new Consolidated School. The one-room schoolhouses were closed and all but one was sold. On the platform are William and John Thornhill.

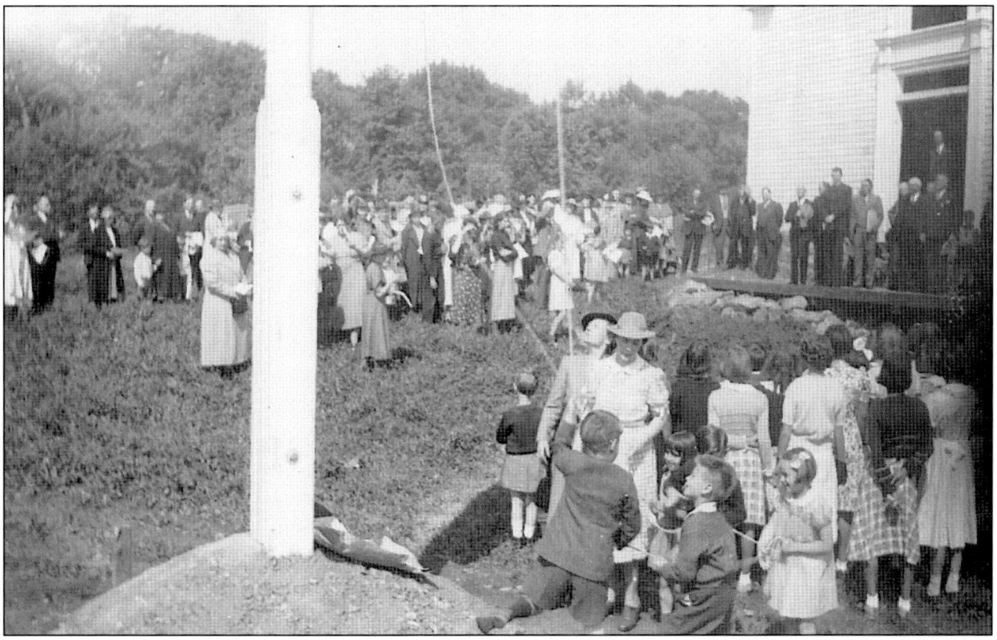

As part of this ceremony, there was the raising of the flag. A first grade student from each school was chosen to participate. Starting clockwise are Mildred Thornhill (blond with the bow in her hair) from the Obtuse School, Andrew Tomascak from Longmeadow School, George Brewer from Center School, Rita Picone from Huckleberry Hill School, Dick Hopkins from the Iron Works School, Lois Tuck (teacher), and Beatrice Wildman.

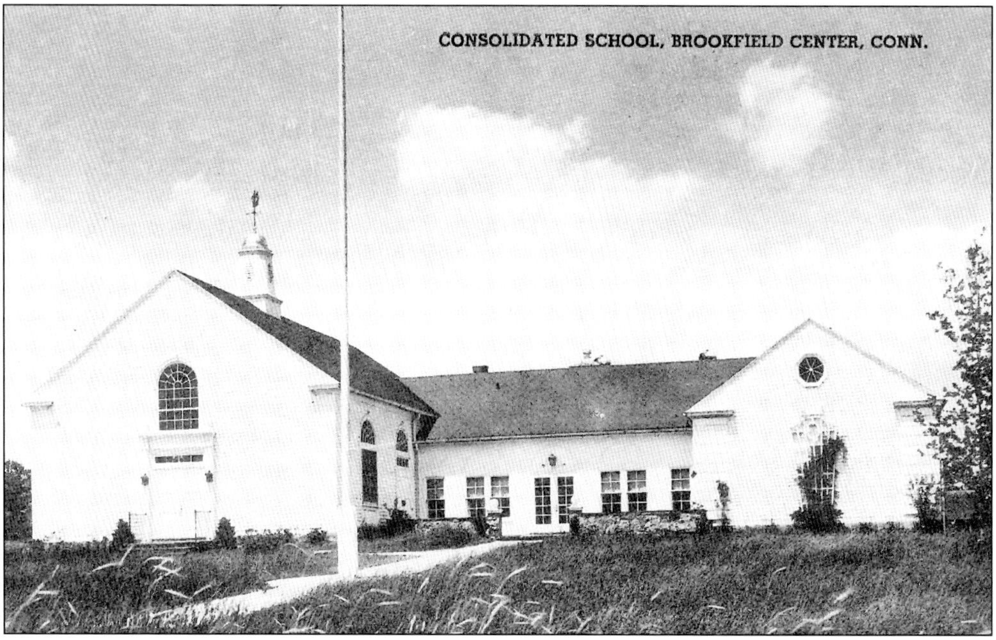

The Consolidated School was finally built in 1938. Many of the town officials didn't want to close the one-room schools. They had been educated in one-room schoolhouses, so they felt that it was good enough for their children. Each year, the vote to close it would come up but was rejected. Finally, it was agreed that a new school was needed and the proposal was passed.

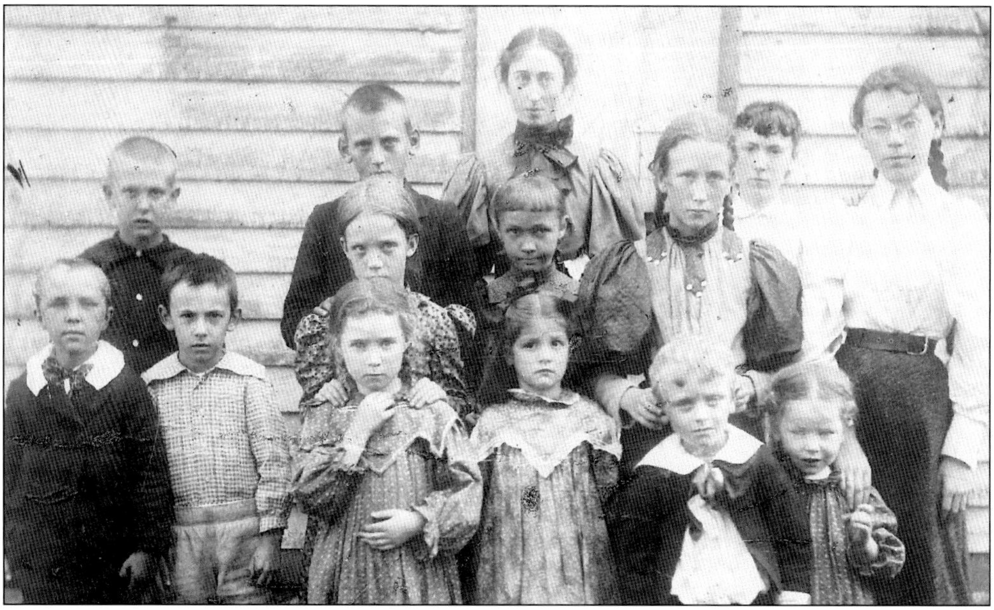

One of the other schools was South Mountain School, which in 1838 changed its name to Whortleberry Hill School. After that, it was called Huckleberry Hill School. The students in this photograph are, from left to right, as follows: (front row) C. Steinhoff, Allan Elwood, Bertha Lee, Ruth Weld, unidentified, and unidentified; (middle row) Edmund Weld, unidentified, unidentified, and Sadie Hill; (back row) William Stapleburg, Miss Florence Sagendorf (teacher), and unidentified.

The young man in the swing is Stuart Terrill. His grandmother, Elinor S. Terrill, is on the right. A friend of his grandmother's, Henrietta Ruggles, is on the left.

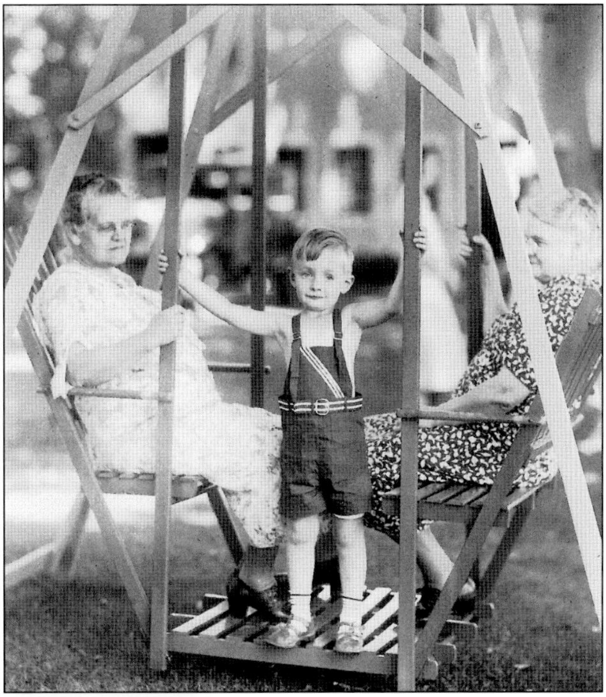

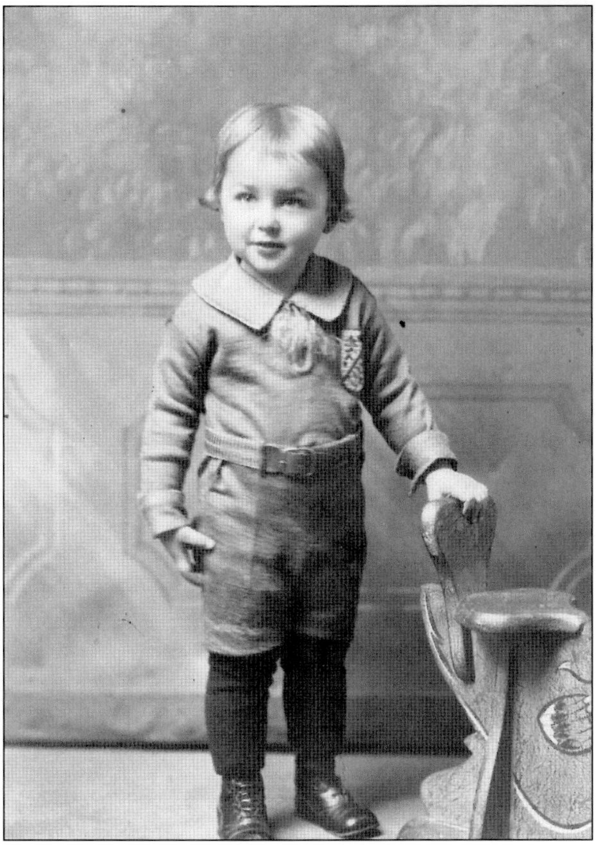

This young man is Raymond Waidelich, the son of George and Viola Waidelich. The photograph was taken on Christmas Day, 1927.

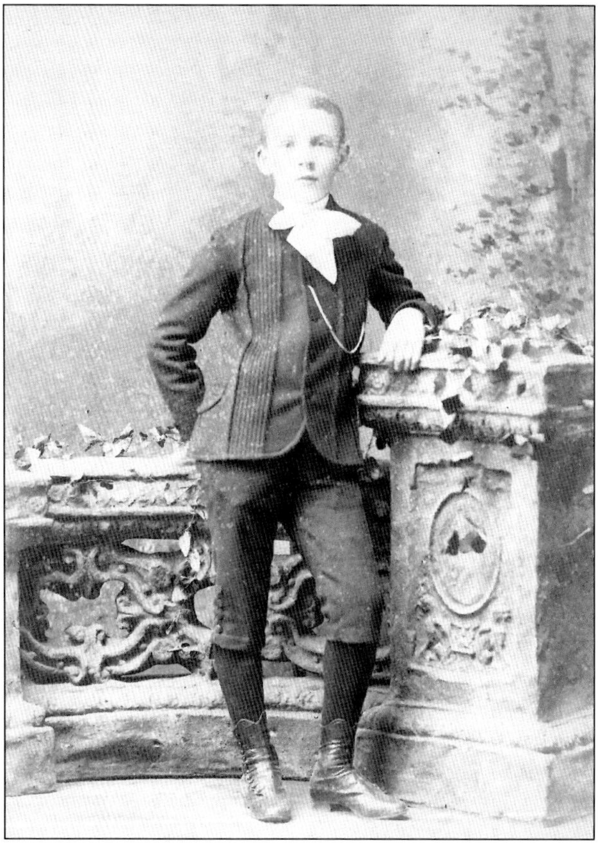

Daniel Clarke Joyce posed for his photograph at the age of 12. In his will, he left the town of Brookfield money to start a public library. The Joyce Memorial Library opened its doors in 1951 in the former town hall on Whisconier Road. Joyce was the son of Daniel D. and Sarah A. (Clarke) Joyce.

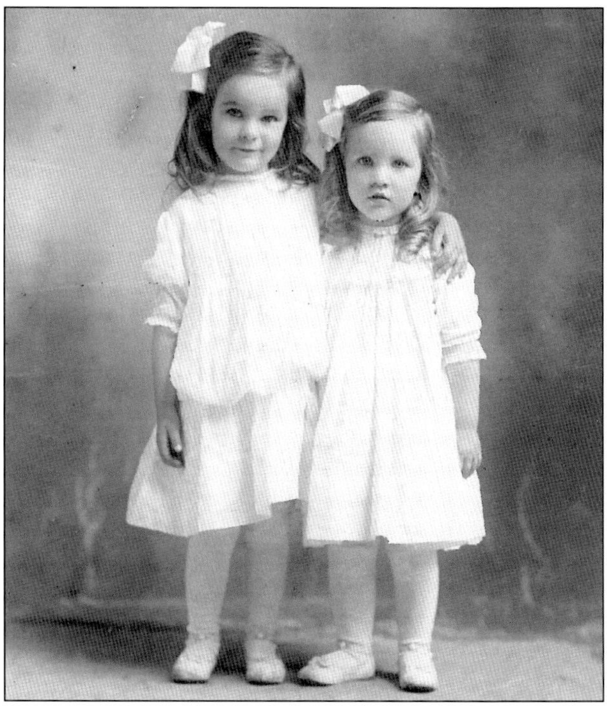

These are the daughters of Percy and Edith (Conkrite) Hawley. Lenore was born in 1903 and Aileen was born in 1904. The family lived on Iron Works Hill.

Bertha Sherwood Alaby holds her daughter, Ethel Louise Alaby. The photograph was taken in 1908. The family lived on Mountain Road.

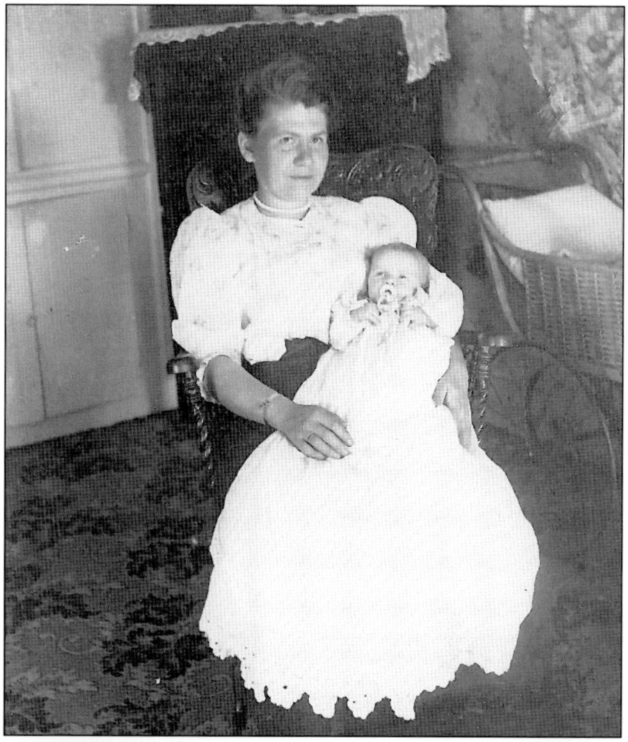

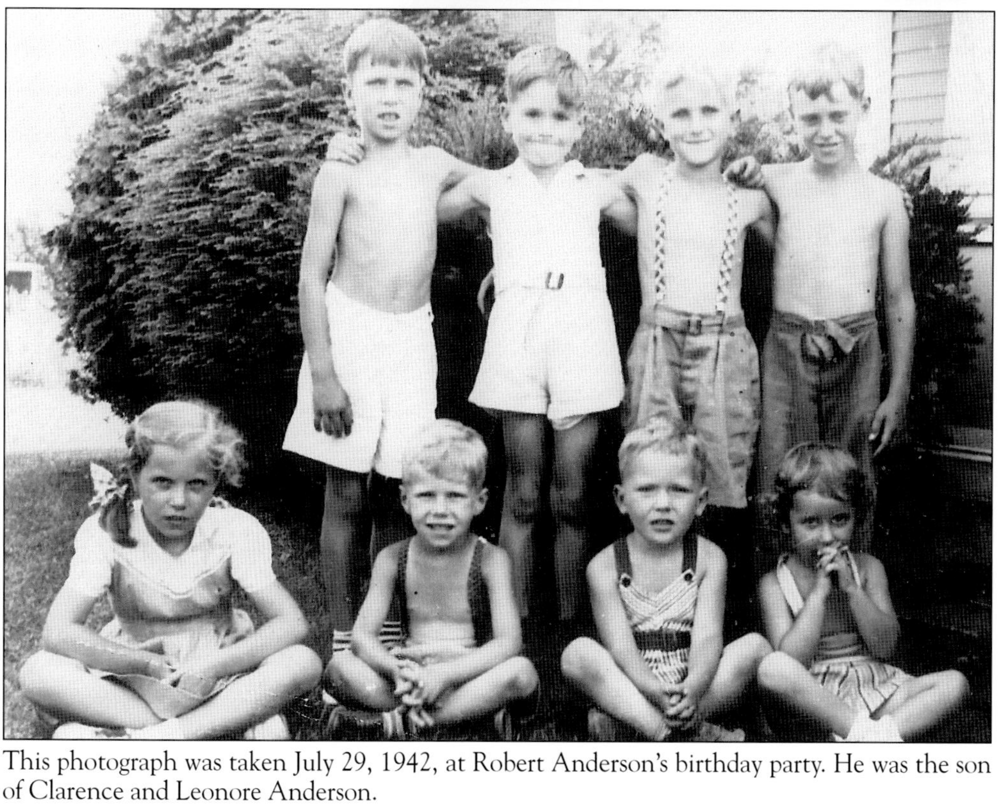

This photograph was taken July 29, 1942, at Robert Anderson's birthday party. He was the son of Clarence and Leonore Anderson.

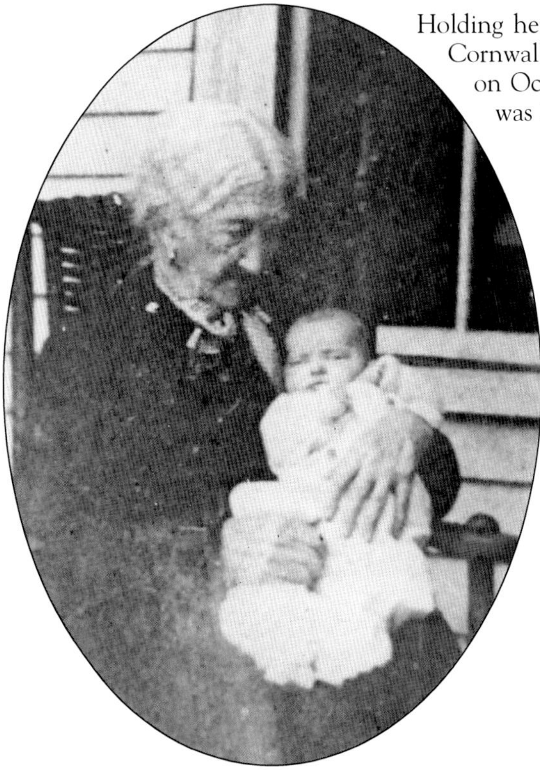

Holding her great granddaughter is Mary (Northrop) Cornwall at the age of 89. The photograph was taken on October 10, 1913. Sallie Campbell Cornwall was 10 weeks old.

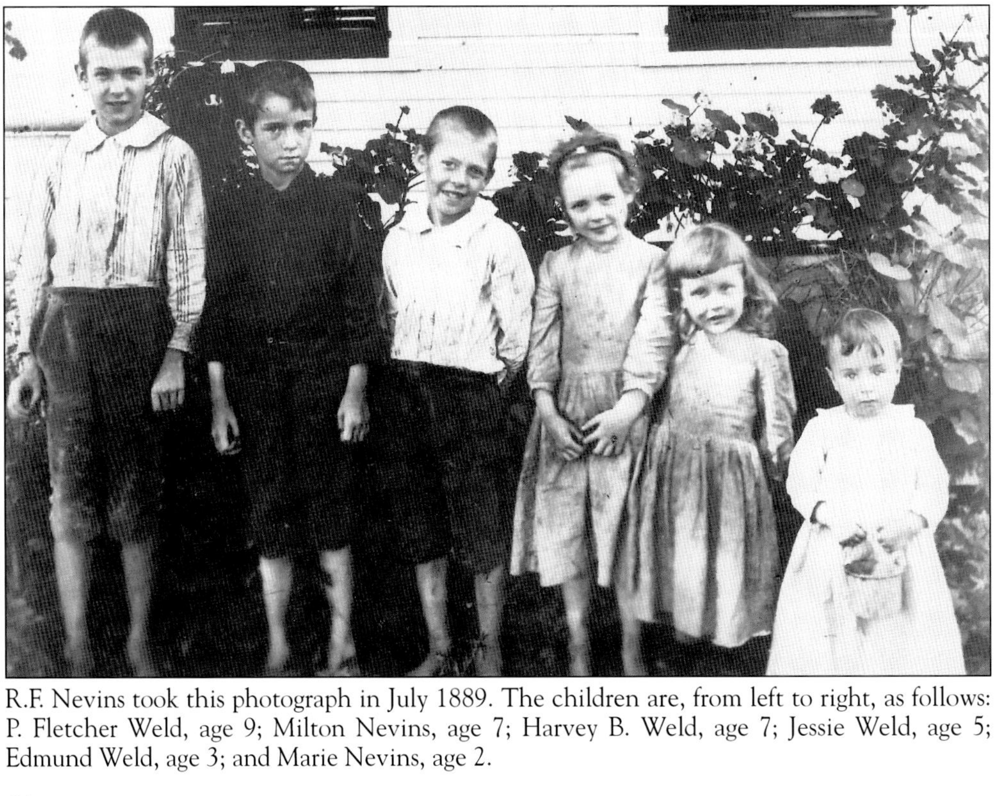

R.F. Nevins took this photograph in July 1889. The children are, from left to right, as follows: P. Fletcher Weld, age 9; Milton Nevins, age 7; Harvey B. Weld, age 7; Jessie Weld, age 5; Edmund Weld, age 3; and Marie Nevins, age 2.

This photograph was taken in 1863 at St. Paul's School for Boys. Many of the boys' schools allowed girls to attend as day students. Shown in this photograph are Angie Kellogg of New Fairfield, Sarah Hazen of Bridgeport, and Eunice Giddings of New Milford. Other students were Fanny Noble, Florie Williams, Addie M. Peck, Sophia E. Beers, Lizzie A. Barnes, Lizzie Joyce, and L.A. Baines, all from Brookfield.

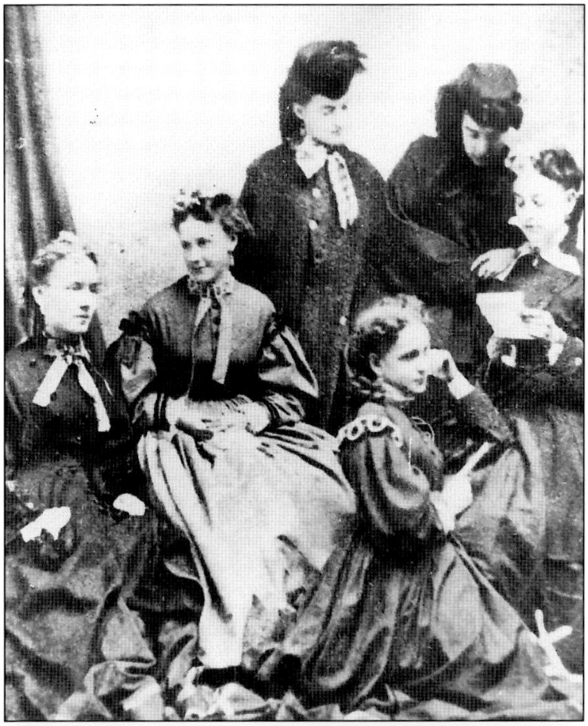

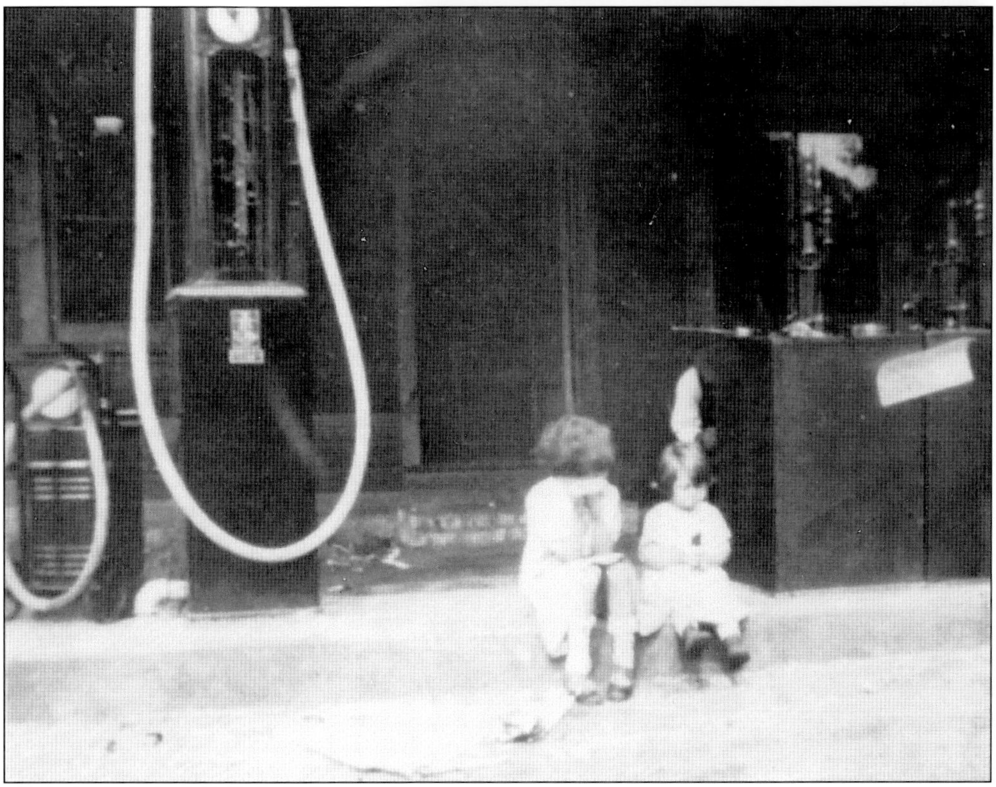

Sitting in front of their parents' gas station are Louise and Jeanette Gruet.

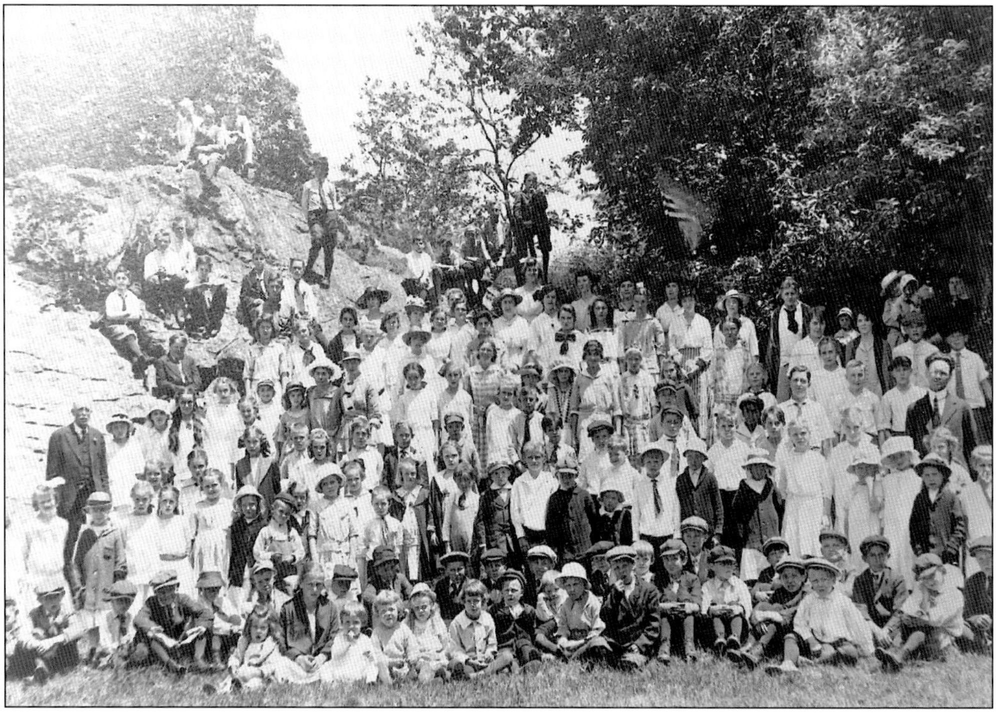

This is a 1916 view of a picnic attended by the Sunday school class of the Congregational Church of Brookfield. The picnic was held at Curtis Grove, a part of the Curtis School for Boys. Fred Curtis is on the left in the third row. He is wearing a suit and has white hair. The parking lot for the Brookfield Library is next to these rocks.

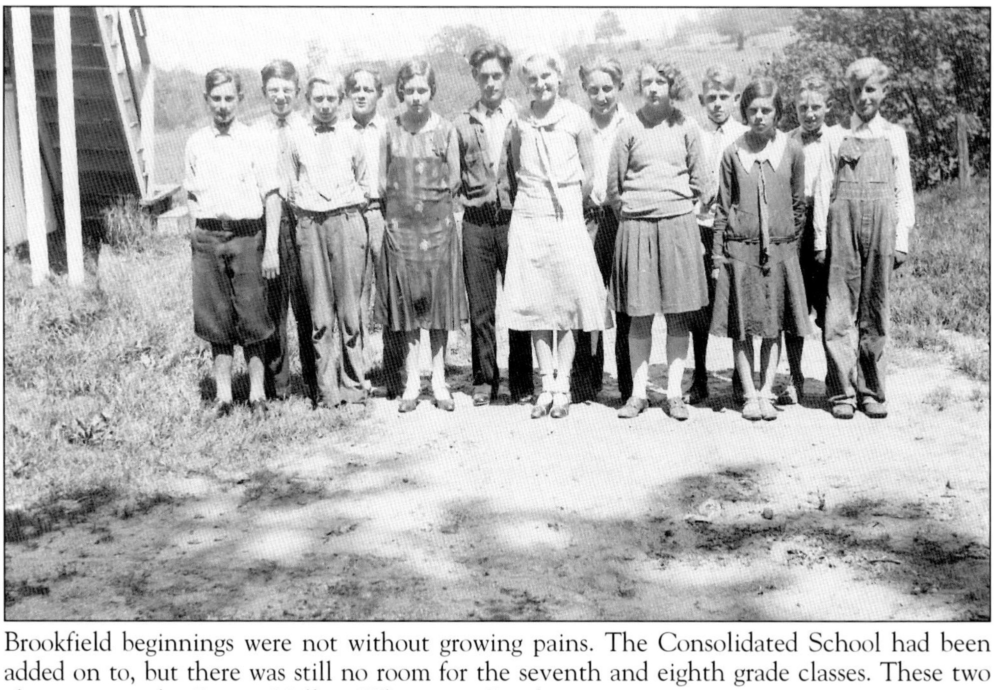

Brookfield beginnings were not without growing pains. The Consolidated School had been added on to, but there was still no room for the seventh and eighth grade classes. These two classes met at the Grange Hall on Whisconier Road.

Five

Candlewood Lake

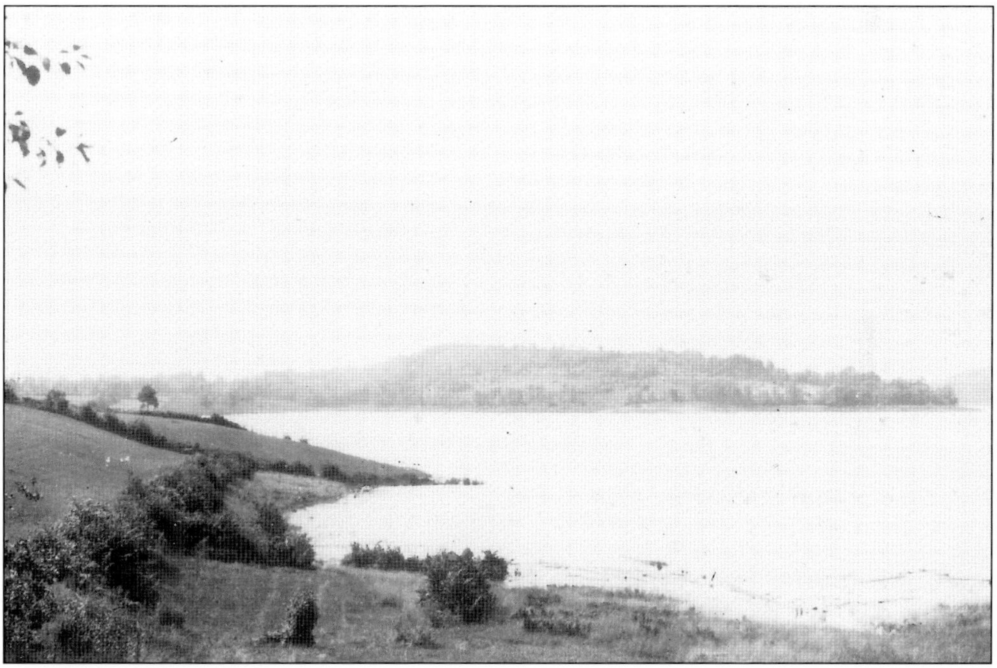

In 1926, the Connecticut Light and Power Company began their plans for a pumped storage facility in the area, the first of its kind in the United States. They began by obtaining public domain over the area. It took 26 months to complete the project. Candlewood Lake, at 11 miles in length, is the largest man-made lake in Connecticut. Brookfield, Danbury, New Milford, New Fairfield, and Sherman all have land on the lake. This photograph was taken while the lake was filling. In the water are some of the trees that were cut down to make way for the lake. The view is looking south from Kellogg Street. The hill on the left would later become Candlewood Orchards and the hill in the distance would become Hawthorne Terrace.

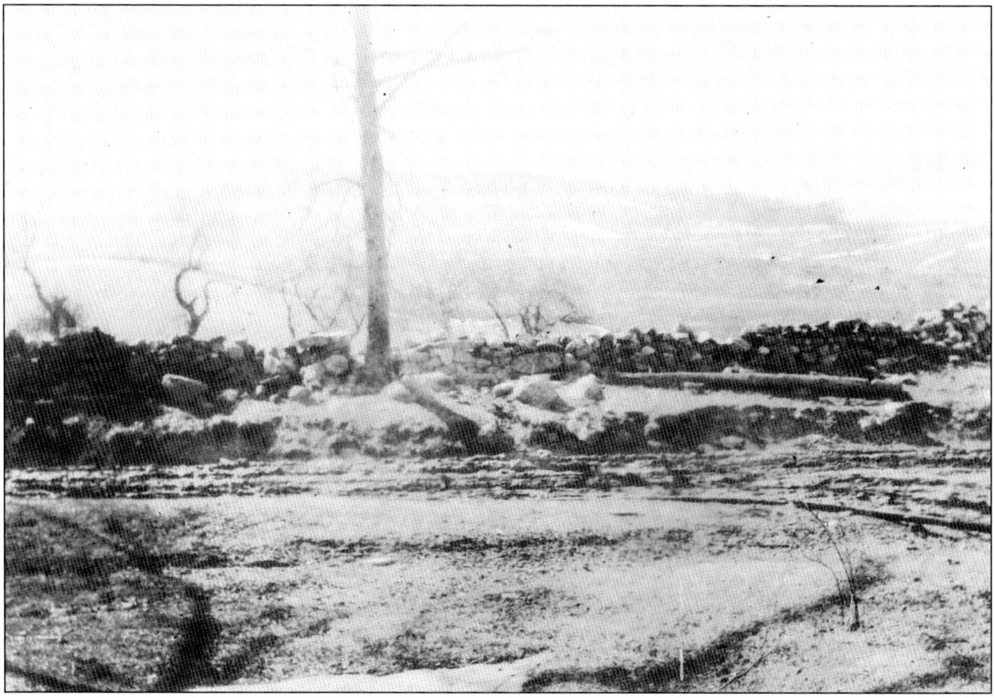

This is a view of the area that became part of the lake. Arrowhead Point is on the right and Pocono Point and Cedar Heights are in the distance.

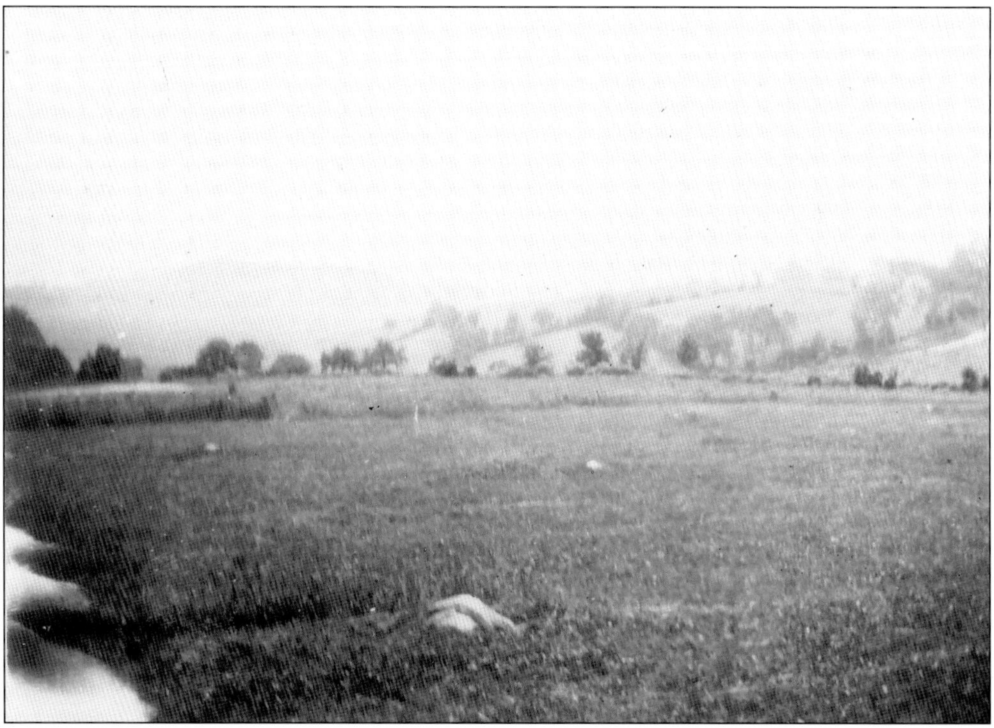

Arrowhead Point (right) is visible in this pre-flood view taken looking south from Hickory Hill. Forty-five thousand acres were flooded.

Mildred Martini is standing on the bridge over Neversink Pond. This photograph was taken in 1922. The bridge is now under the lake.

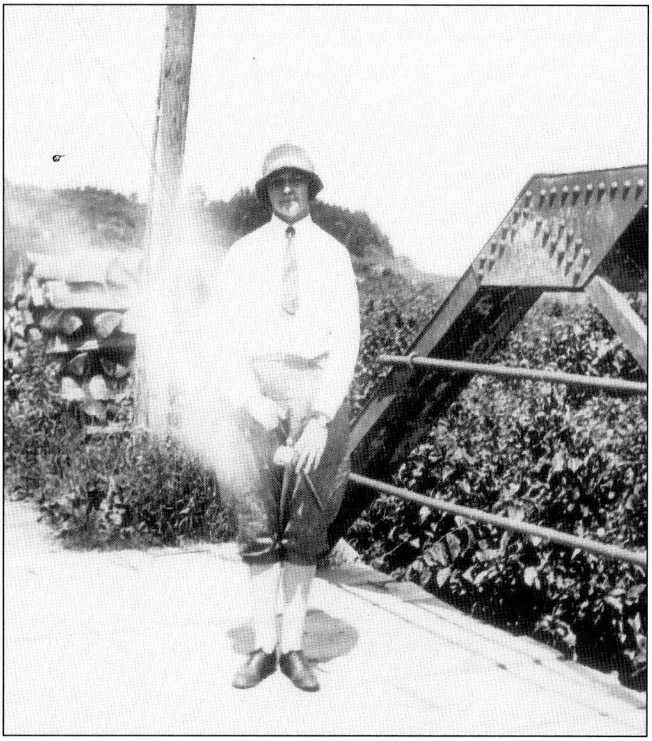

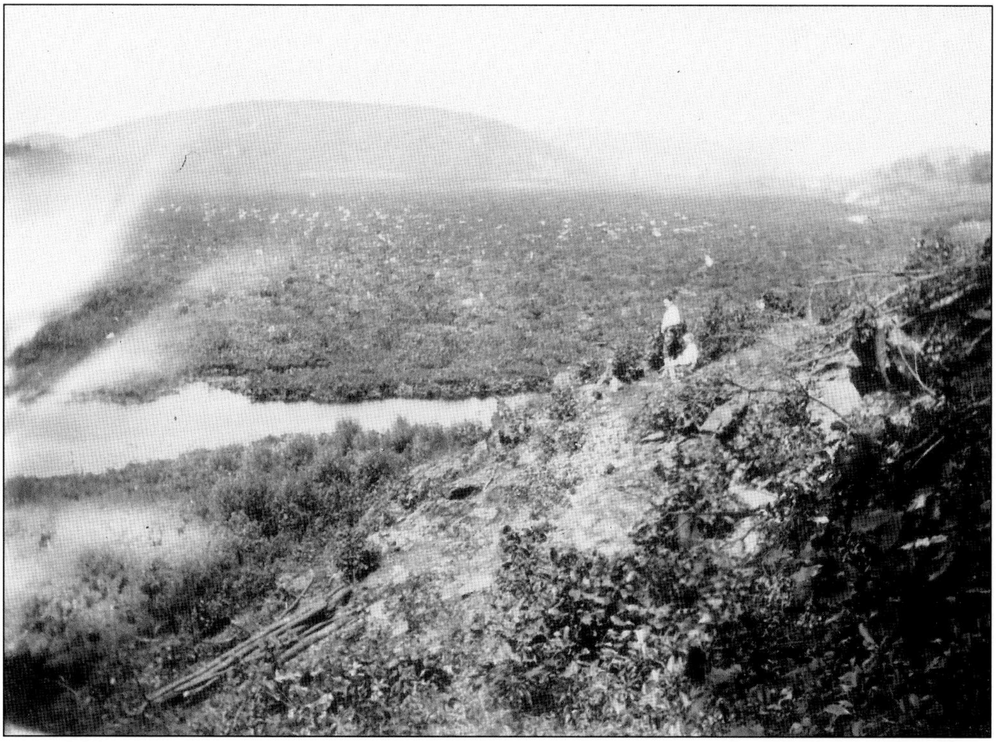

There were five ponds that made up Candlewood Lake. Neversink Pond is shown here. This area is said to be 50 to 60 feet deep and is the deepest spot in the lake.

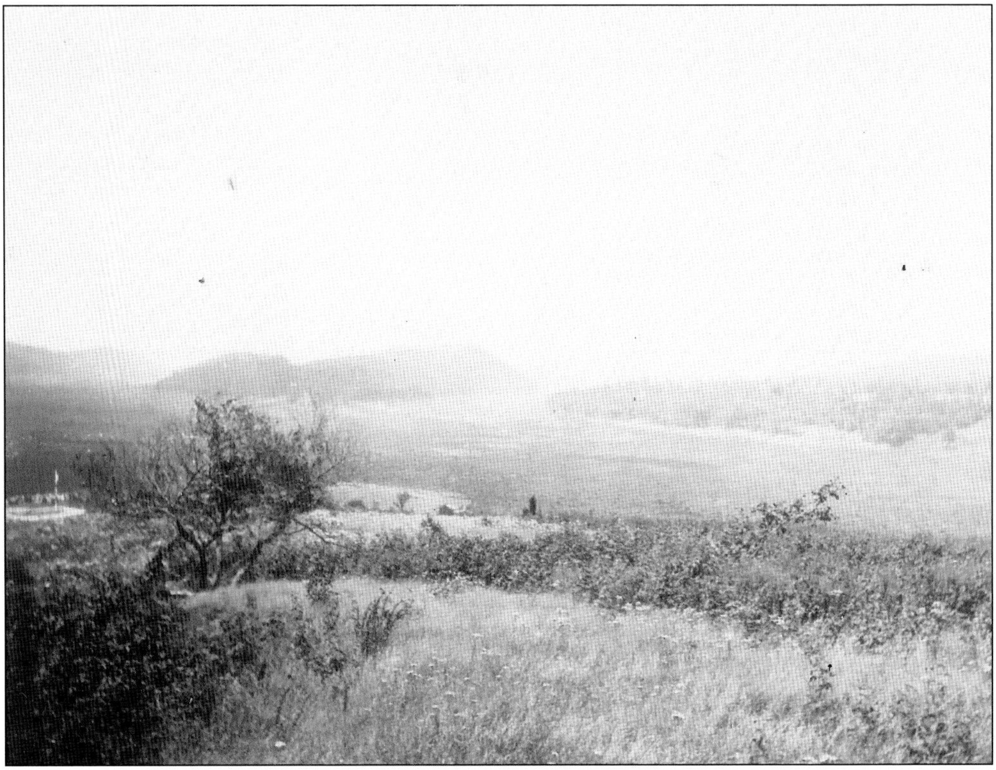

This is the area that was called Hatch's Point before it became known as Candlewood Lake. It is now called Candlewood Shores. The mountain due north is Candlewood Mountain and Vaughns Neck. The hill on the right is presently used by Candlewood Lake Club.

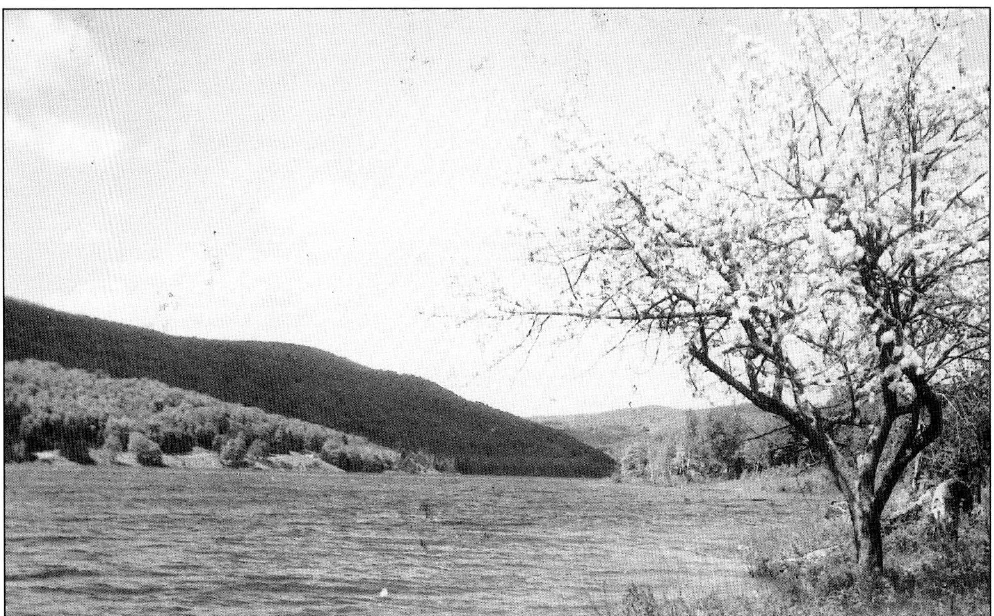

This view looking north was taken from Hatch's Point after the area was flooded.

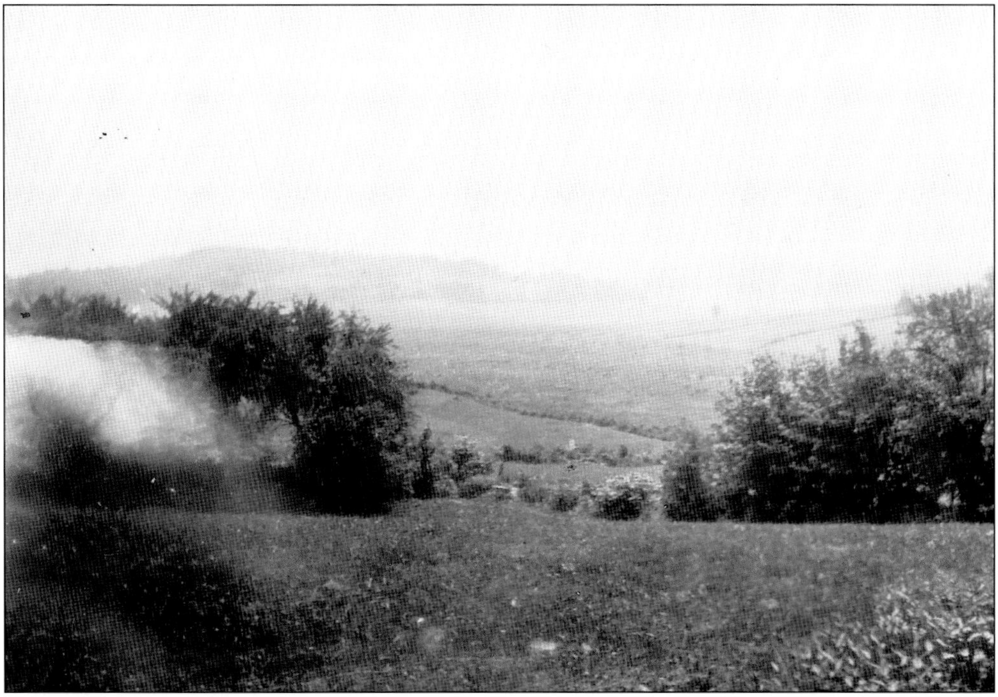

This view is looking west over the area that was flooded to form Candlewood Lake. Before the area was flooded, farmhouses, stone walls, barns, orchards, bridges, a cemetery, and farms were located here. Some of the remains (now under water) can still be seen when scuba diving. The majority of the bodies in the cemeteries were removed to cemeteries in New Fairfield and Brookfield, but some families chose not to move their loved one's remains to another cemetery.

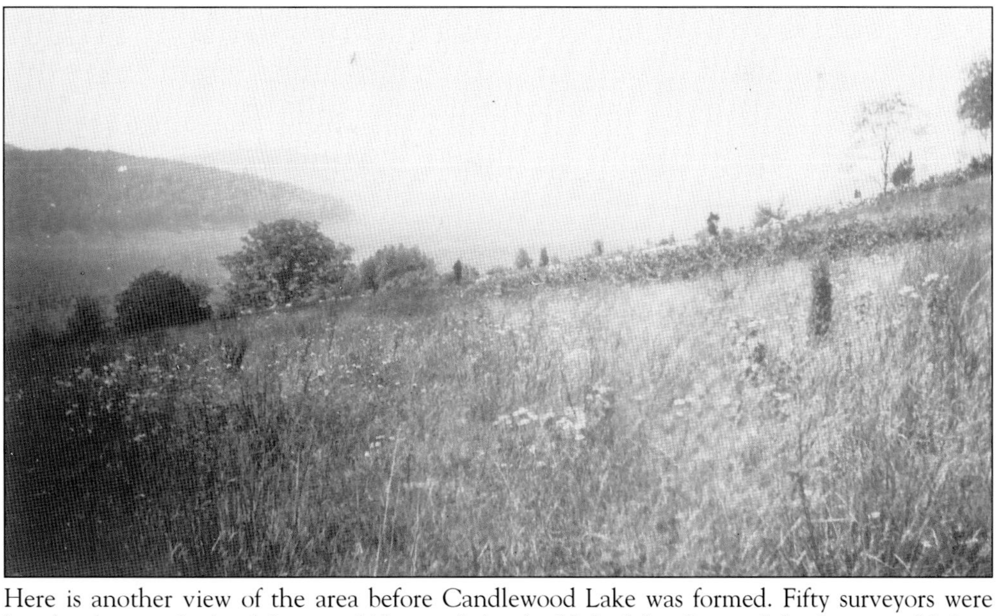

Here is another view of the area before Candlewood Lake was formed. Fifty surveyors were hired to lay out the land that would be needed to build the lake. Some of the farmers sold their land for very little money—$2,356 for 53 acres and $100 for 3 acres. Other landowners traded land with the power company and ended up with lake-front property.

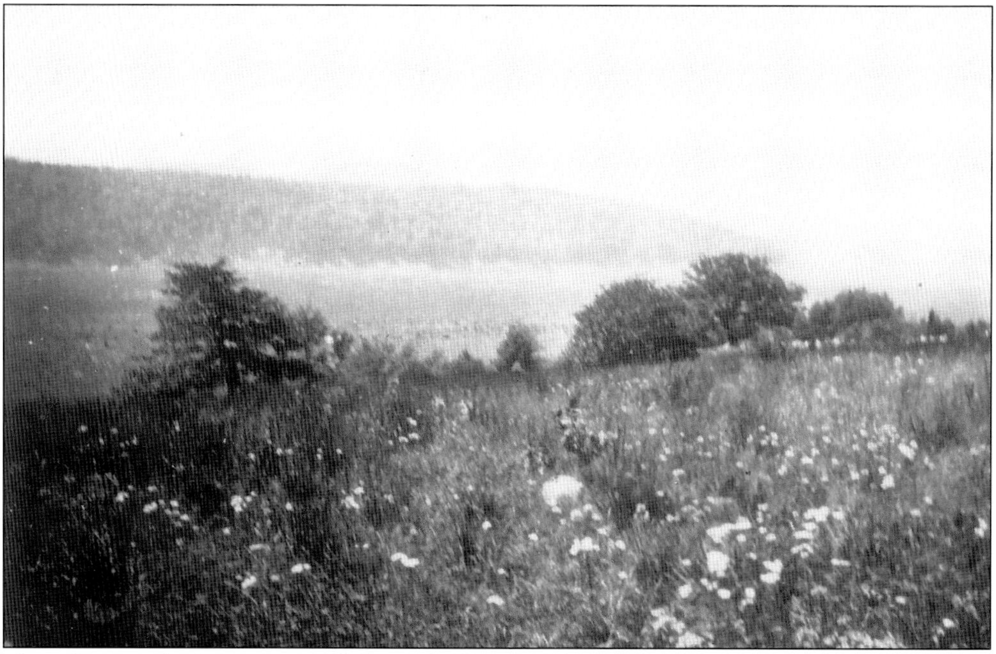

This photograph shows more of the area that would be filled for Candlewood Lake. About 1,400 men were hired to help create the lake. Connecticut Light & Power brought in about 500 men from Canada and Maine to work on the project. The trees and brush were burned in massive bonfires.

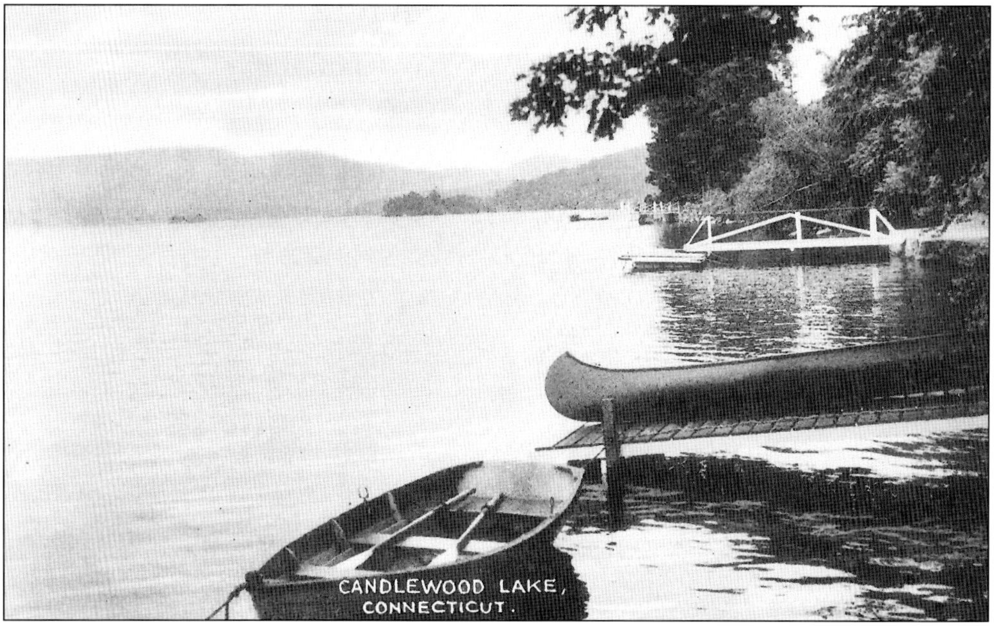

A name for the lake became a problem. Many people wanted to call it Lake Danbury. Others argued that it needed a name that would be identified by the area. It was finally decided to name the lake in honor of the candlewood trees that grew on the Candlewood Mountain. The name Candlewood comes from early times, when the settlers would cut down the saplings, light them, and use them as candles.

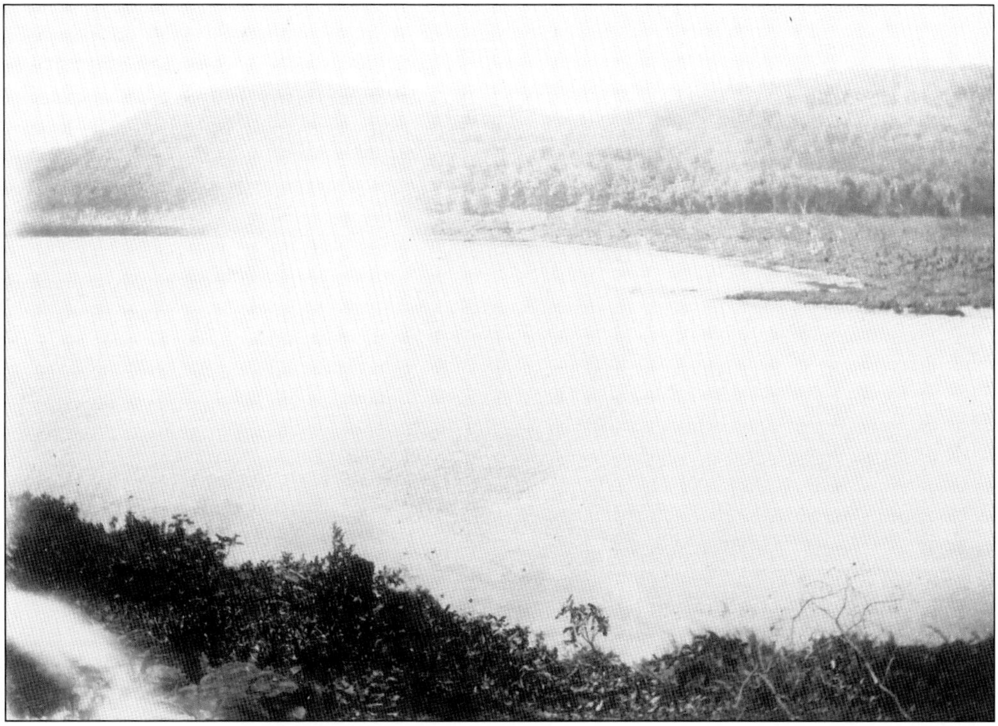

Several dams were built, with the largest being at the north end of the valley. When this dam was completed, it measured 952 feet in width and 100 feet in height. The photograph was taken looking west from Arrowhead Point. The lake is shown 75% filled.

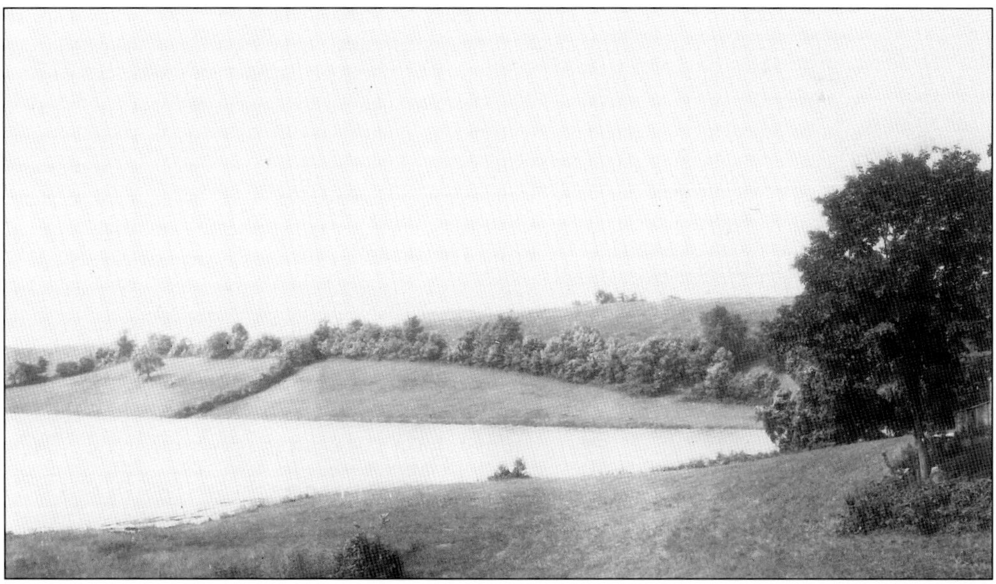

Before Candlewood Lake was created, most of the area around Kellogg Street was a part of New Fairfield. Once the valley filled, New Fairfield became a divided town. In 1961, Brookfield and New Fairfield voted to have this area annexed to Brookfield. The area includes Candlewood Shores, Arrowhead Point, Hickory Hills, Candlewood Orchards, and the Brookfield Town Park.

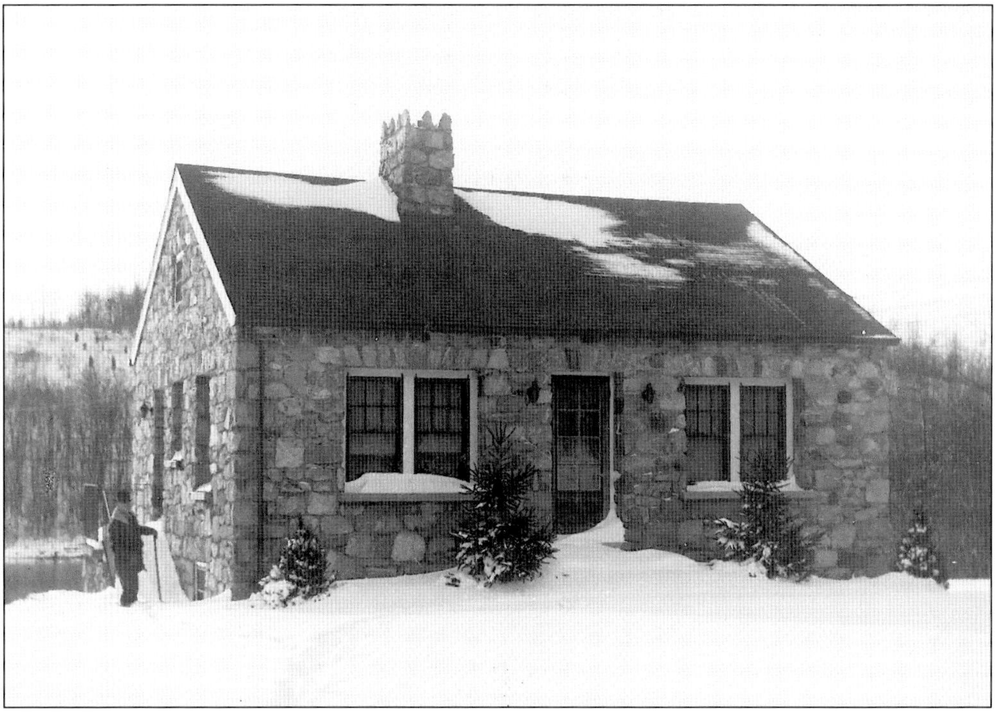

This stone house is located on Candlewood Lake Road next to the Brookfield Town Park. In the background is Candlewood Shores. Shown in this November 26, 1938 photograph is Frank Waidelich, the owner of the house.

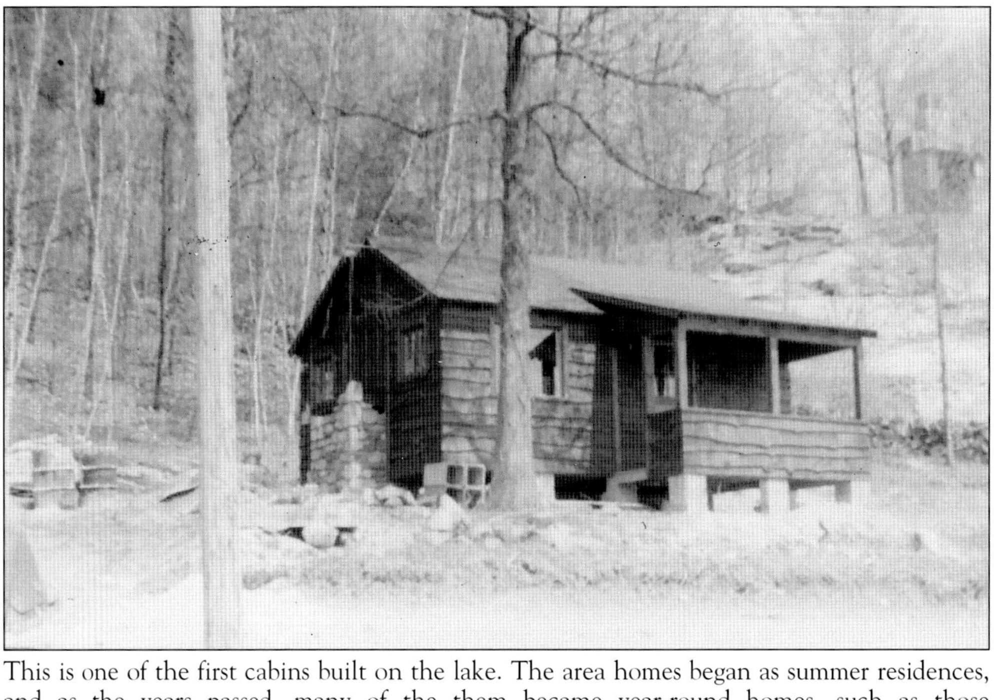

This is one of the first cabins built on the lake. The area homes began as summer residences, and as the years passed, many of the them became year-round homes, such as those in Candlewood Shores.

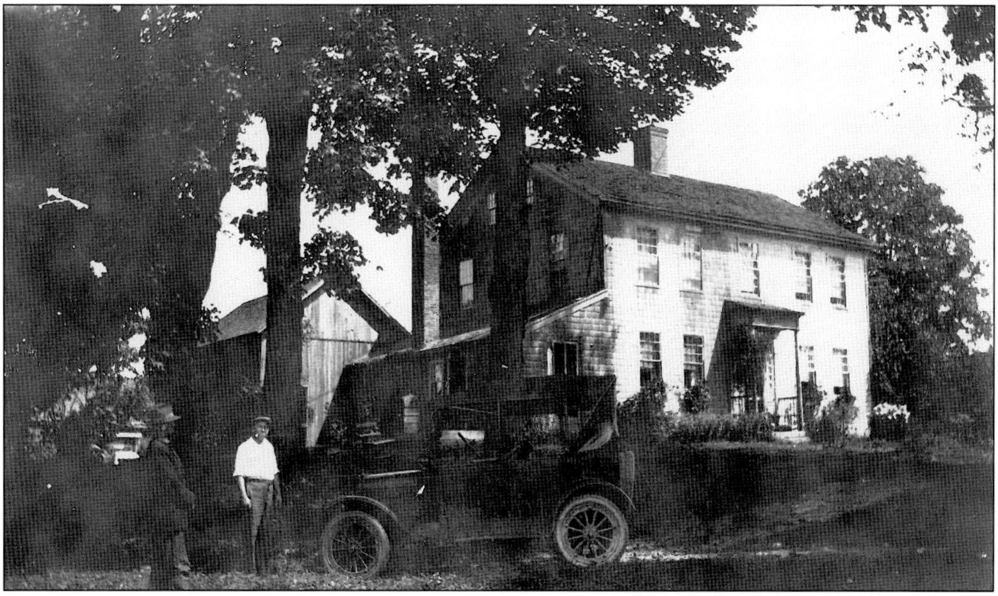

Built by Martin Kellogg in 1750, this house stayed in the Kellogg family for many years. Shown here is the Martini family, one of the many owners of the house.

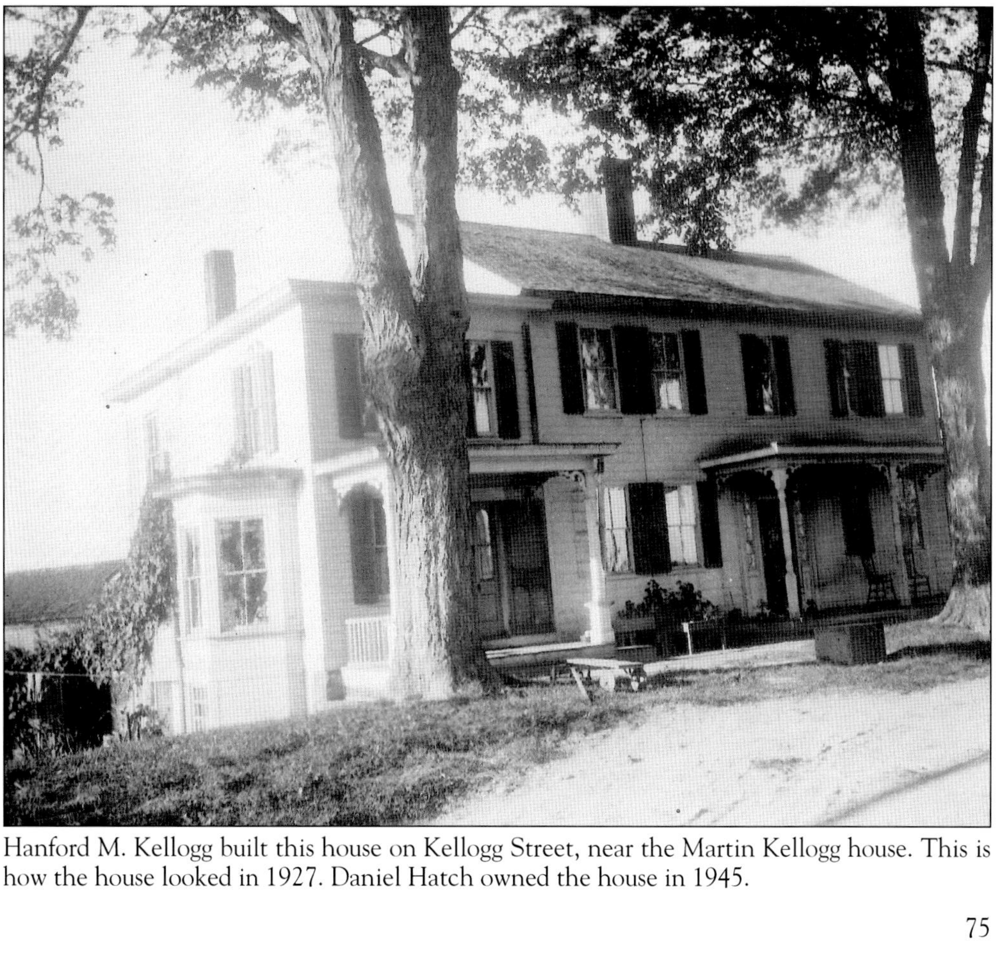

Hanford M. Kellogg built this house on Kellogg Street, near the Martin Kellogg house. This is how the house looked in 1927. Daniel Hatch owned the house in 1945.

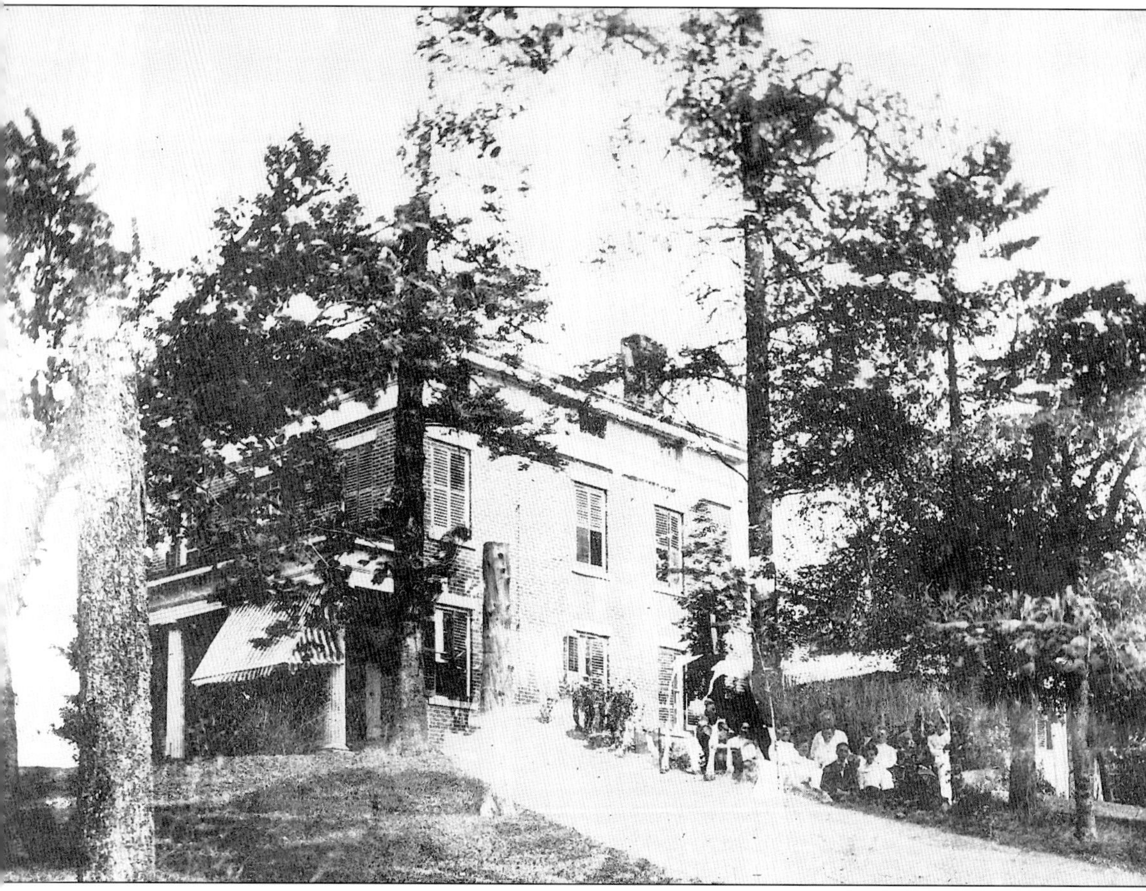

Brazillai Bulkley Kellogg built this brick house *c.* 1845. The land was originally in New Fairfield but became part of Brookfield after Candlewood Lake was formed. Kellogg owned a large farm and made bricks here. His first wife was Emeline Johnson and his second wife was Florida Merwin; both were Brookfield residents. The house was called Breezy Top because of the location at the top of Kellogg Street. The area is now called Arrowhead Point. Burton A. Bugbee restored the house when Leopald Nathans owned it. Mr. Nathans changed the name to Brick Top. When Marie Guglieri bought a small house at the top of Barrett's Hill, she named her new home Breezy Top, after the Kellogg house.

Six

PRIVATE SCHOOLS

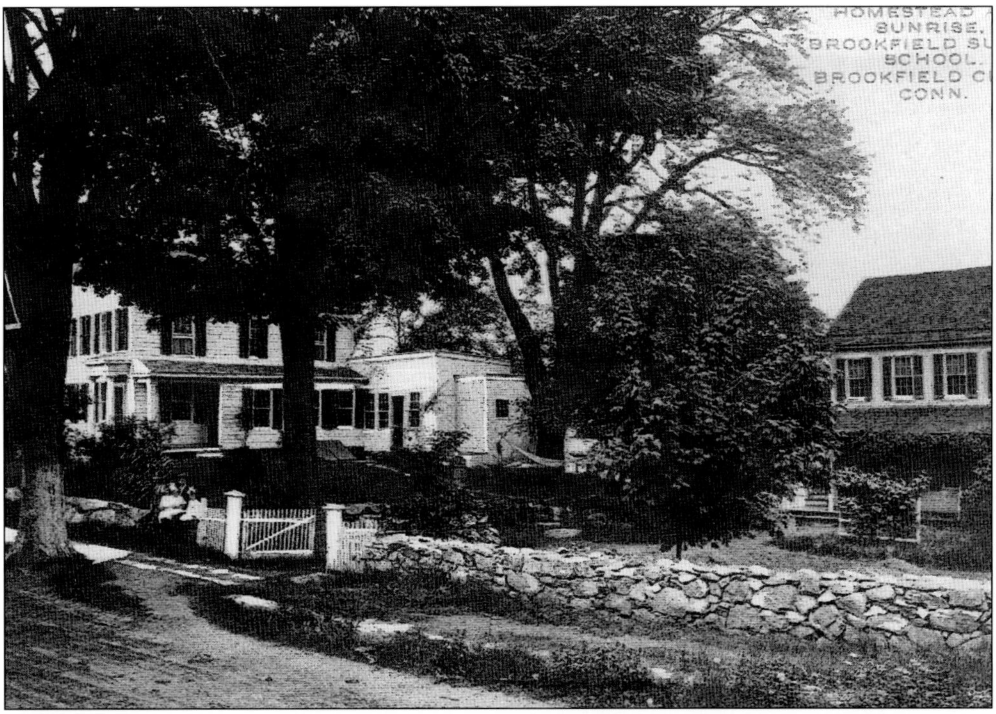

Herbert Wilber Greene founded the Brookfield Summer School of Singing in 1900. The school closed when he died in 1924. The focus of the school was to enhance the pupils' performances in music. This was accomplished by private lessons, lectures, performance, and study in voice and piano. The school consisted of eight buildings. Two of the buildings that made up the school were the Homestead (on the left) and Sunrise, which contained the dining hall. When "The Group Theater" stayed here, they used Sunrise as a rehearsal and performance hall. The school was also called the Greene School of Music.

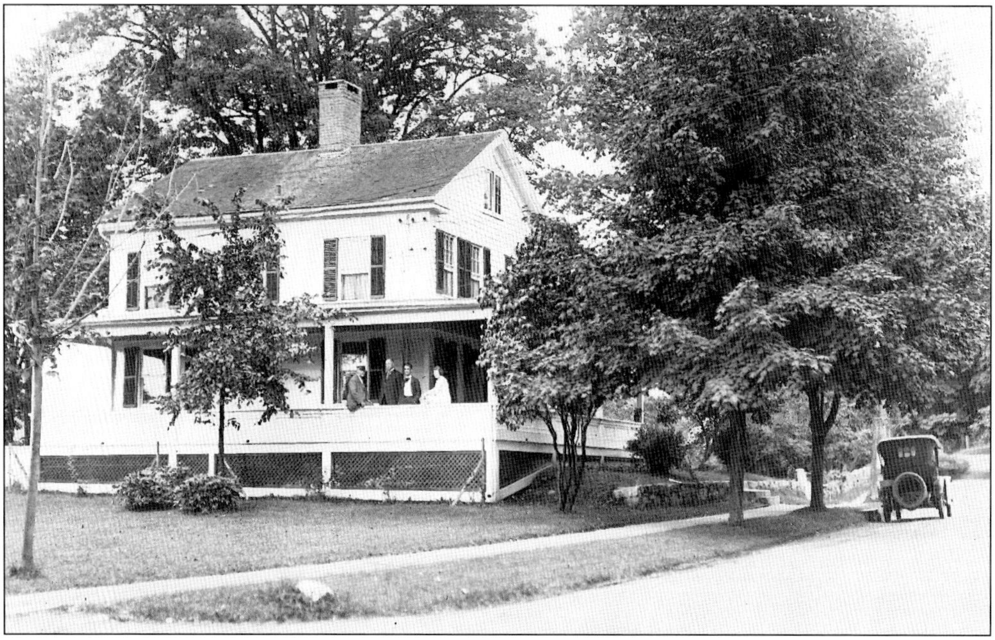

The Homestead was the residence of Professor Herbert and Mrs. Greene. The house was built as the first parsonage of the Congregational church. After the school closed, it became the Hillside Brook Inn. In the summer of 1931, "The Group Theater" stayed at the inn. The "Group" met to enhance their acting skills. Some of the actors in the group were Clifford Odets, Elia Kazan, Stella Adler, and John Garfield.

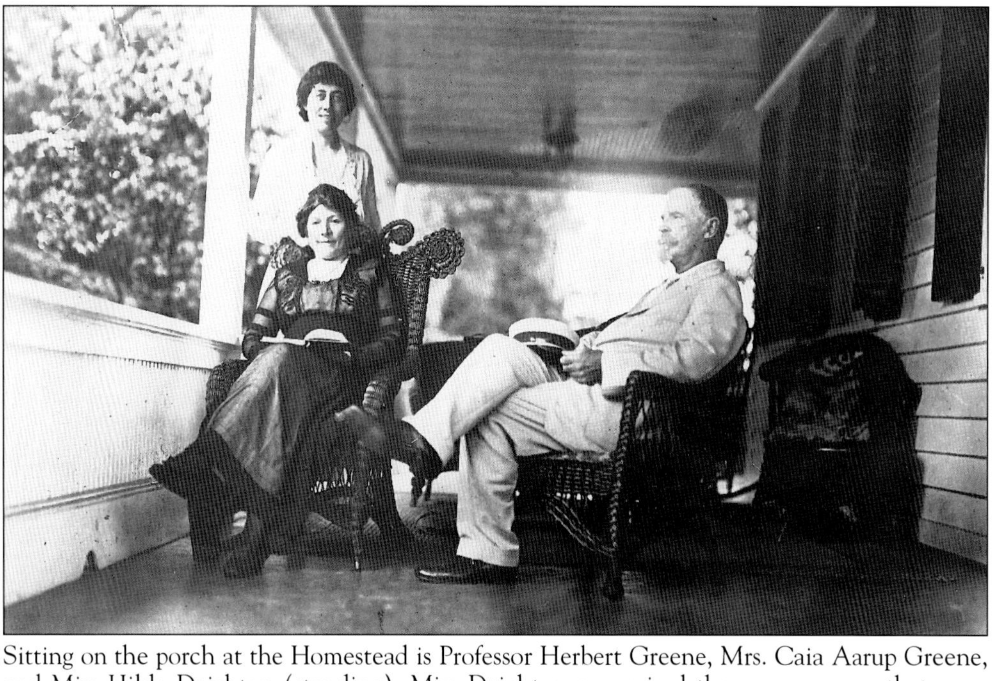

Sitting on the porch at the Homestead is Professor Herbert Greene, Mrs. Caia Aarup Greene, and Miss Hilda Deighton (standing). Miss Deighton supervised the many operas that were performed by the students. The Homestead later became the home of Constantine Fabian, who invented a way to make hats without using mercury.

The Farm, another one of the buildings used in the music school, contained the secretary's office and a sitting room.

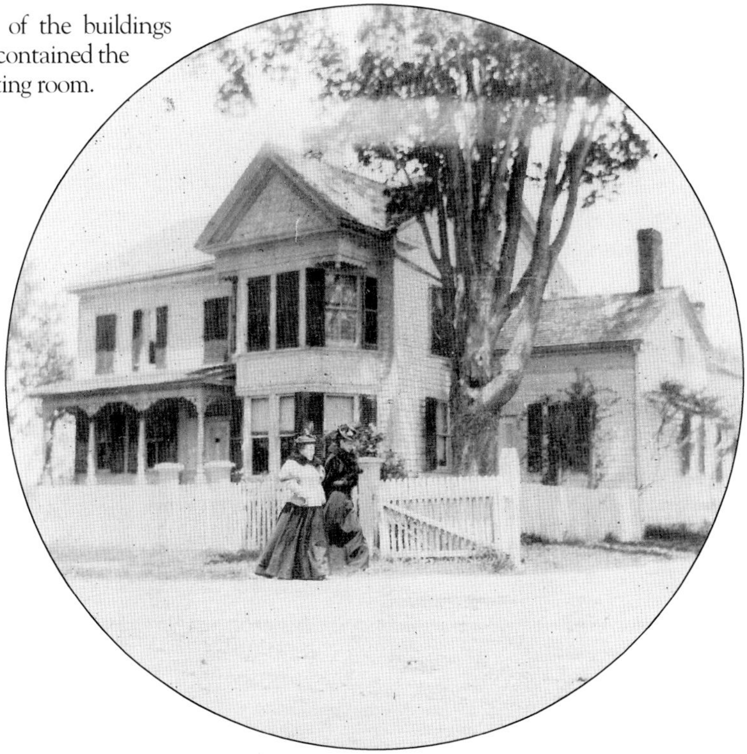

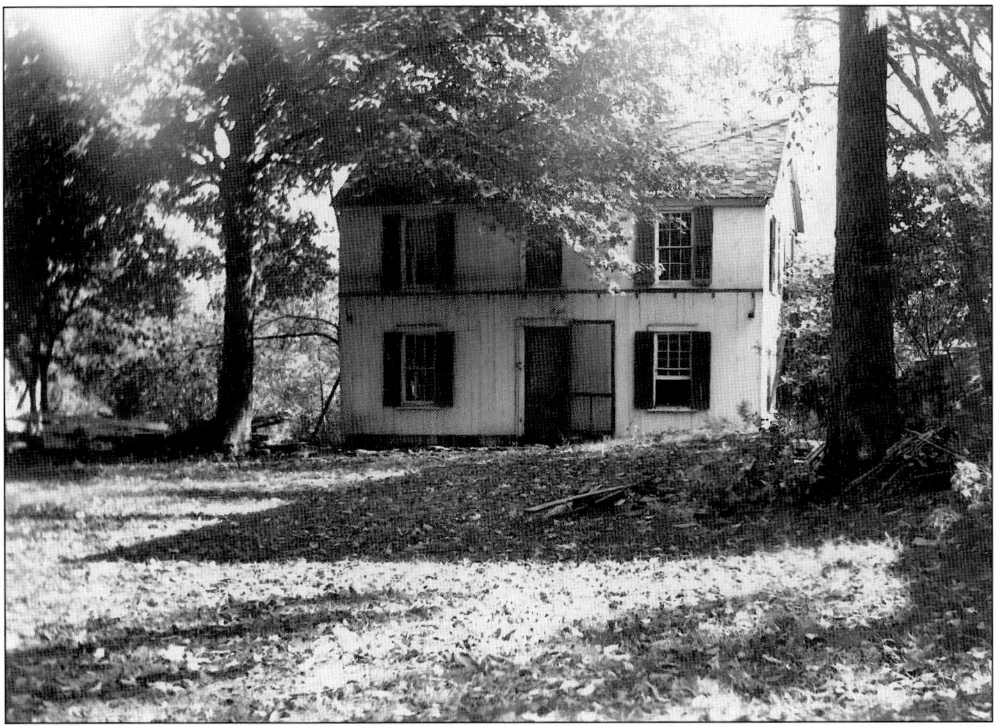

This building was called the Wigwam. It has since been taken down. Besides the many buildings, there was a swimming hole and Echo Rock, which produced a perfect echo.

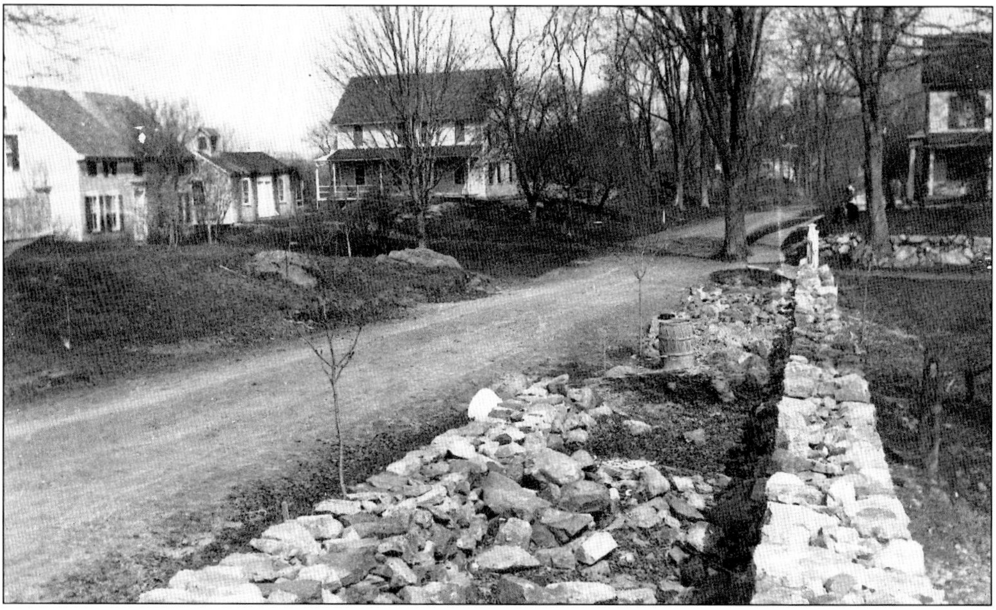

The building in the forefront was called Backlog and the rooms were used as a place for recreation. The small building next to it was the first opera house. The next building was originally built as a barn c. 1870. The barn was eventually turned into a summer dormitory and reading room for the students. The school buildings were located on both sides of Whisconier Road. John Lee built the stone wall.

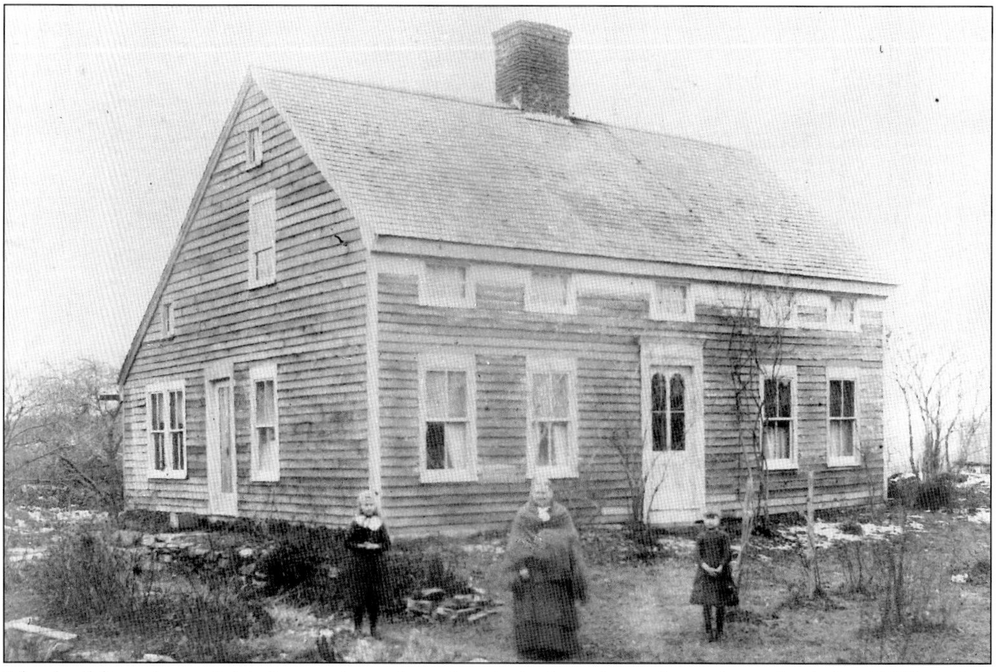

The building date of this house is unclear, but it is thought to have been built by 1730. It has had many names over the years, including Backlog, Appleyard, and Sunclad Acres. Besides being a private home, it was part of the Greene School of Music. The name Backlog comes from a large log that is in the back of a large fireplace.

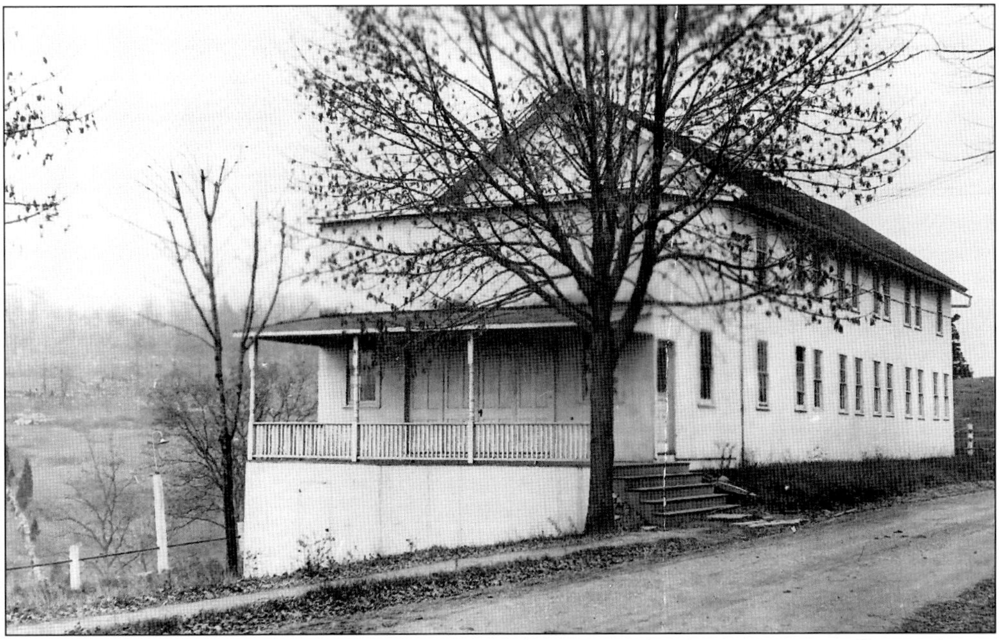

Hillcrest Hall was the second opera house for the music school. It was originally a tobacco barn. This building has had many uses over the years. Besides being a barn and opera house, the Pocono Grange called this building home. At one time, the volunteer fire company, post office, and seventh and eighth grades used this building. It eventually became an apartment building on Whisconier Road.

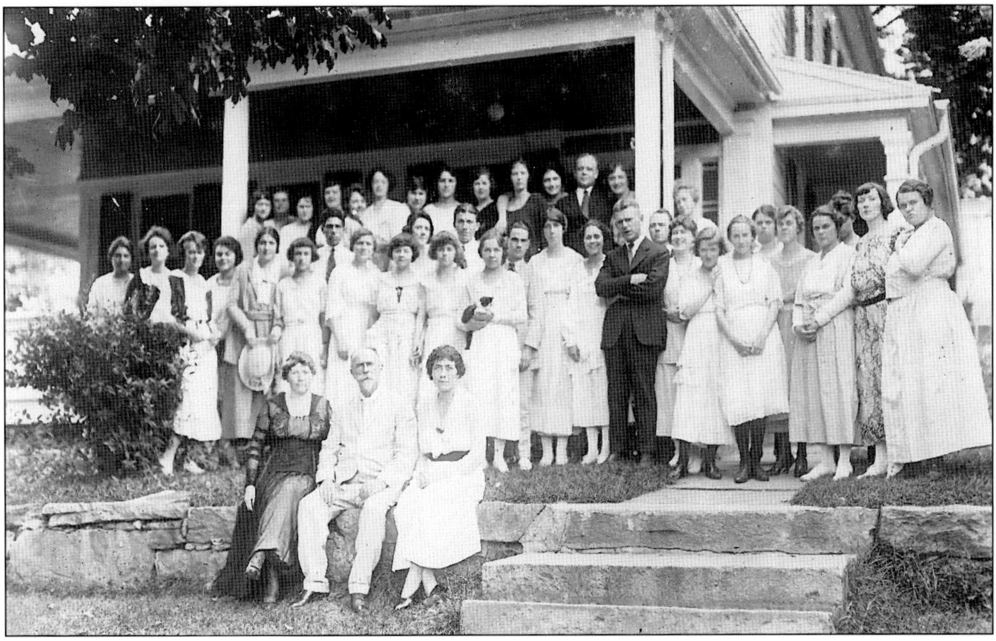

Sitting on the stone wall is Caia Aarup Greene, Herbert W. Greene, and Hilda Deighton (right). Standing in back are the students from the school. These students were in the choirs for both the Congregational church and the Episcopal church. They also performed such operas as *Faust*, *Hansel and Gretel*, *Carmen*, *Madame Butterfly*, and *Rigoletto*.

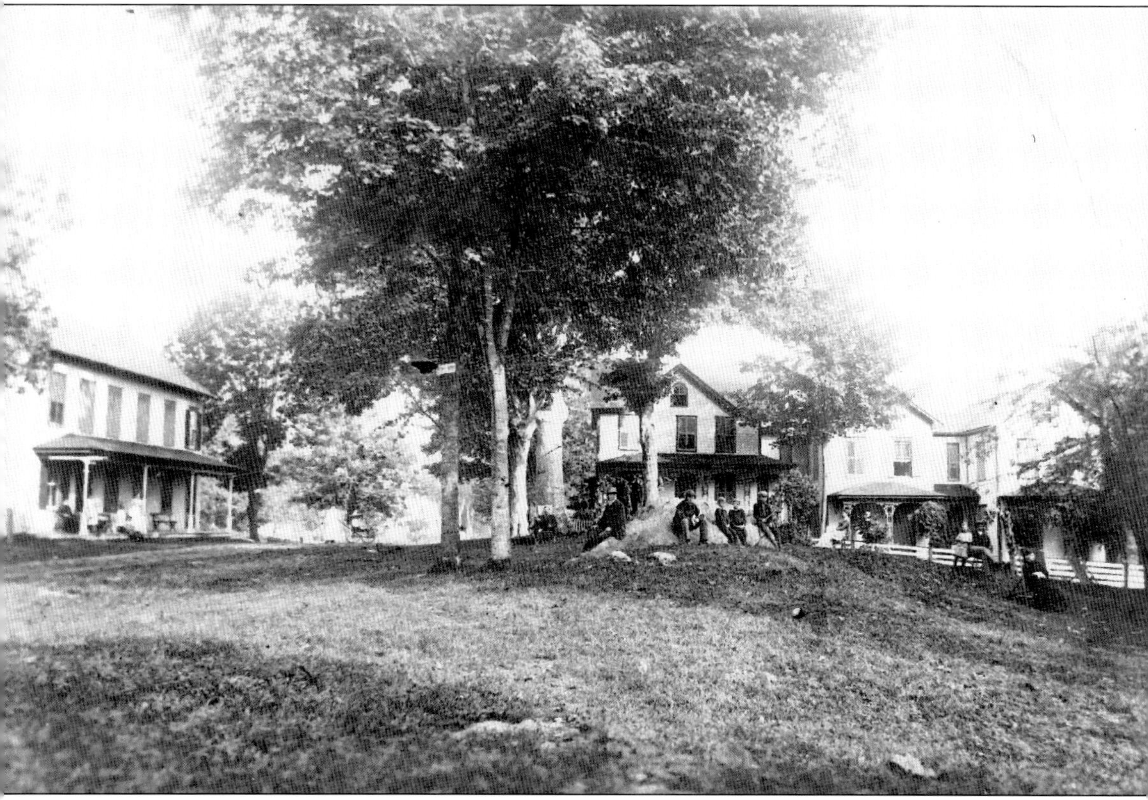

Frederick S. and Ida Curtis founded the Curtis School for Boys in Bethlehem, Connecticut, in 1875. In 1883, Professor Curtis moved the school to Longmeadow Hill in Brookfield. Three years later, he purchased the Goodsell estate and moved the school to Whisconier Road. Professor Curtis and his wife ran the school until the late 1920s, when his son Gerald and Gerald's wife, Martha, took over. The school was called a sub-preparatory school for boys aged 9 to 13. Classes consisted of correspondence, Latin, French, English history, reading, writing, German, geography, finance, U.S. history, oral spelling, ancient history, and the building of good moral character.

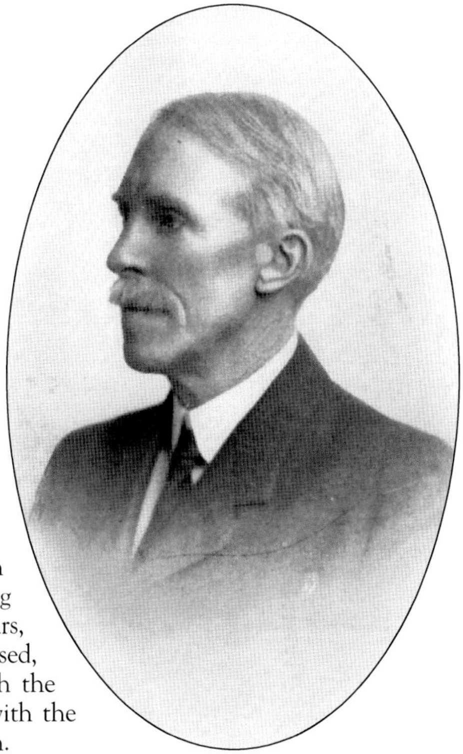

Frederick Smillie Curtis was the founder of the Curtis School for Boys. He was born February 8, 1850, in Stratford, Connecticut, to Calvin and Elizabeth Wicks Curtis. After graduating from Yale University, he taught at Westchester Normal School and Swarthmore College. He married Ida J. Whiting and they had three children: Chloe, Gerald, and Lawrence. Fred died on February 9, 1930.

The school building for the Curtis School is on the left in the photograph below. The large building was the dormitory for the school. Over the years, the dormitory was enlarged. After the school closed, it became an inn. Whisconier Road went through the property before Professor Curtis exchanged land with the town and the road was moved to its present location.

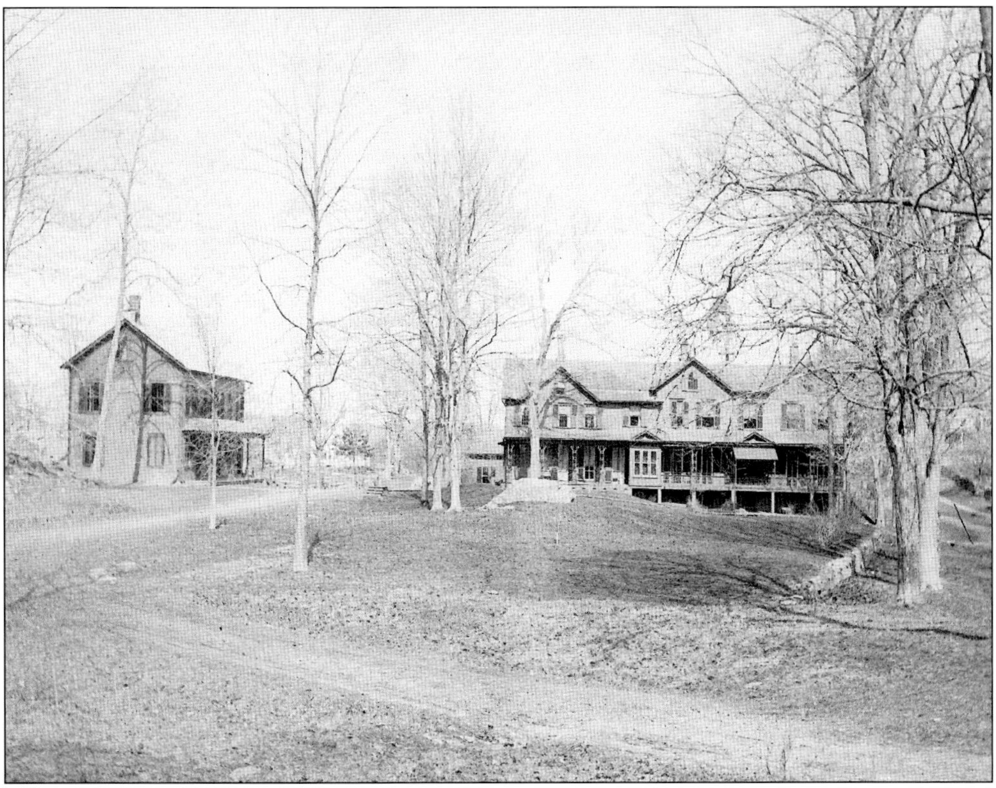

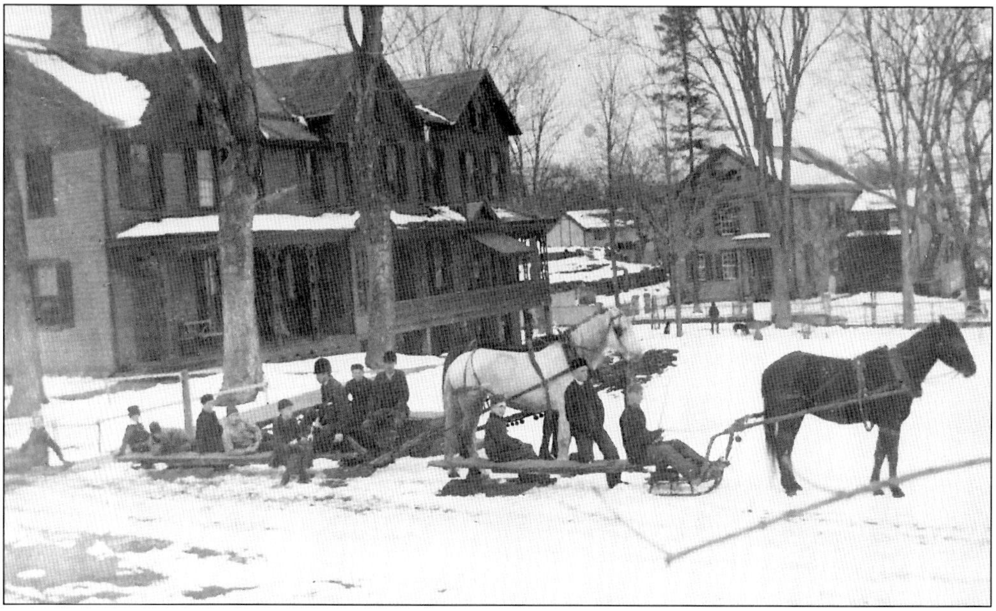

These boys are shown with the school's horses, Maude and Belle. The house across from the dormitory is the home of Dr. Amos Williams. The photograph was taken in 1900, before any remodeling of the dormitory was done.

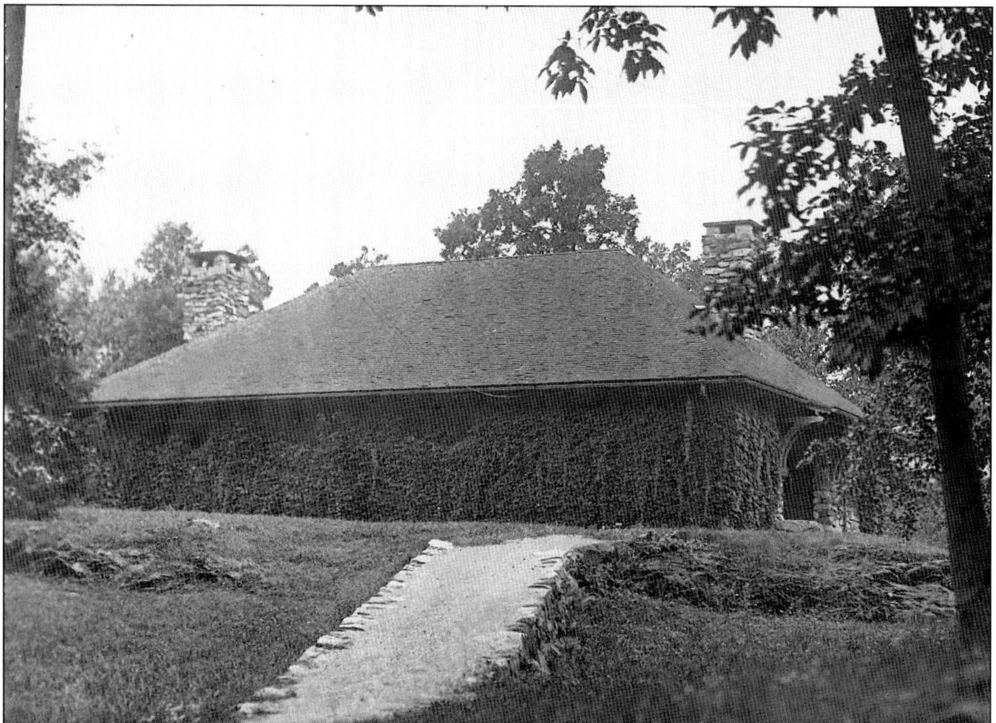

This is the second gymnasium for the Curtis School for Boys. The first was destroyed by fire. This stone building was built in 1907. In 1959, the Country Players of Brookfield purchased the building and it is used as a theater.

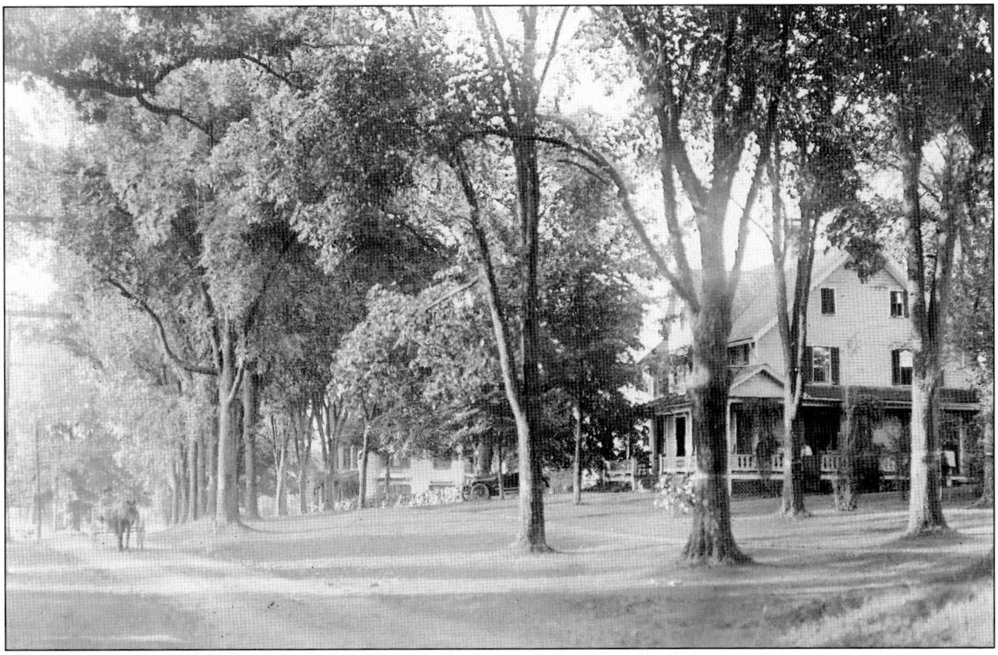

In 1789, this house was built for Urania and Samuel Merwin on Longmeadow Hill Road. Another owner was Rev. Henry D. Noble. He had been the rector of St. Paul's Episcopal Church and became the headmaster of St. Paul's School for Boys in 1858. In 1868, he died and his wife took over running the school for a short period of time.

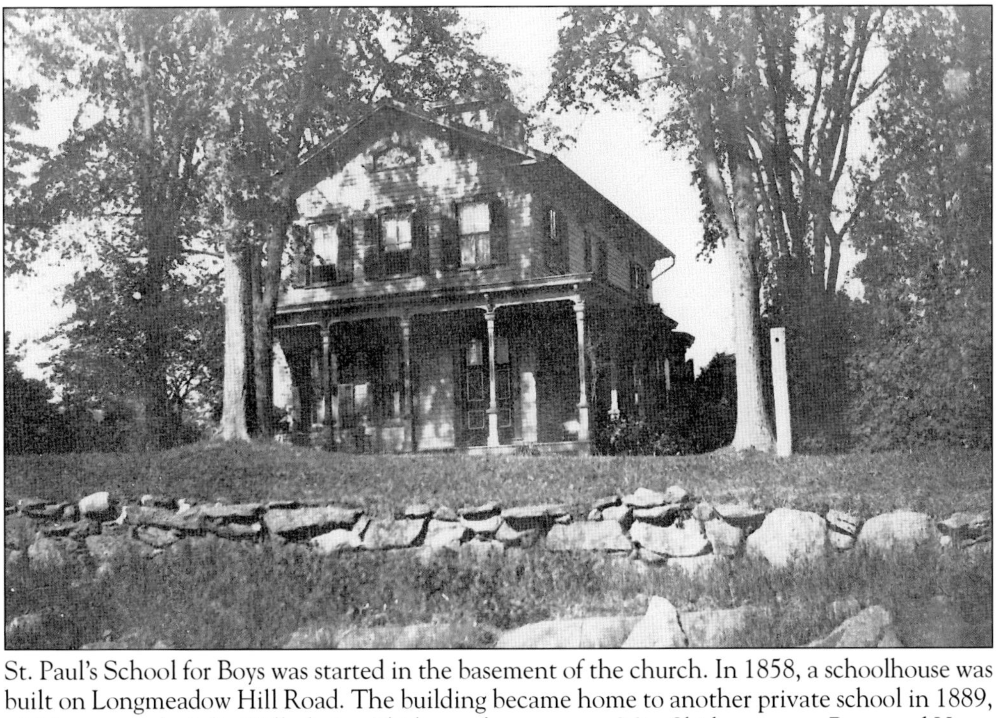

St. Paul's School for Boys was started in the basement of the church. In 1858, a schoolhouse was built on Longmeadow Hill Road. The building became home to another private school in 1889, which was run by Julia Wilhelmine Skidmore for ten years. Miss Skidmore gave Reverend Harry and Rose Martin this home, shown here in 1909, after their missionary tour in China.

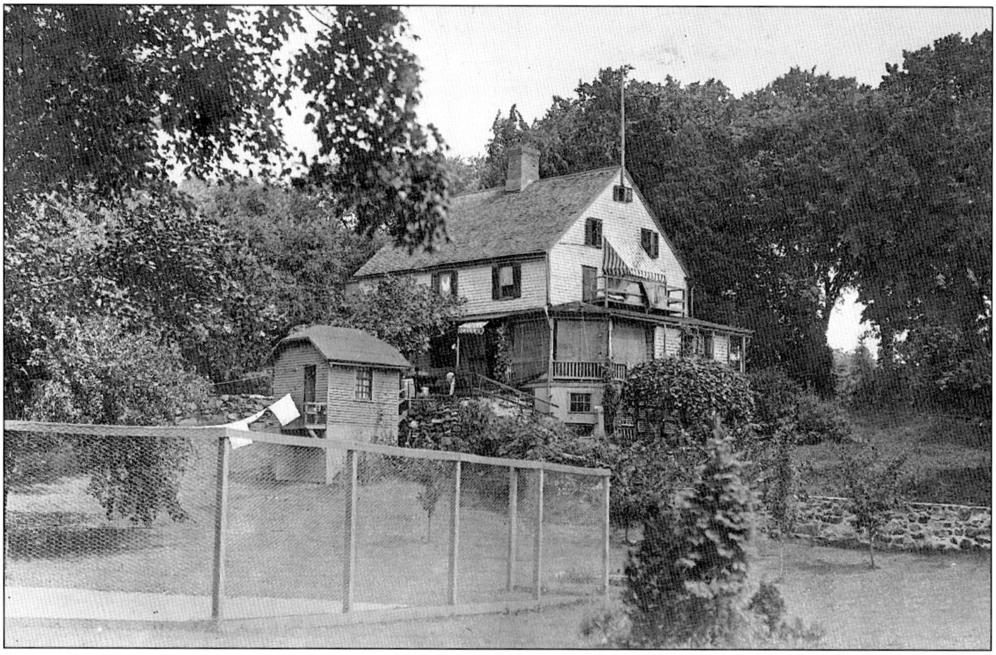

From 1908 to 1918, there was another music school in Brookfield. The founder was Madam Anne E. Ziegler of the Ziegler Institute of Normal Singing, New York City. The school was located on Longmeadow Hill Road in a house built by Peter Hubbell. Dr. Noah Lacy, another owner of the house, attended the state's 1818 Constitution Convention. In the 1930s, Edna Ferber lived in the house while she wrote the book *American Beauty*.

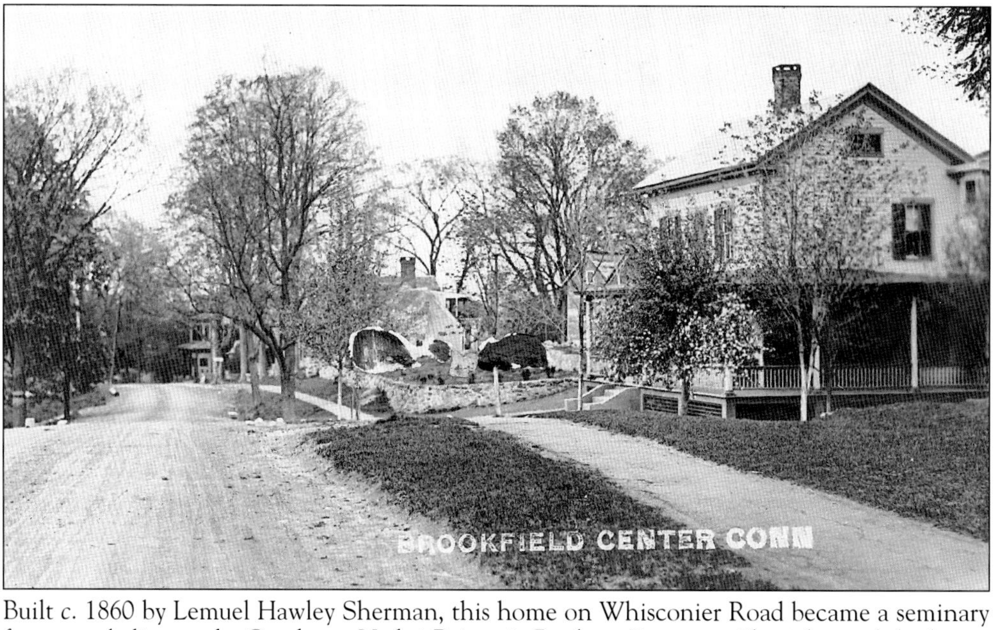

Built *c.* 1860 by Lemuel Hawley Sherman, this home on Whisconier Road became a seminary for young ladies run by Candance Vashti Brittania Benham Booraem. She inherited the house from her Aunt Britannia, for whom she was named. Candance was the daughter of the Reverend Benjamin M. Benham, rector at St. Paul's Episcopal Church. In 1909, William Pinckney, owner of the Village Store, purchased the property.

Seven

Home Sweet Home

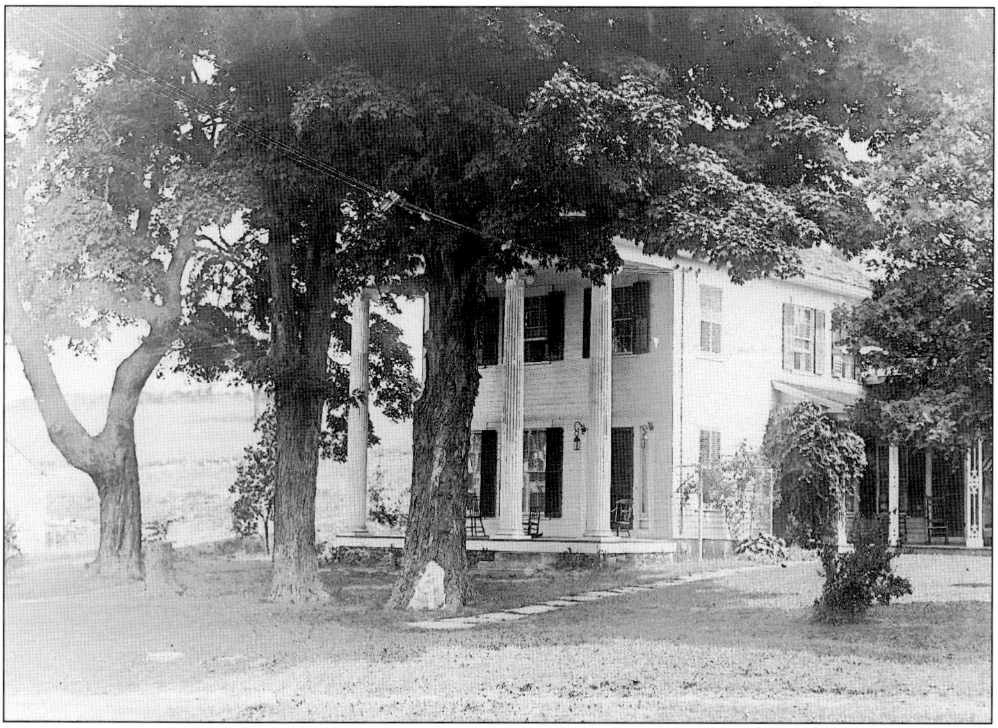

Frederick and Levi Jones built this house *c.* 1858 at the corner of Hillandale Road and Farview Road. Between 1914 and 1918, Harrie Coburn renovated much of the home. It was at this time that the pillars were added to the front of the house. He also named the farm Newbury Farm. In 1921, Samuel A. Smith purchased the property and raised cattle here. His grandson, Sam Smith, sold this home and built a new home next door, where he raised sheep. There is still a sheep farm there; it is one of the few farms left in Brookfield.

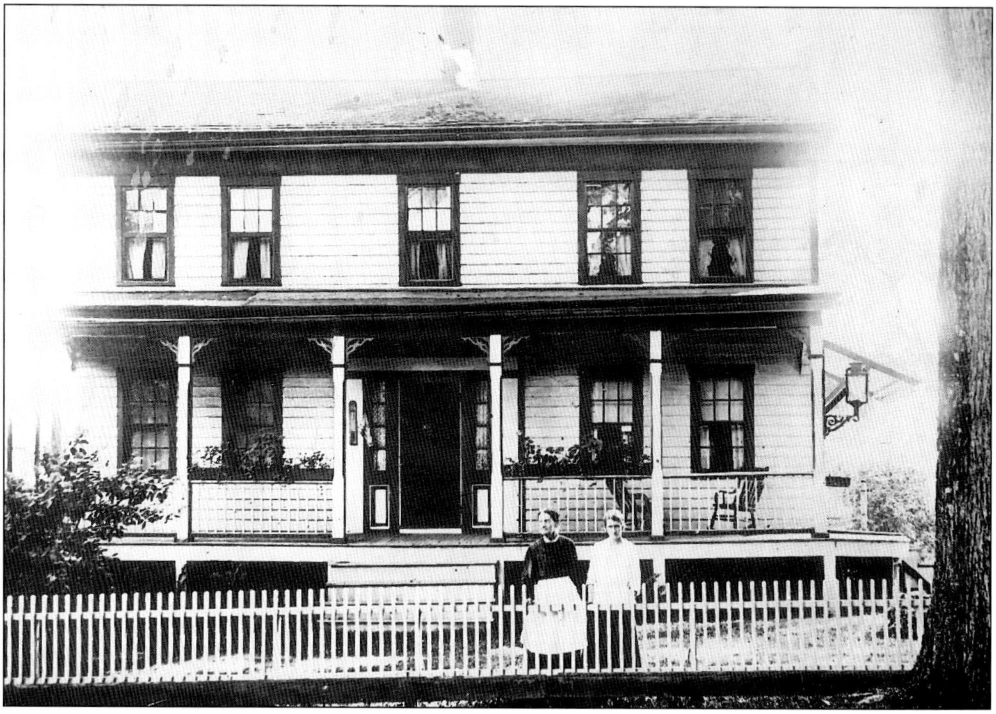

This was the home of James Bateman, who owned the shear factory across the Still River. The house, now Merle's Barbershop, is located on Federal Road.

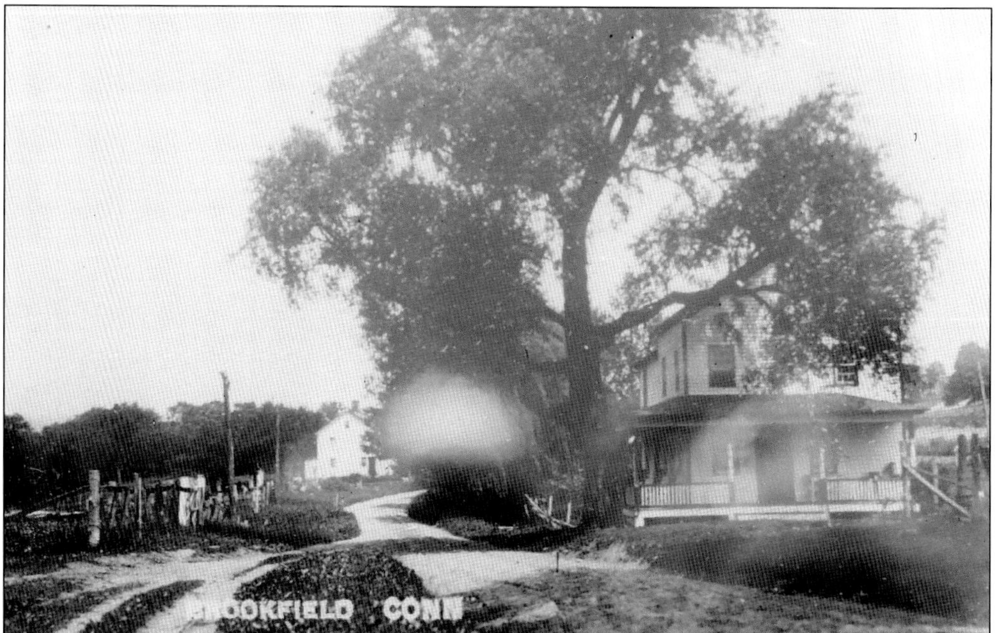

The south side of this house, located on Pocono Road, was built in the 1700s. At one time, there was a button factory located here. In the 1800s, an addition was built. In 1952, on Halloween, the house was moved back from the road to its present location. This was the Pflomm homestead.

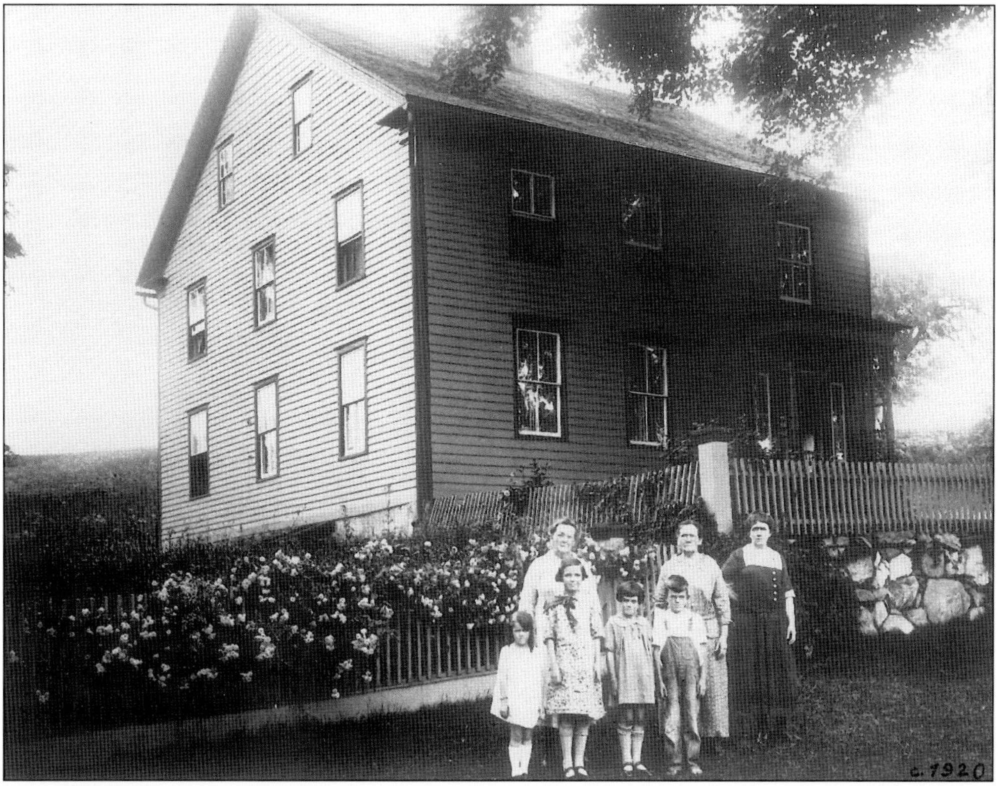

Samuel Ruggles, the youngest son of Capt. Joseph Ruggles, built this home in 1797. Samuel and Huldah had nine children. Two of their children were missionaries in the Sandwich Islands in 1819. This photograph was taken *c.* 1920. The family members are, from left to right, as follows: (front row) Mary Clark, Helen Clark, Elizabeth Clark, and Robert Clark; (back row) Margaret Meaney, Bridget McMahon, and Helen McMahon Clark.

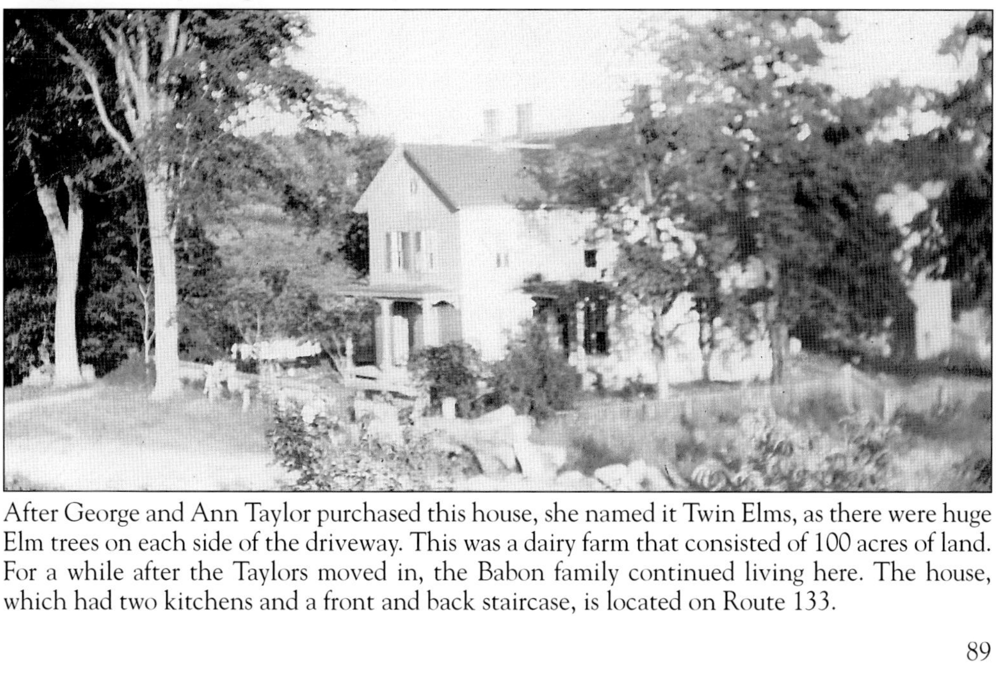

After George and Ann Taylor purchased this house, she named it Twin Elms, as there were huge Elm trees on each side of the driveway. This was a dairy farm that consisted of 100 acres of land. For a while after the Taylors moved in, the Babon family continued living here. The house, which had two kitchens and a front and back staircase, is located on Route 133.

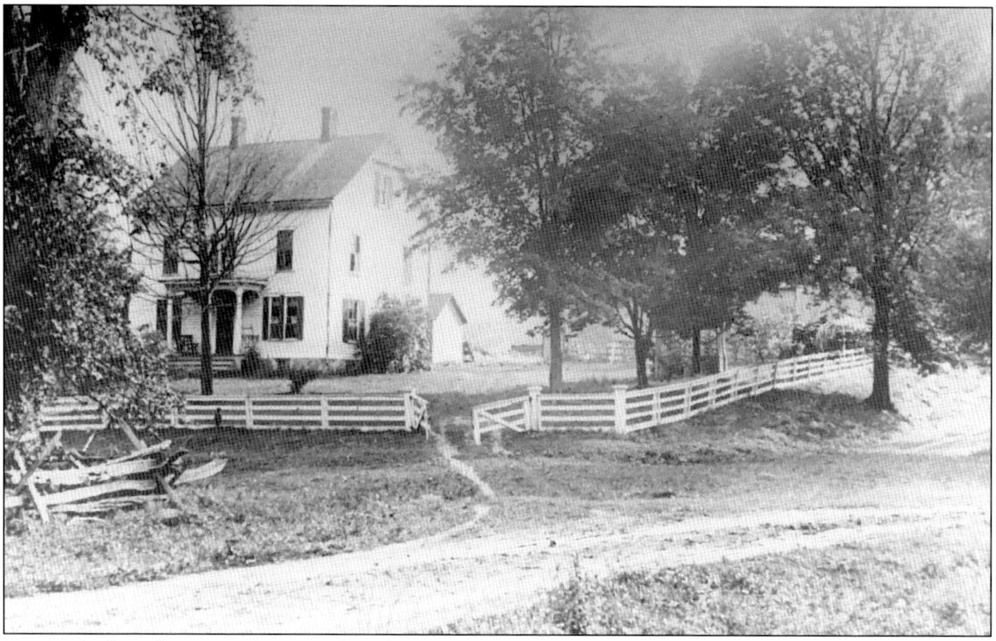

In 1915, this photograph was taken by Paul Fletcher Weld of the Camp residence, located at the corner of the Old Sherman Turnpike and 40 Acre Mountain Road.

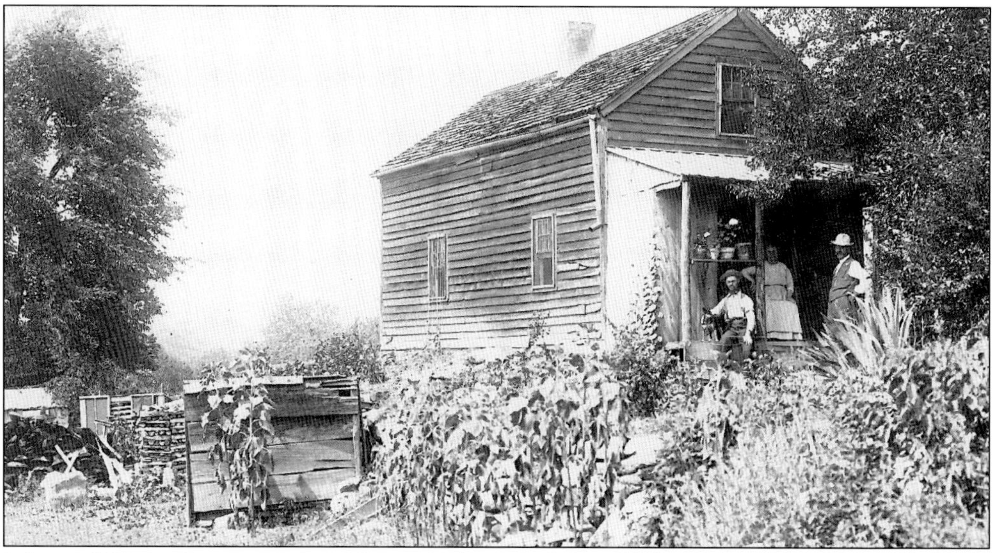

Julia and Henry Demaris sit on their porch, visiting with an unnamed guest. The house is located on Candlewood Lake Road and has had several additions over the years.

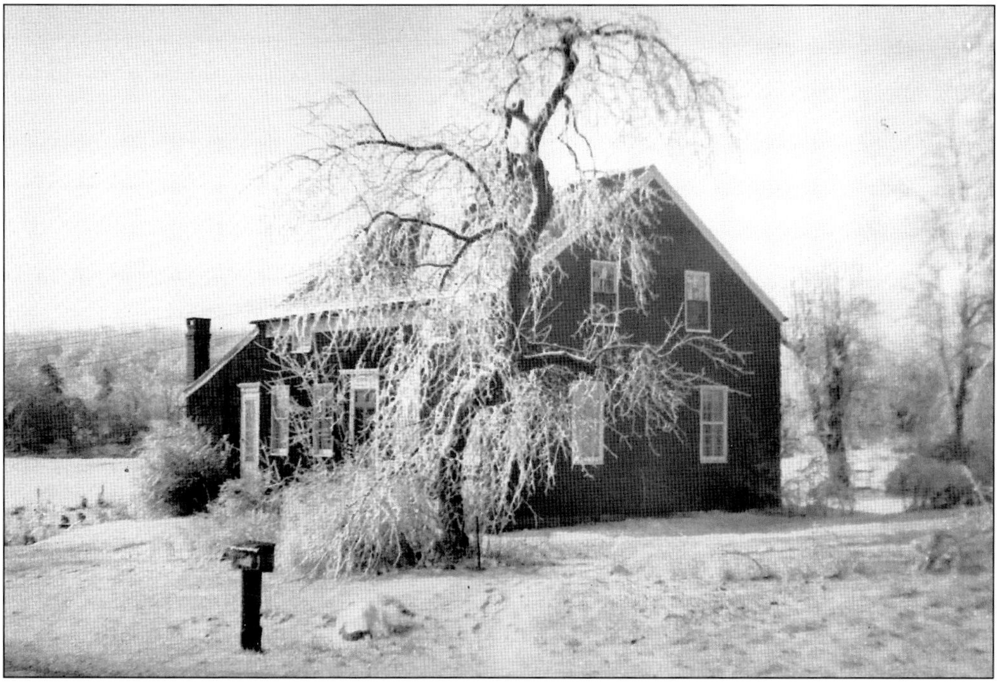

Capt. Benjamin Dunning built this house *c.* 1746 on Obtuse Road, South. An addition was put on for his son Jared. Captain Dunning served on the building committee for the first meetinghouse in the Newbury Parish. Mary Dunning married Isaac Babbitt and, upon her death, he married Mary's sister Eunice. Marcus Babbitt, the son Issac and Eunice, was living in the house in 1870.

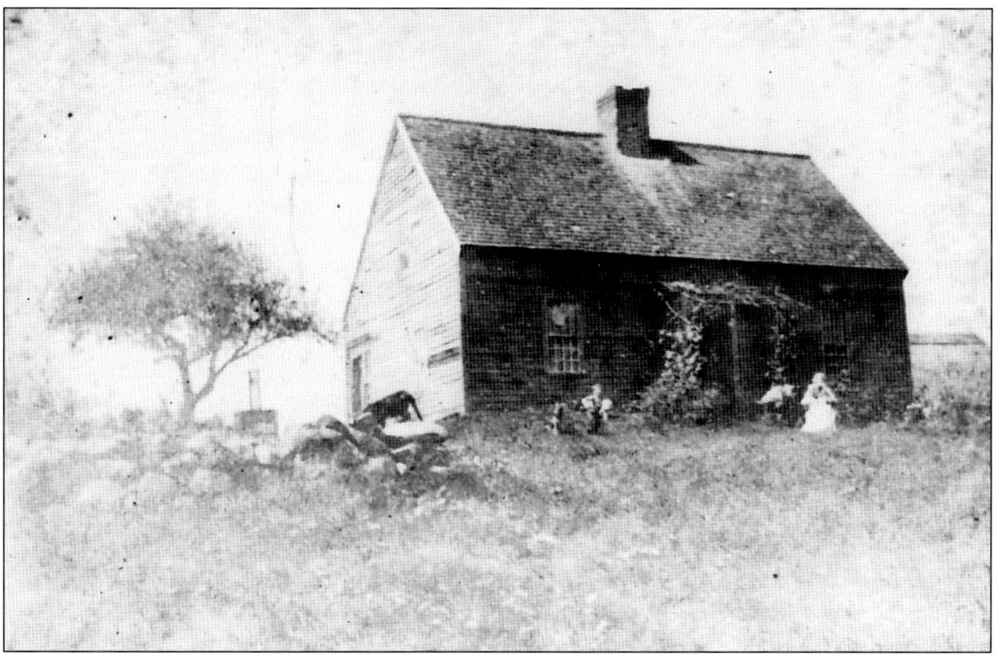

This building was the Sherman Foote homestead. A more recent owner was Wendell Davis. The house, once located on Pocono Road, has been taken down.

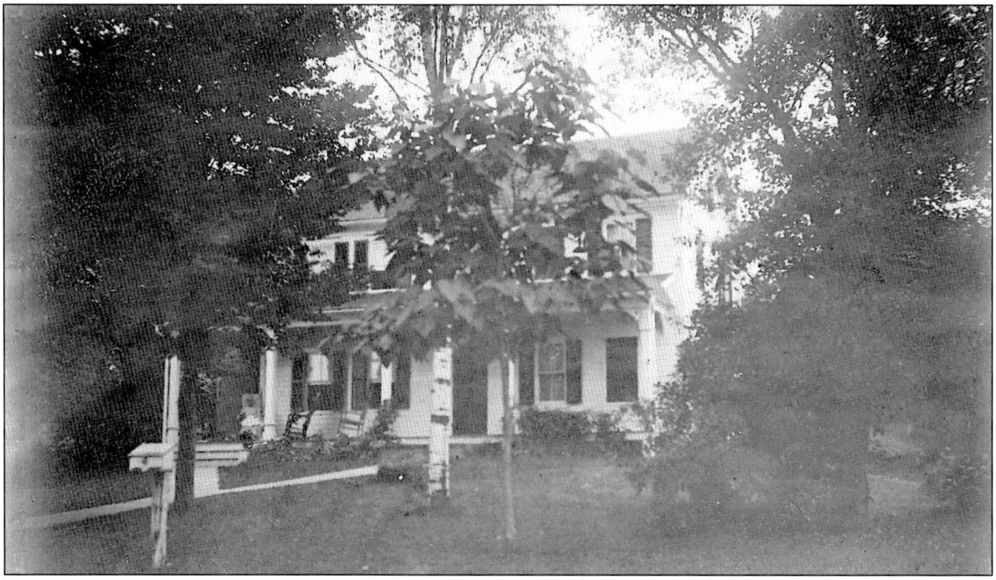

The Starr family of Huckleberry Hill built this home. It stayed in the Starr family for many generations until it was purchased by Daniel Joyce. It then stayed in the Joyce familyfor many years. The property, which included the Huckleberry Hill Cemetery and an orchard, was located on Federal Road, near Joyce's C orner. The house eventually burned and was taken down.

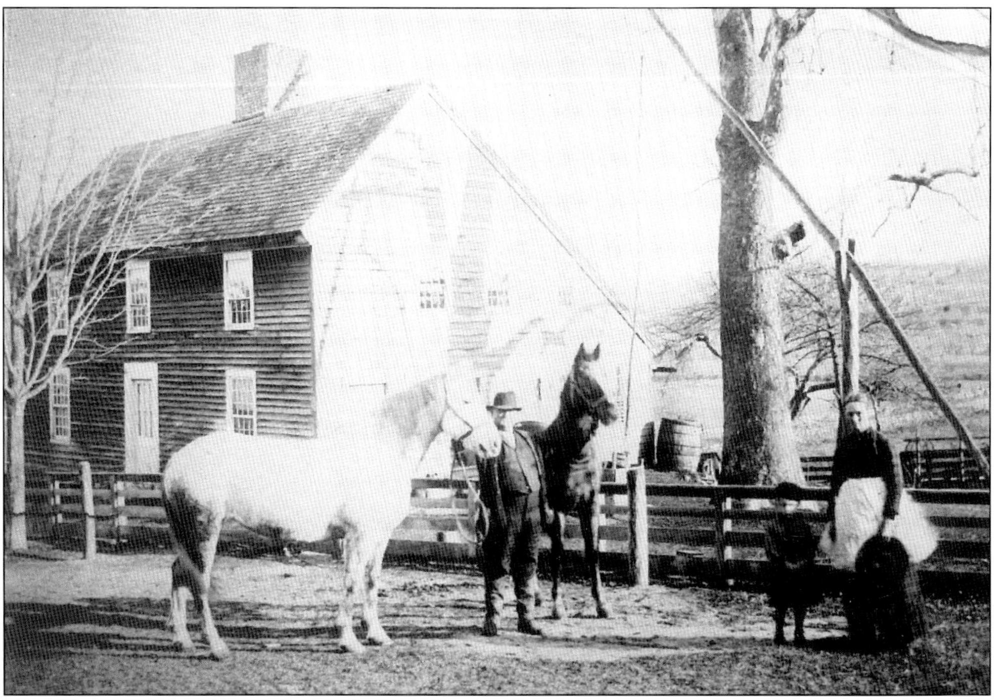

The Wildman homestead was located across the street from the Huckleberry Hill Cemetery. It was called the "Pest House" because those with smallpox were treated here; when they died, they were buried in the old cemetery. The house was taken down and moved to another state. The Sycamore tree seen here stills stands at the corner of Federal Road and Route 133.

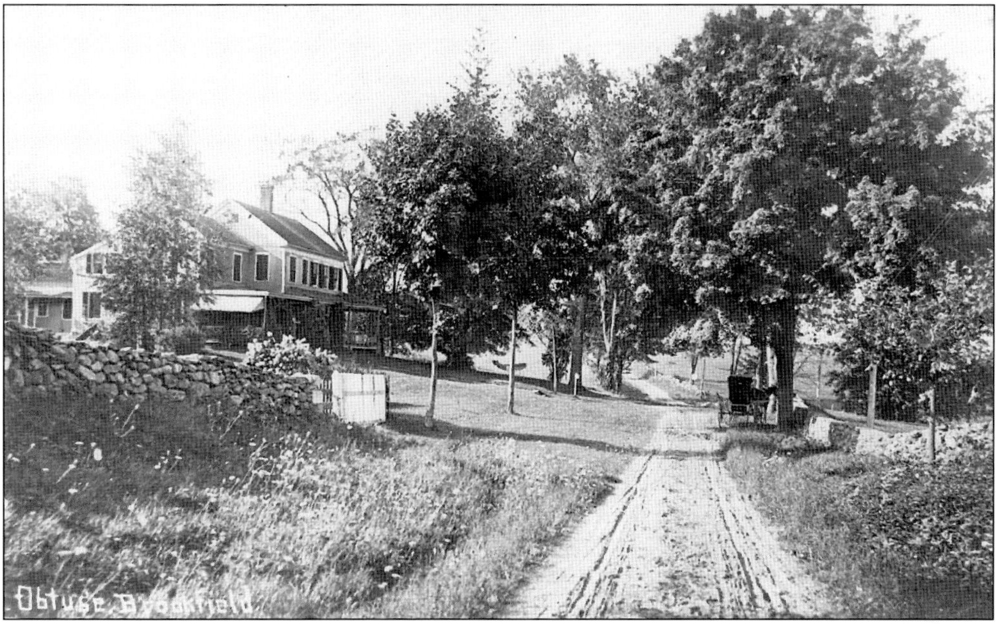

Horace and Emily Beers lived in this home on Obtuse Road, South. It became knows as Beersford. Their son Fred raised his family here. In 1930, he sold the house after building a new one in Brookfield Center. He received honorary recognition as a leader in agriculture from the Connecticut Agricultural College (now the University of Connecticut).

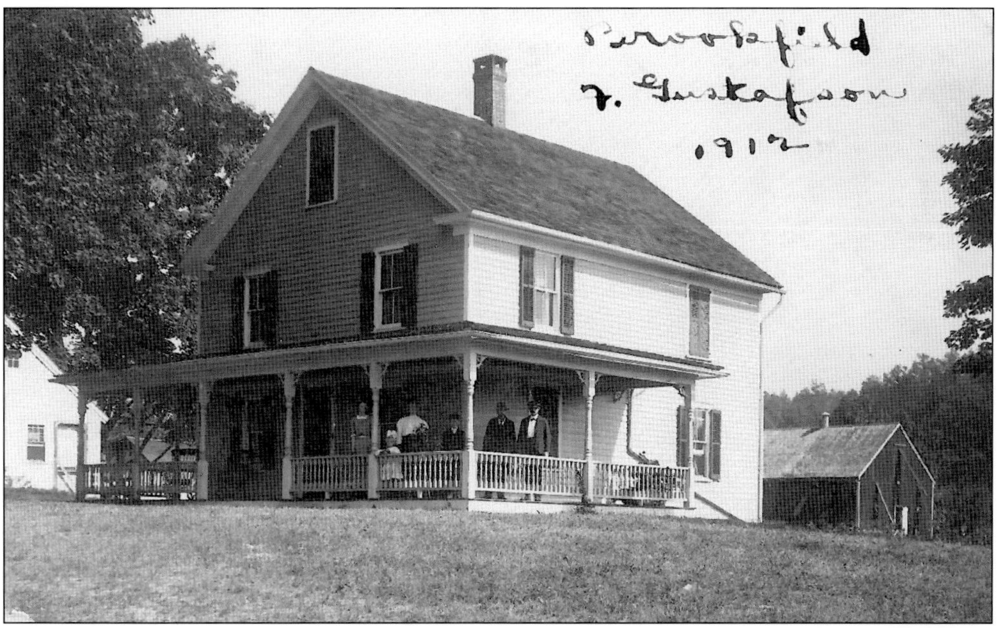

The Frank Gustafson house, shown here in 1912, is located on Whisconier Road. Frank was born in Ekyby, Sweden. In 1893, he married Johanna Carlson of Hogstad, Sweden. They built this home and had four children, Christine, Frederick, Eric, and Gertrude, all born in Brookfield. When Gertrude was a child, the family used to sit on the front porch and listen to music school students rehearse.

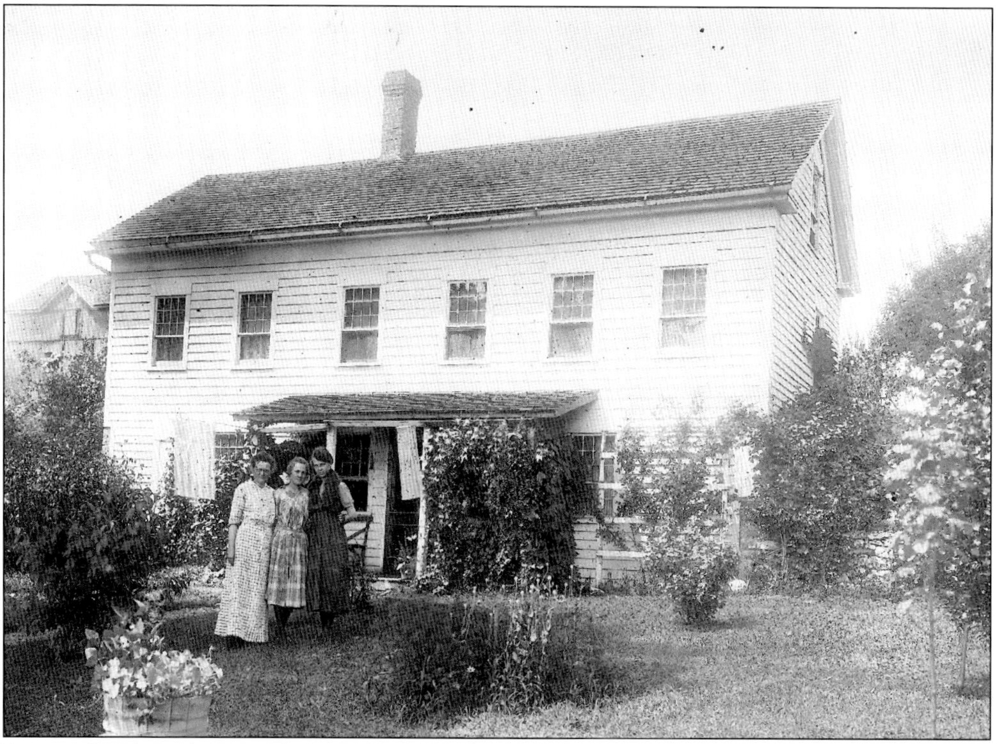

Posing for this photograph is Louise Bowdy and her daughters, Hilda and Mable. Their home was located on Federal Road, near the end of Super 7 highway. The house has since been taken down.

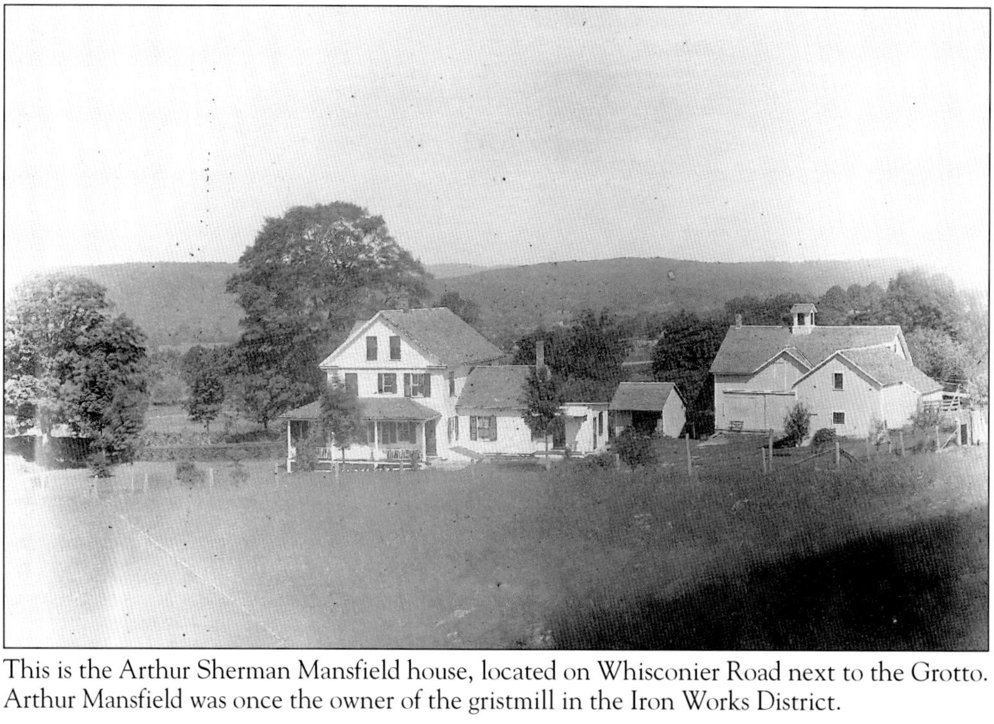

This is the Arthur Sherman Mansfield house, located on Whisconier Road next to the Grotto. Arthur Mansfield was once the owner of the gristmill in the Iron Works District.

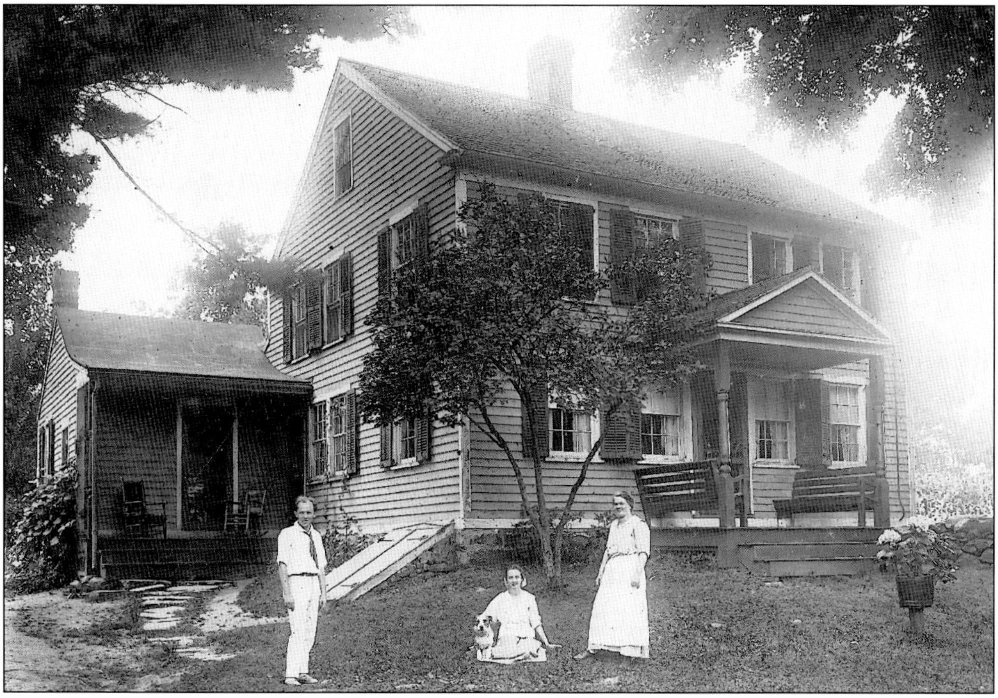

This house was a wedding gift to lawyer Bryant Smith and his bride, Caroline Blackman, from his father, Joseph. It was built *c.* 1810. Fred Curtis purchased the house, and the caretaker of the Curtis School for Boys lived here. Seen here is Florence Johnson on her 16th birthday (sitting with the dog), her mother, Mamie, and a family friend, Arthur Bows. The house is located next to the Brookfield Library.

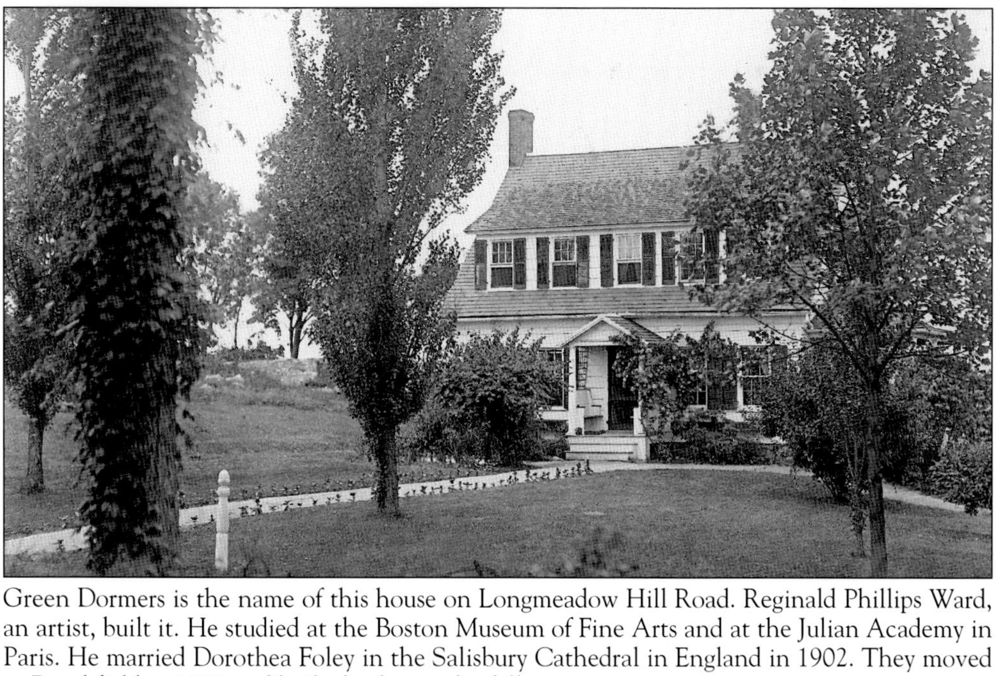

Green Dormers is the name of this house on Longmeadow Hill Road. Reginald Phillips Ward, an artist, built it. He studied at the Boston Museum of Fine Arts and at the Julian Academy in Paris. He married Dorothea Foley in the Salisbury Cathedral in England in 1902. They moved to Brookfield in 1912 and built this house the following year.

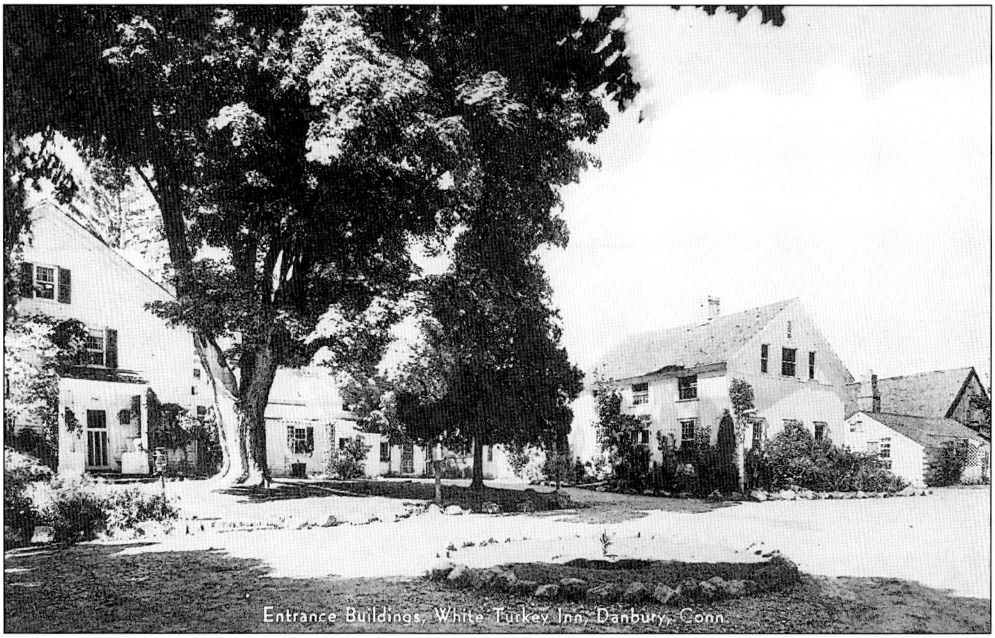

The White Turkey Inn was a landmark for many years. John Gregory Sr. built it in 1760 as a wedding present for his son John and John's bride, Hannah. They ran a farm here, but by the 1900s, it had been abandoned. In 1904, Charles and Mary Morgan purchased the farmhouse, and after a year of renovation, the inn reopened in 1905. They ran the inn here for 30 years.

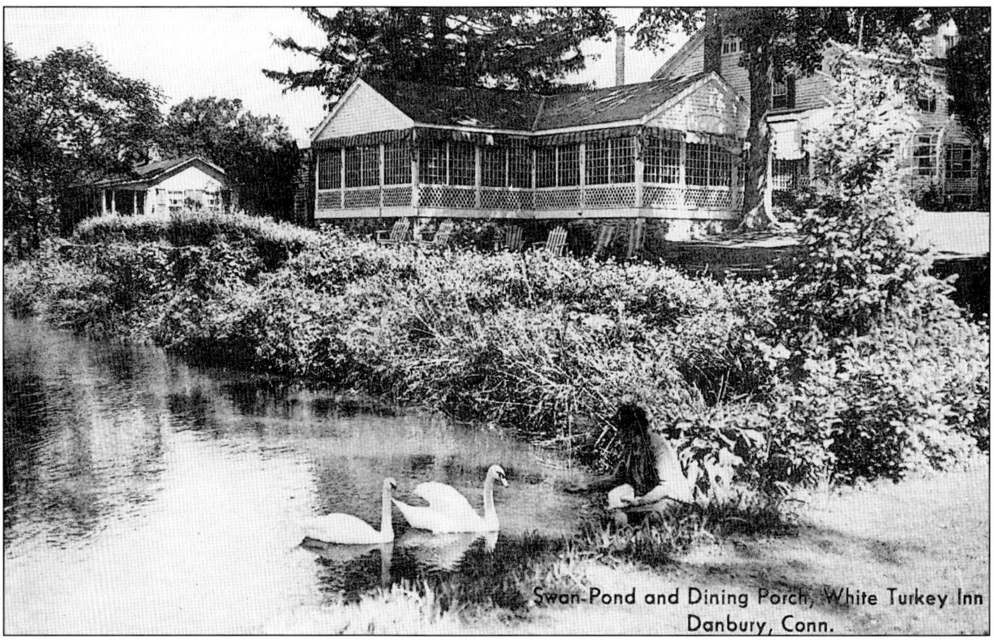

Over the years, there were swans, white turkeys, and beautiful gardens on the property. There was also a honeymoon cottage. Mrs. Morgan created the name, following the English tradition of naming teahouses after animals. Harry and Dorothy Davegas purchased the inn in 1935. The inn and pond were removed in 1971 and a shopping center was built on the site.

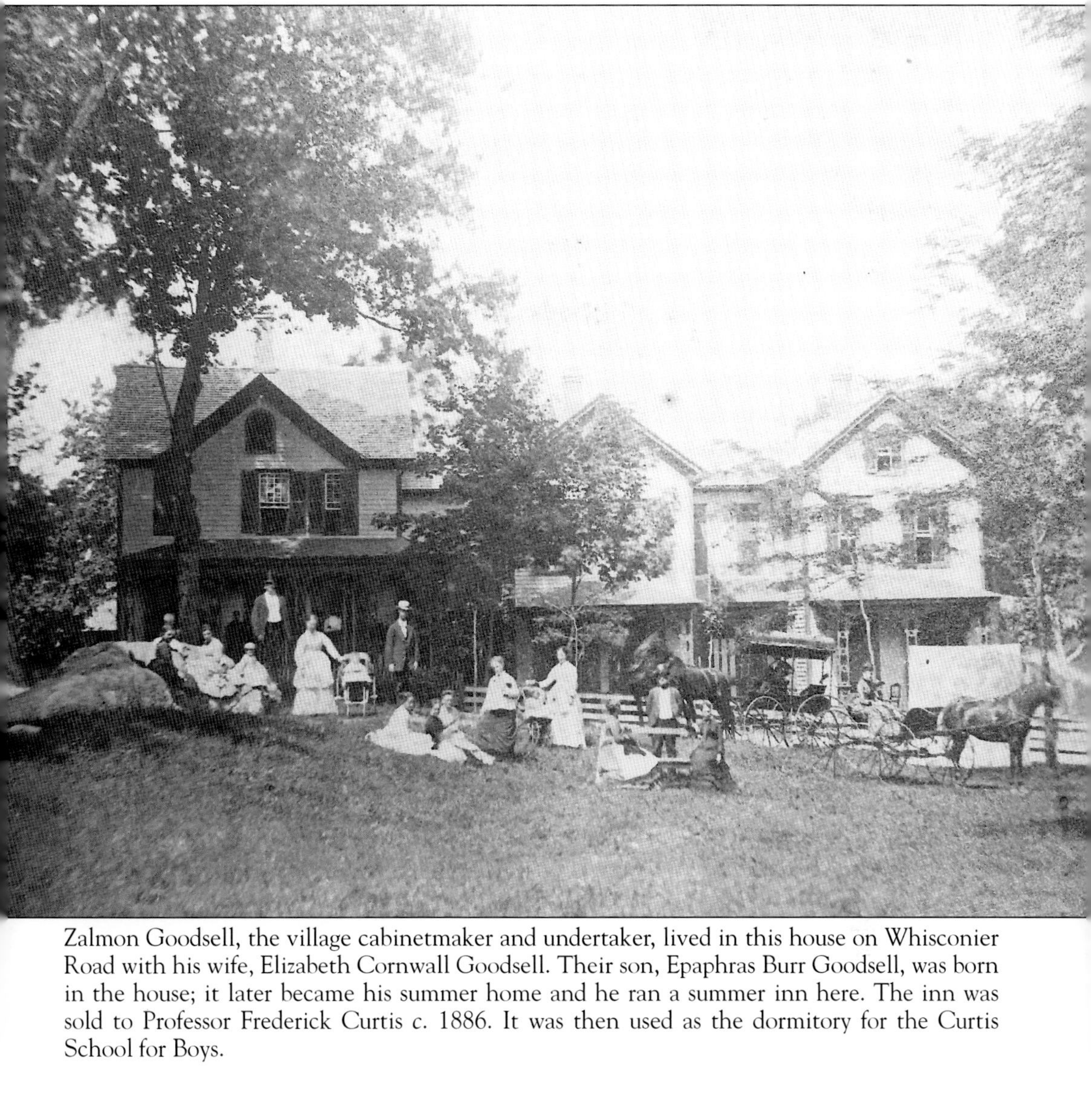

Zalmon Goodsell, the village cabinetmaker and undertaker, lived in this house on Whisconier Road with his wife, Elizabeth Cornwall Goodsell. Their son, Epaphras Burr Goodsell, was born in the house; it later became his summer home and he ran a summer inn here. The inn was sold to Professor Frederick Curtis *c.* 1886. It was then used as the dormitory for the Curtis School for Boys.

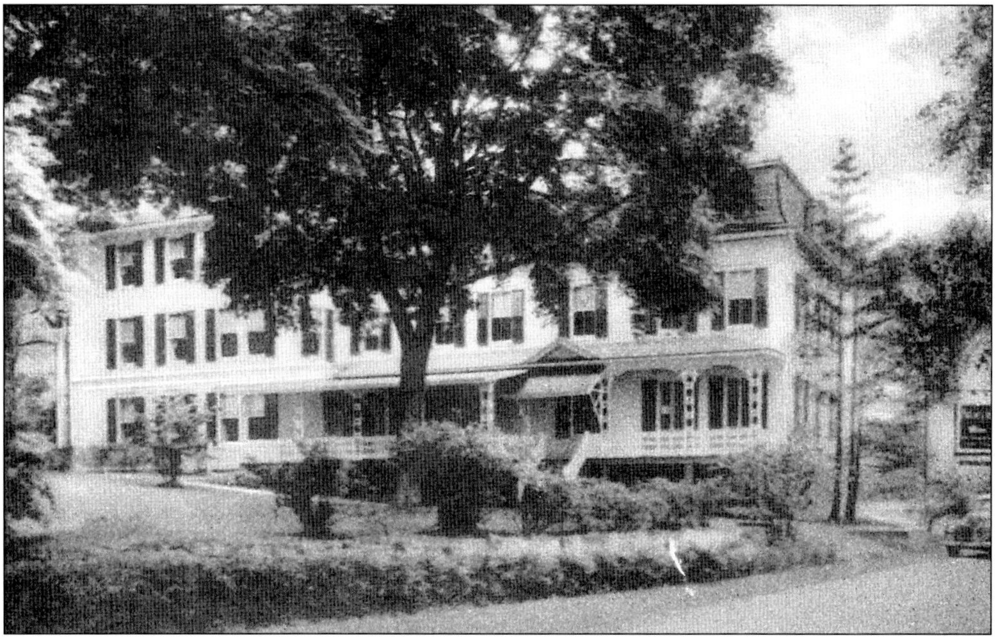

In 1943, the Curtis School for Boys closed and George Najjar purchased the property. The dormitory became the Nutmeg Inn, also known as Najjar's Inn. In 1959, the inn caught fire and burned to the ground. The Brookfield Library occupies this site, now called Curtis Crescent.

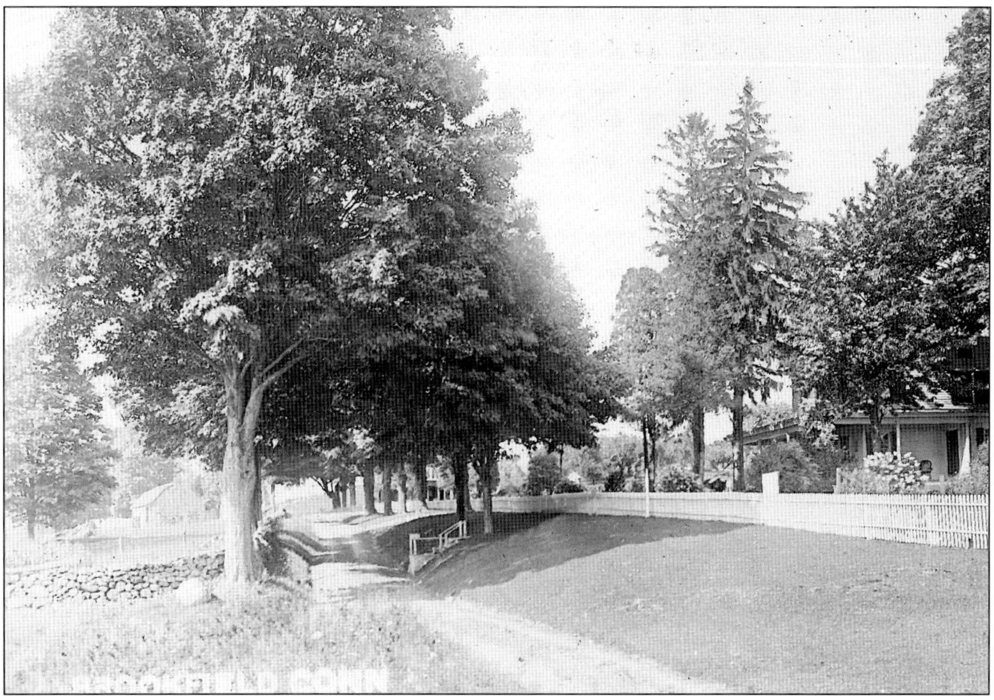

Benjamin Hawley built Farview Inn on Farview Road. Hawley was born in 1794 and died in 1877. He married Betsey Peck, and together, they built the house. Their son Emmon inherited it. Over the years, it has had many owners. By the 1930s, it was an inn managed by Marcel Gaits.

Eight

Back to the Land

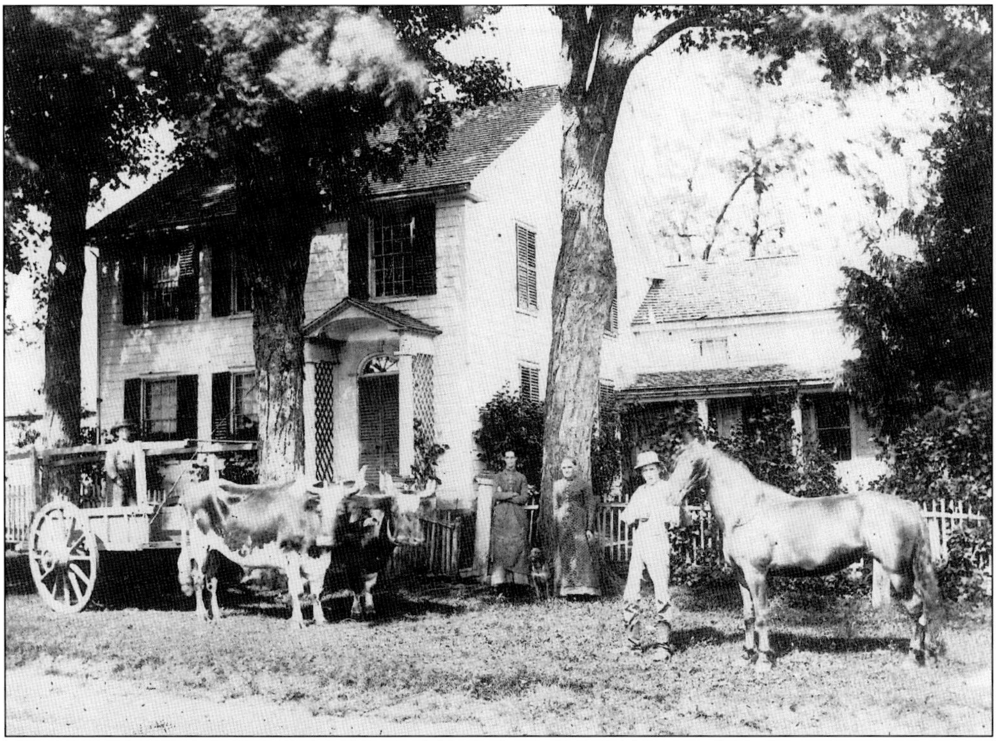

This photograph was probably taken before 1875, while the Rufus Skidmore family owned the farm. Howard and Ruamy Peck also owned the farm, located on Obtuse Road, South, for many years. In 1925 Howard's nephew, Lawrence Burr, and Lawrence's wife, Helen, moved to Brookfield to work here. When Howard died in 1935, Lawrence inherited the diary farm. For the next 40 years, Lawrence and Helen raised their family here. After Lawrence Burr retired in 1978, the farm became the Burr Farm Garden Center. Lawrence died in 1978 and Helen died in 1997 at the age of 93. They both were very active in town and church activities.

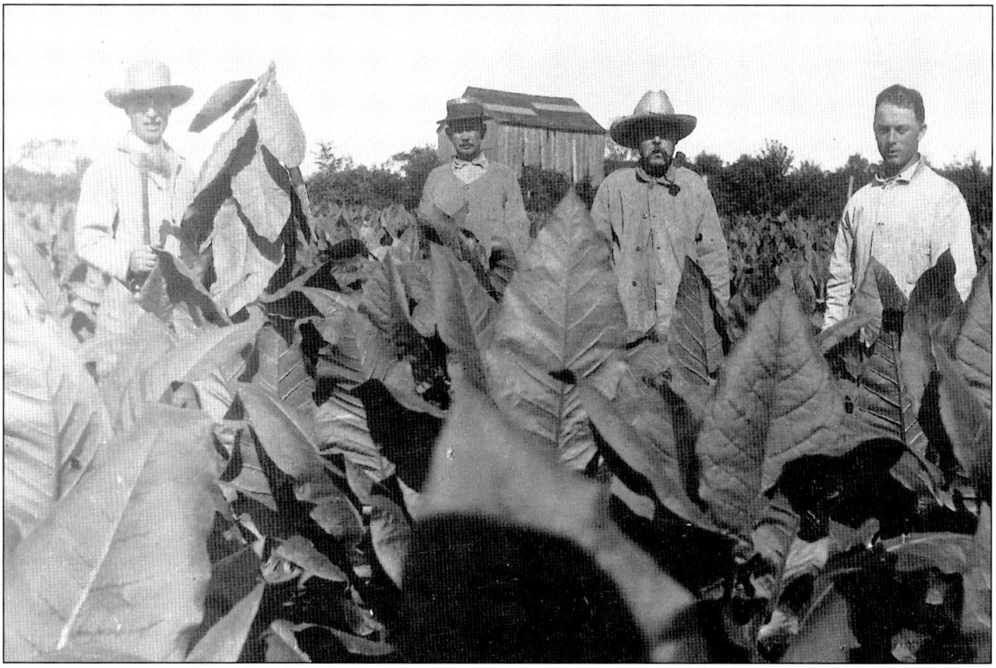

Tobacco was a large crop in the town of Brookfield. Seen working in the tobacco field, from left to right, are Frank Waidelich, Martin Martini, George Adam Waidelich Sr., and George Waidelich Jr.

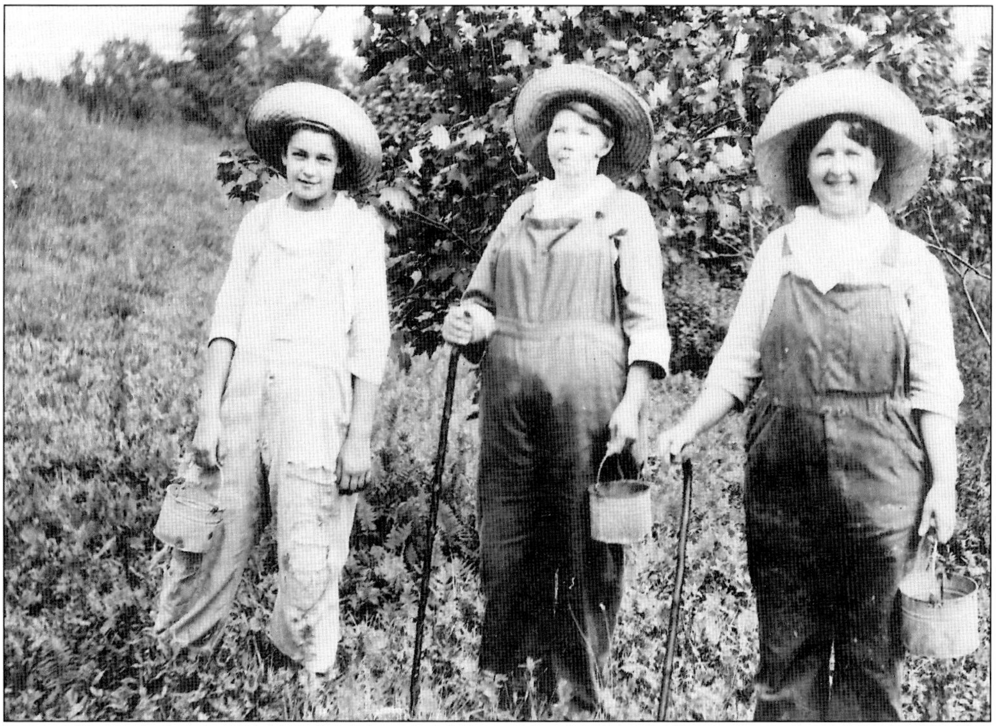

Out to do some berry picking, from left to right, are Viola Martini, Minnie Martini, and Della Martini.

Huldah Lucy Stevens lived on her father's homestead on Kellogg Street. Her parents were Captain Elias and Lucy Stevens. She was one of ten children.

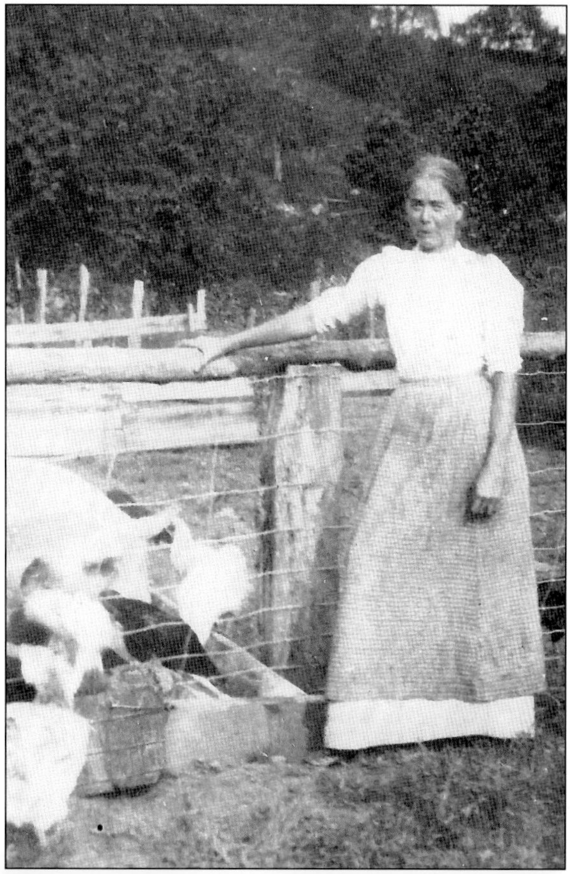

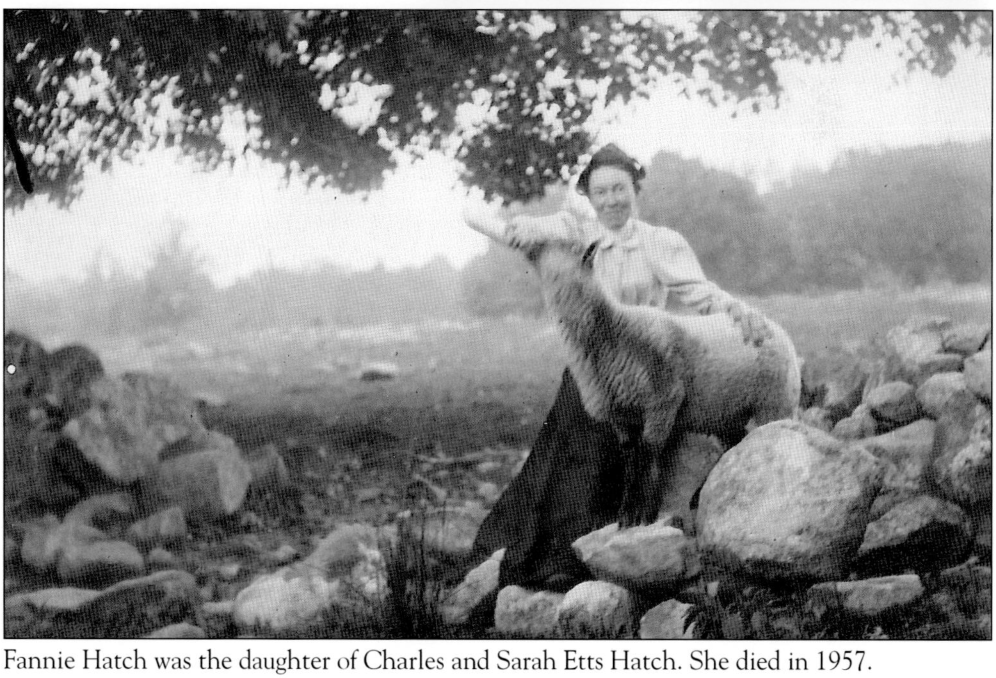

Fannie Hatch was the daughter of Charles and Sarah Etts Hatch. She died in 1957.

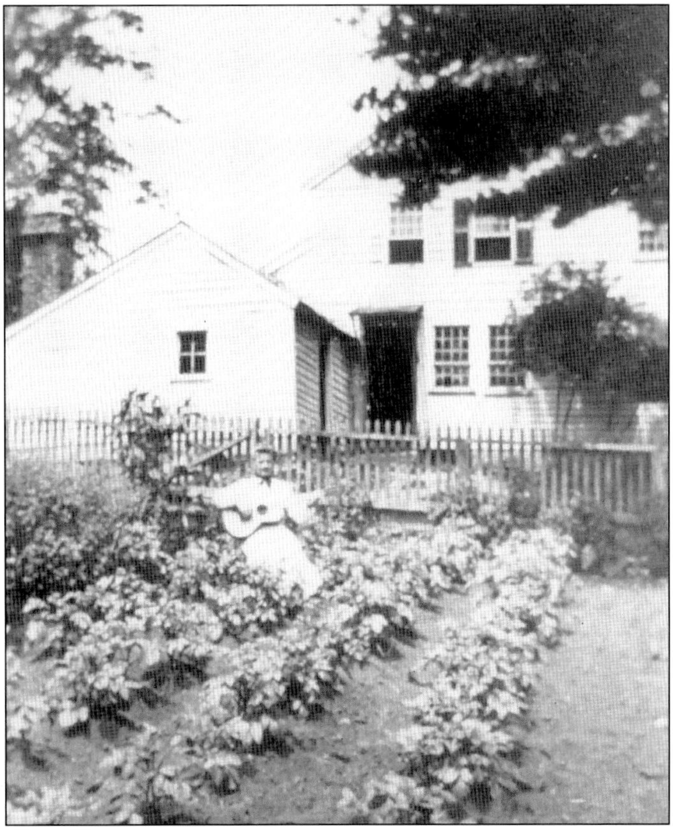

Mamie Nelson Johnson was the wife of Frank Oscar Johnson, the caretaker for the Curtis School for Boys. They lived in the caretaker's house seen in the background. The couple had three children: Florence, Frank and Edward. One of Ed's jobs was to pick up students, parents, and visitors at the train station and bring them to the school. The photograph was taken in 1905.

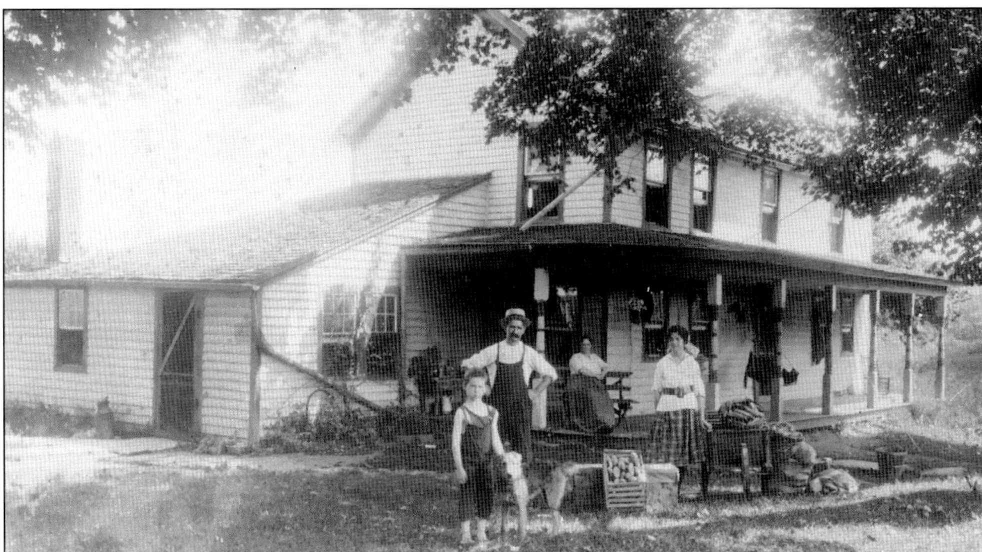

The site was purchased from local Native Americans in order to build this house, which was a saltbox originally. The members of the Peter H. Fennell family shown here are, from left to right, Joe, Peter, Hattie, and Emily. Peter ran a market garden in the 1920s. The produce grown on the farm was taken to market in Waterbury and Danbury by train. The photograph was taken *c.* 1918.

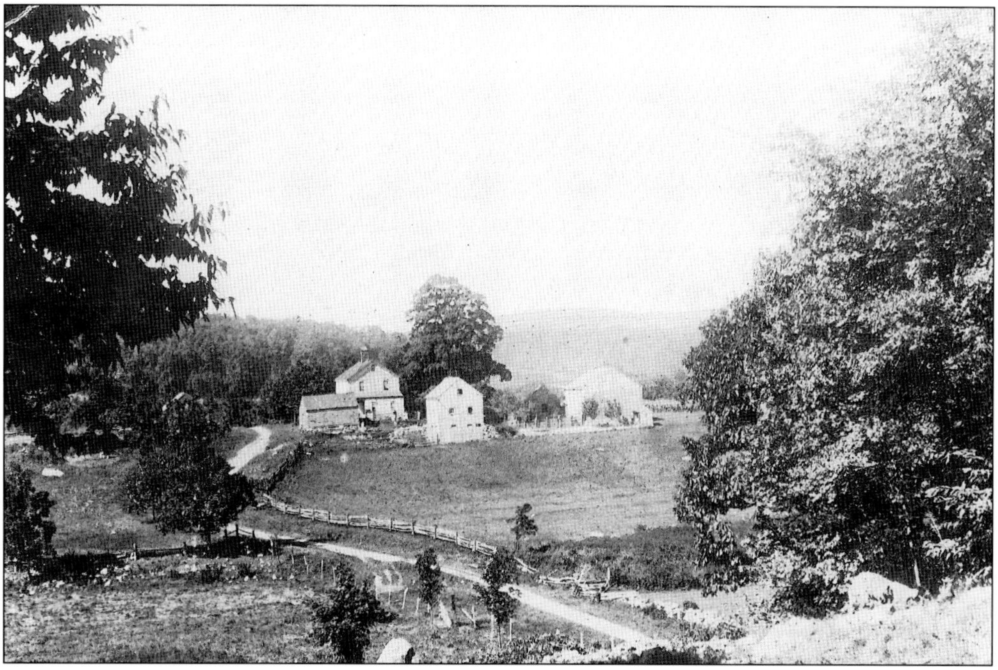

This was the Miles Alaby farm, located at the end of North Mountain Road. There was a pond on the property that allowed animals to drink and provided ice in the winter. Mr. Alaby found arrowheads and other Native-American artifacts while plowing the fields. Part of this area is now called Cadigan Park.

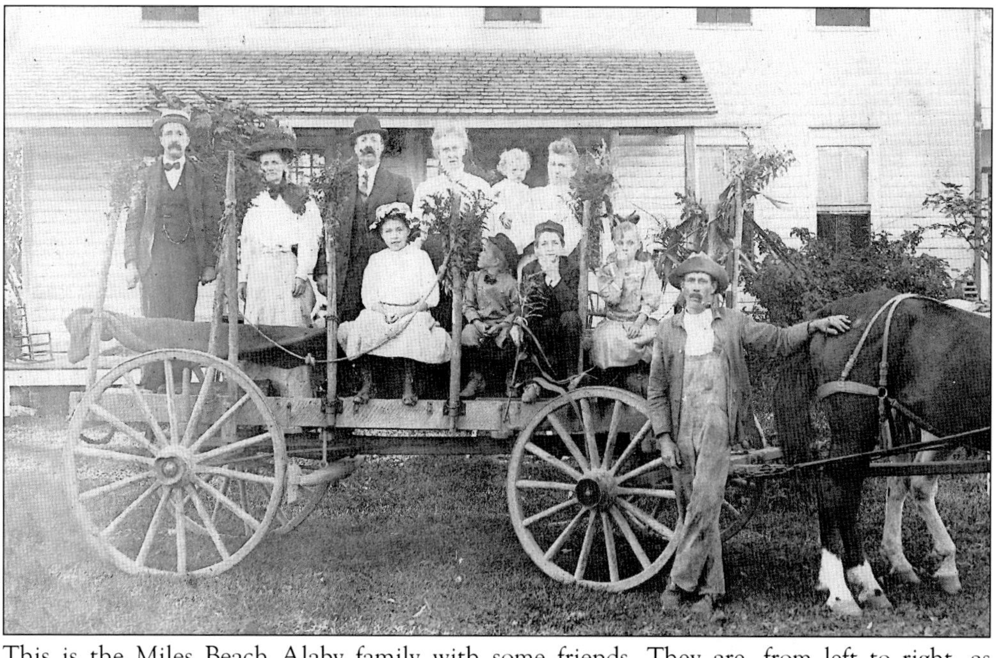

This is the Miles Beach Alaby family with some friends. They are, from left to right, as follows: (front row, seated) Alice Alaby, Ward Alaby, a guest, and Helen Alaby; (back row) Charlie Parker, Annie Parker, two guests, Ethel Alaby, and Bertha Alaby. Miles Alaby stands with the horse. The wagon was decorated for a special occasion in 1909.

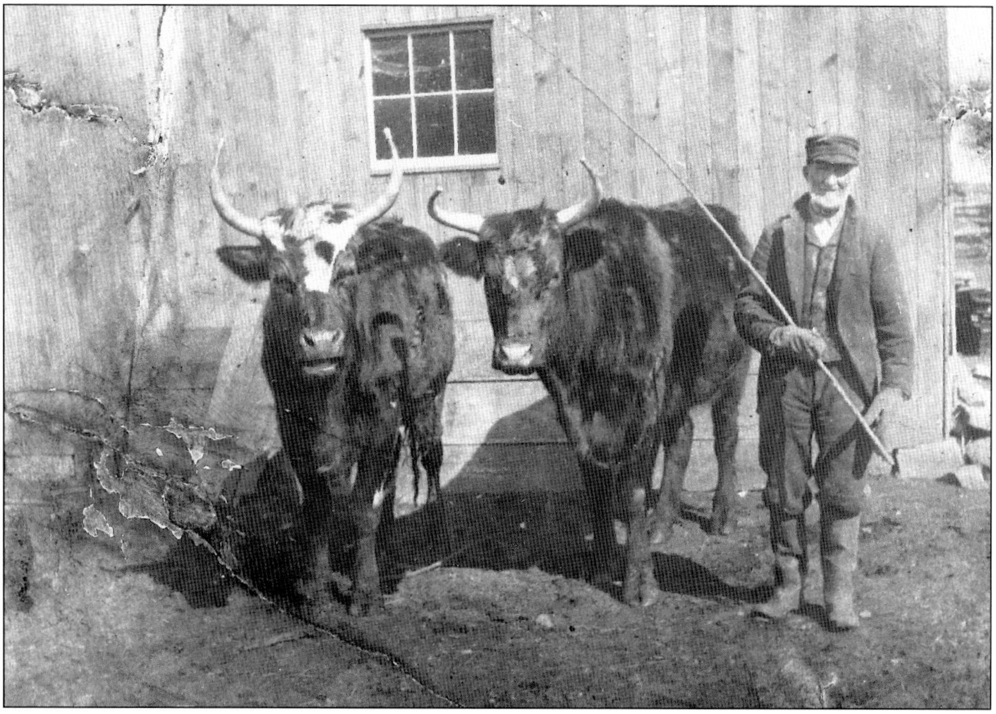

George Smith poses with his oxen.

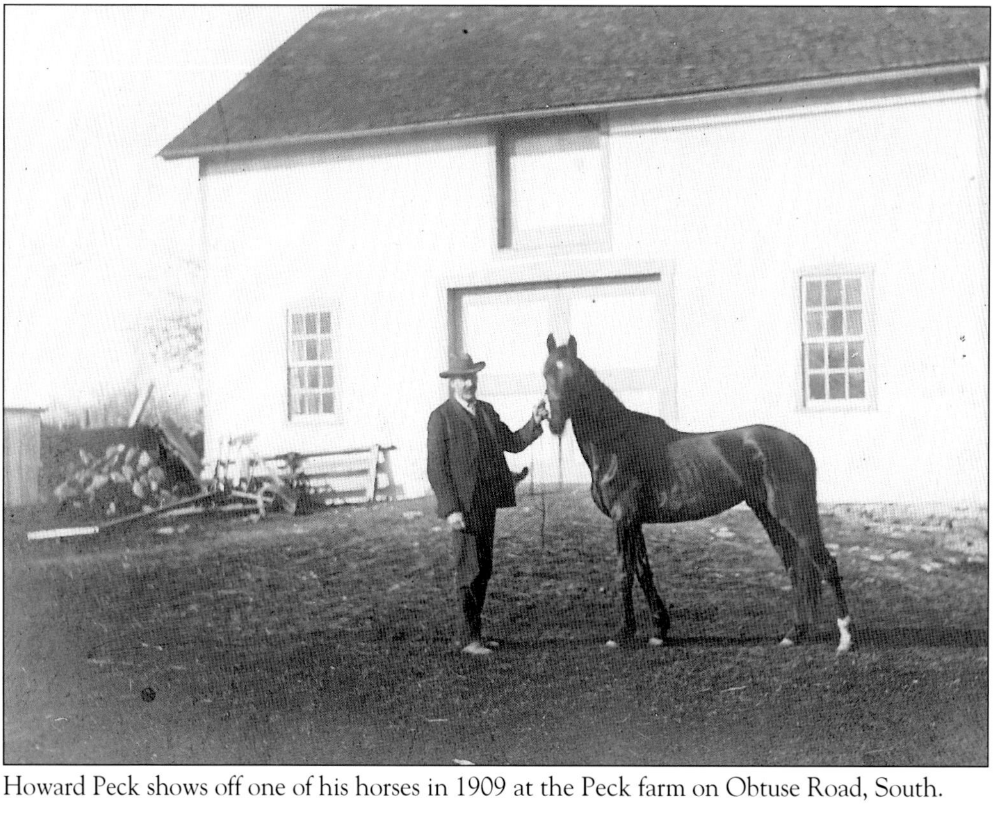

Howard Peck shows off one of his horses in 1909 at the Peck farm on Obtuse Road, South.

Charles Henry Camp was the son of John and Eliza Camp of Brookfield. He was born February 19, 1862, and died in 1938. He was the town representative from 1916 to 1918, and served as the first selectman in 1911, 1912, and 1913. This photograph was taken in 1914.

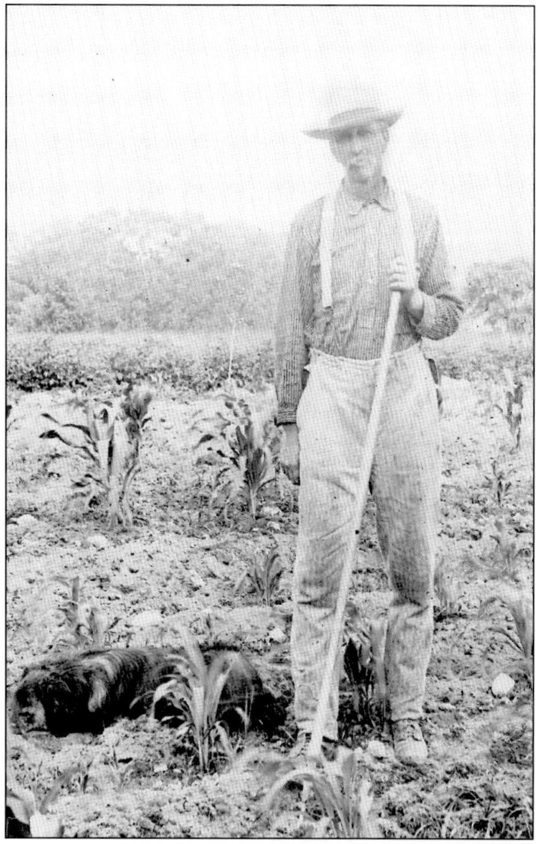

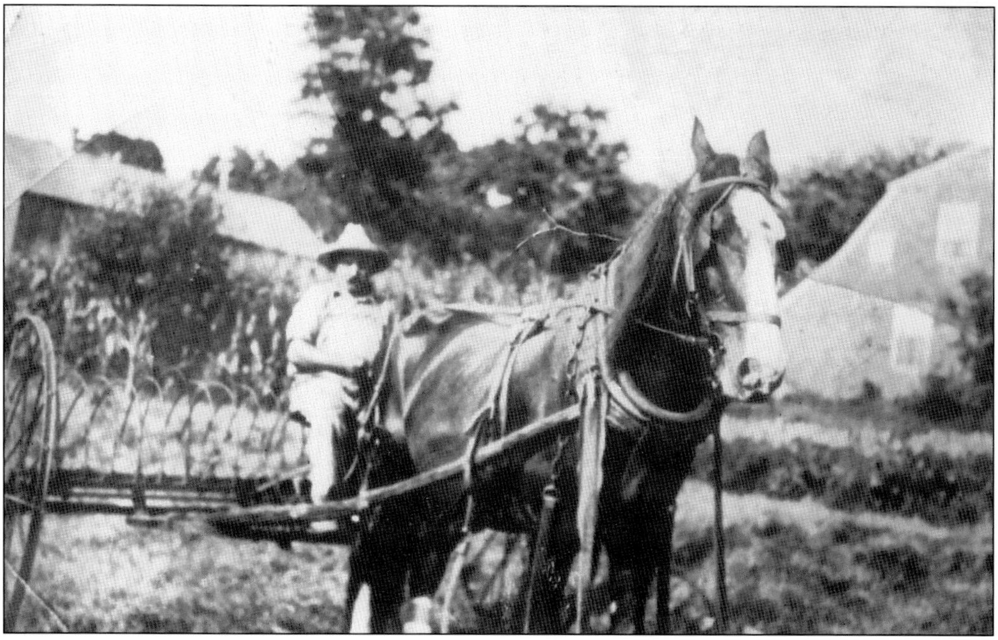

Francois Weigle and "Charlie" were photographed in front of the Weigle home, which still stands on Station Road.

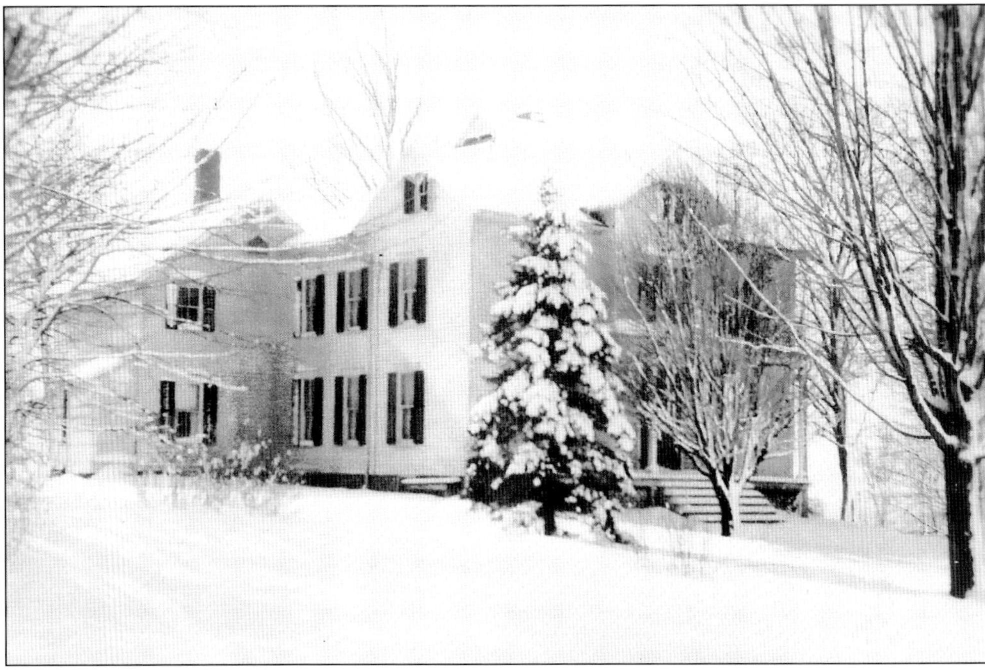

Thomas Halpin built this house on Whisconier Hill. Later, when Merritt M. Clark owned it, he planted a large number of fruit and ornamental trees on the property. In 1928, Donald L. Thomsen purchased it. It has been called Donnie Brook Farm.

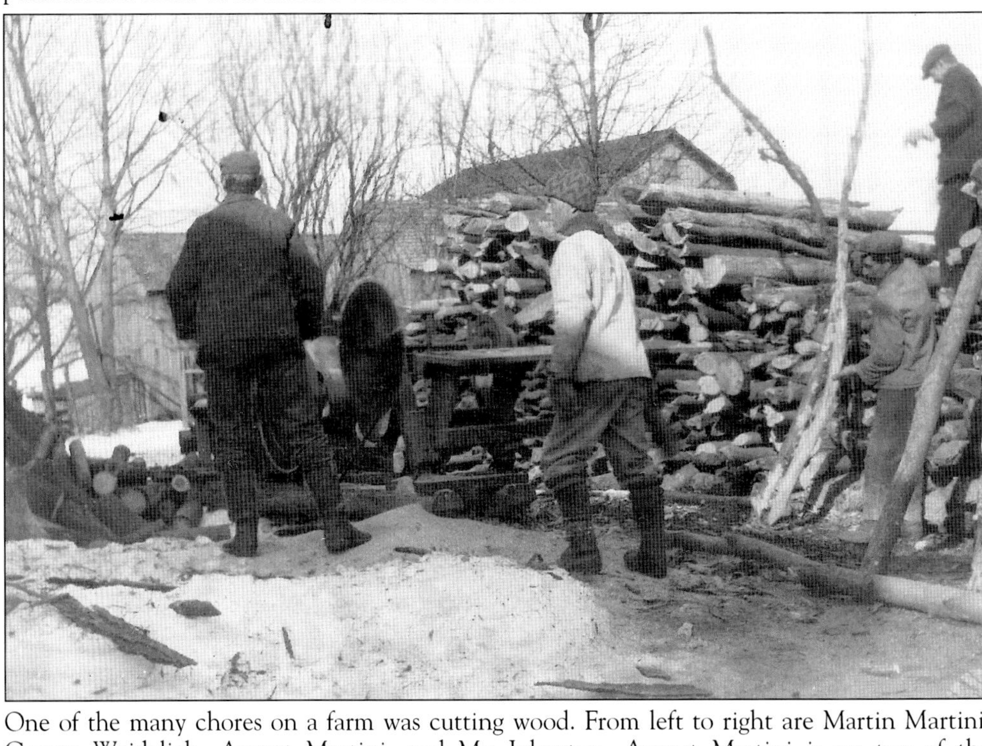

One of the many chores on a farm was cutting wood. From left to right are Martin Martini, George Waidelich, August Martini, and Mr. Johnston. August Martini is on top of the pile of wood.

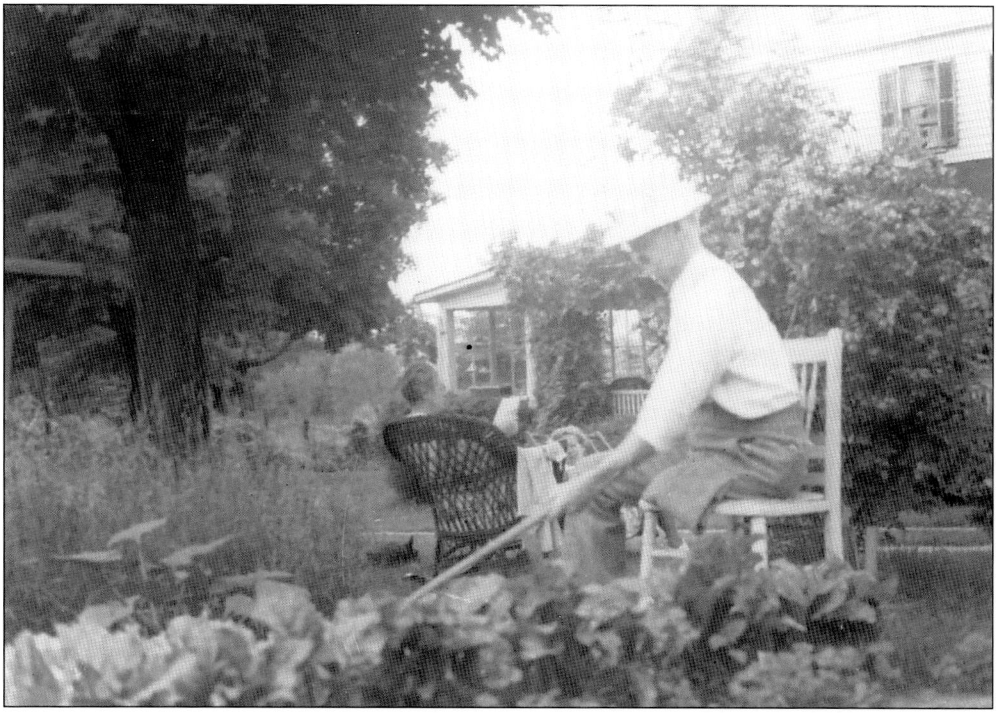

Arthur Sherman Mansfield was born May 28, 1861, in Brookfield. He married Florence Emily Kellogg. He was the miller at the gristmill in the Iron Works District for many years. His daughter Lina remembers him falling into the sluiceway when he was cleaning it.

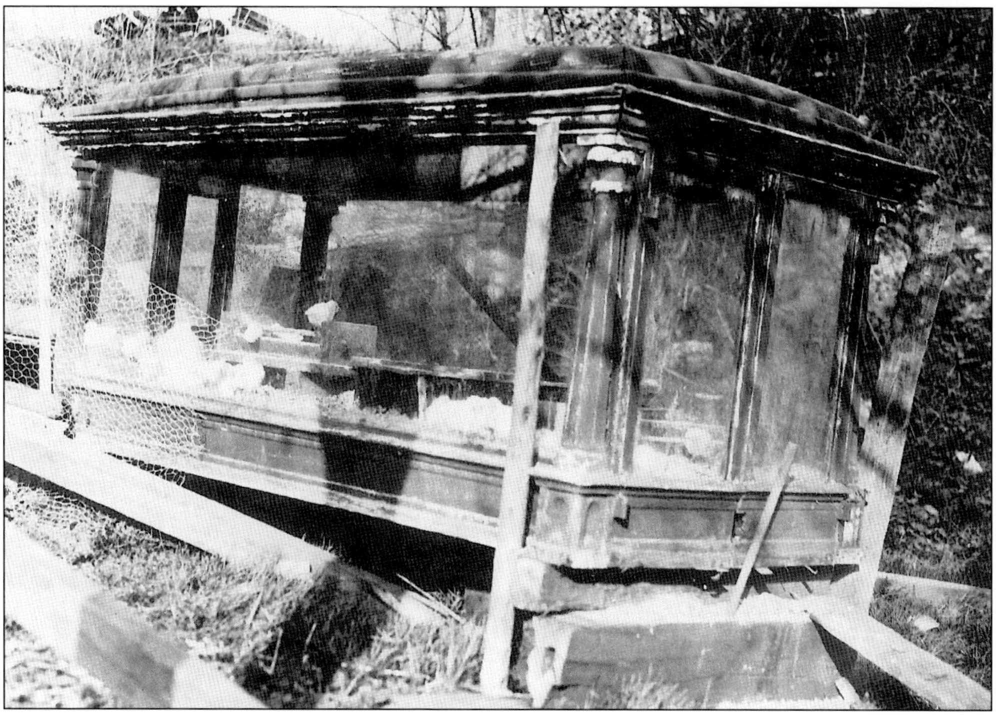

This horse-drawn hearse was turned into a chicken coop.

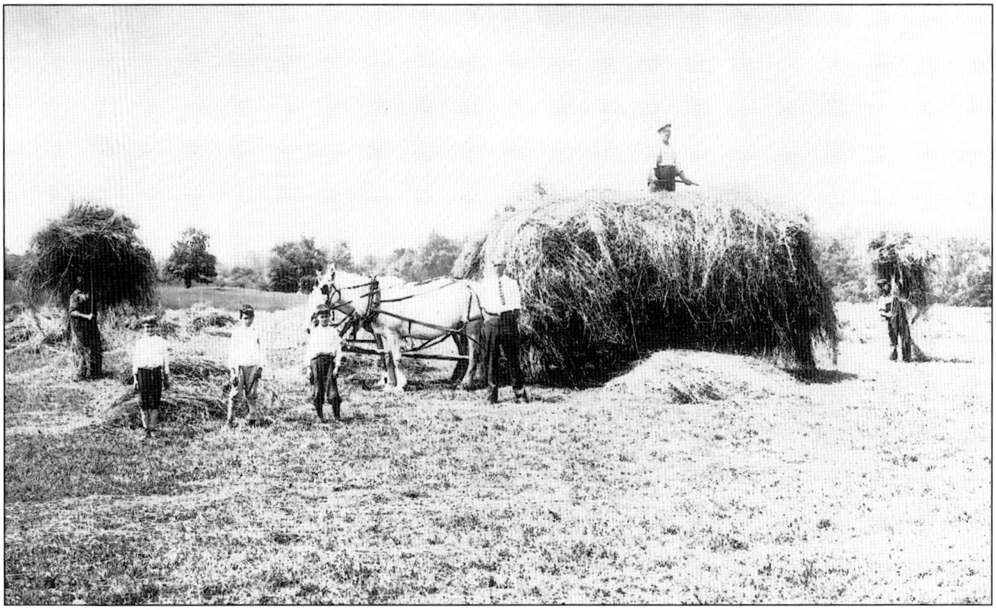

The Joyce farm was located on the northwest corner of Federal Road and Route 133. From left to right are Ralph Joyce, Clarence Joyce (the son of Clarence Joyce), ? Case (the son of James Case), Ralph Joyce (the son of Ralph Joyce), James Case, Arthur Joyce (on the wagon), and Clarence Joyce. Hay and corn are still grown in this field.

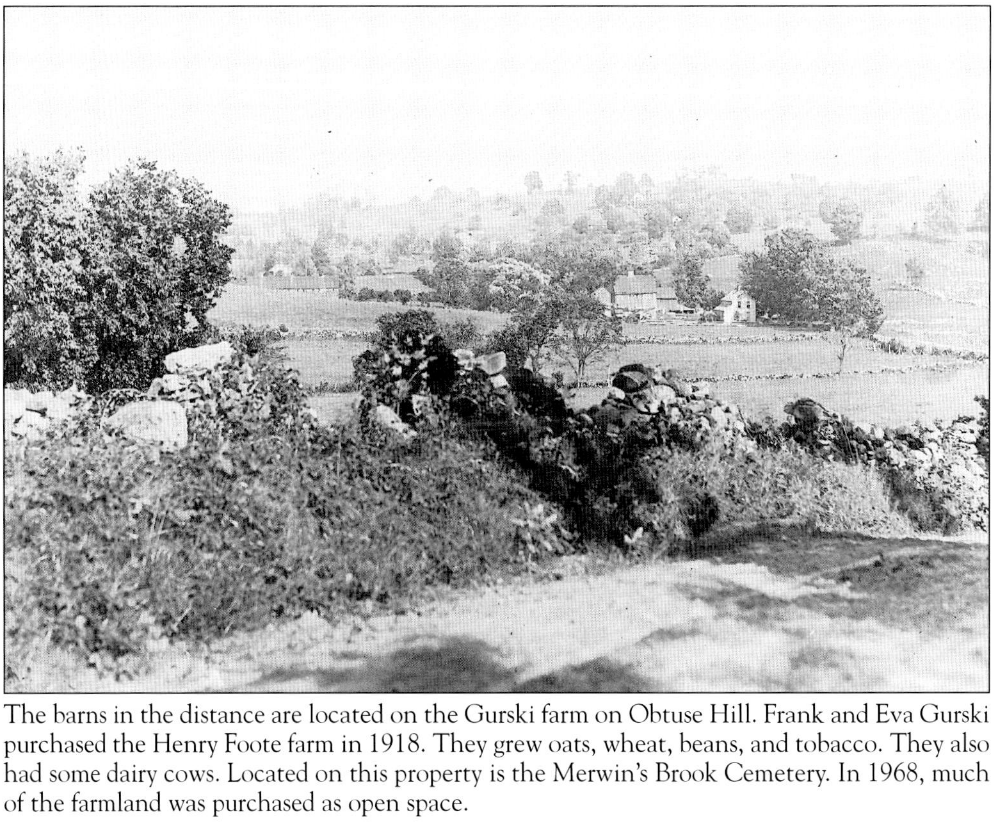

The barns in the distance are located on the Gurski farm on Obtuse Hill. Frank and Eva Gurski purchased the Henry Foote farm in 1918. They grew oats, wheat, beans, and tobacco. They also had some dairy cows. Located on this property is the Merwin's Brook Cemetery. In 1968, much of the farmland was purchased as open space.

Nine

Friends and Neighbors

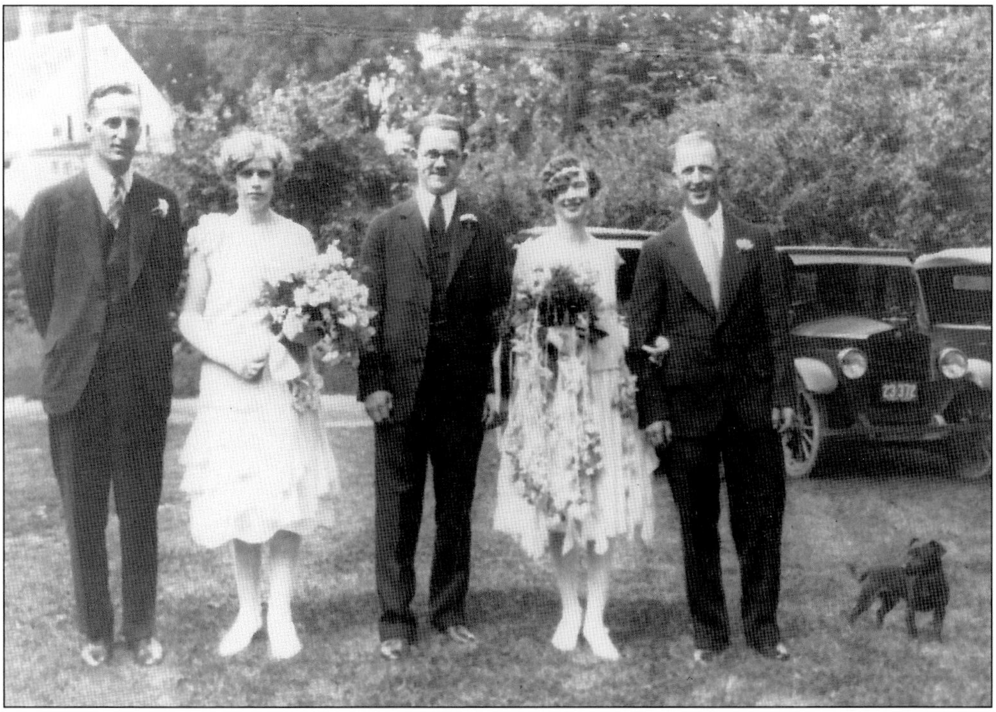

On June 16, 1928, Florence Johnson married John Jensen. They were married in the Congregational Church of Brookfield by the Reverend Archie Hook. The bride's parents were Frank Oscar and Mamie Johnson. The photograph was taken on the lawn of the caretaker's house of the Curtis School for Boys, where her father was the caretaker. From left to right are Aaron Jensen, Marilyn Jolson, Rev. Archie Hook, Florence Johnson, and John Jensen.

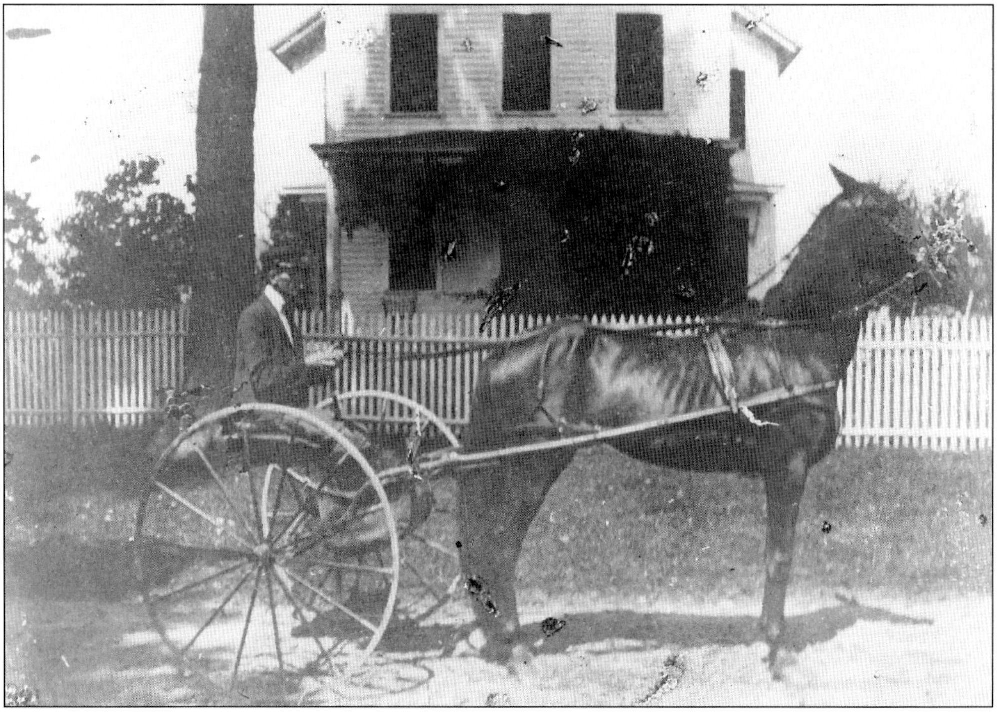

Mr. Herbert Lake was the first RFD postman in Brookfield. He lived in the Obtuse District.

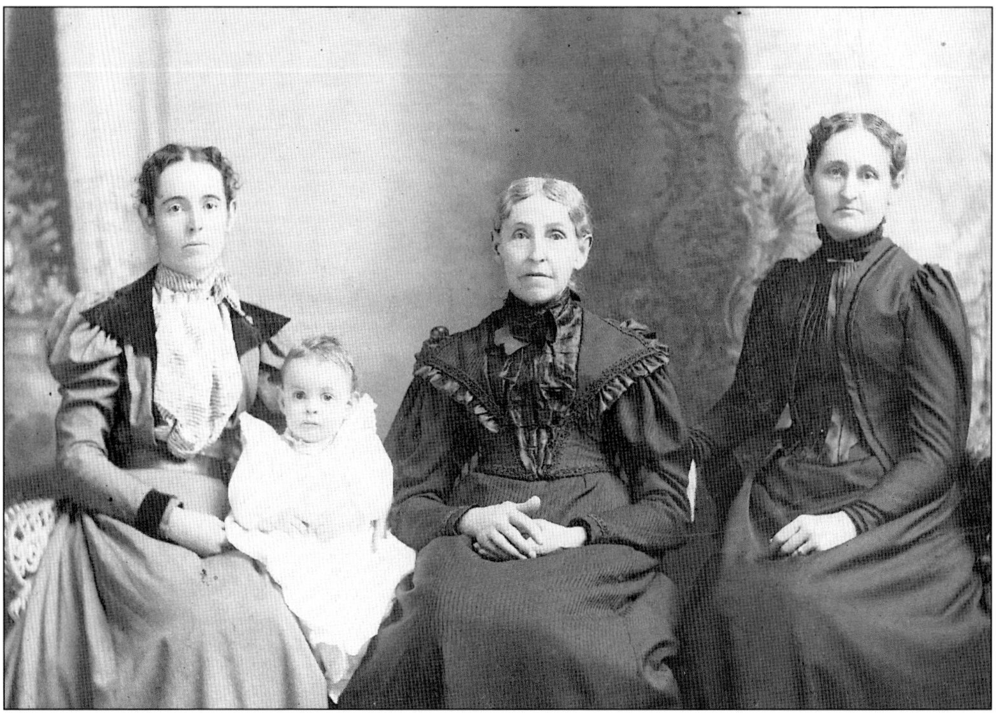

In this photograph are, from left to right, Florence Emily Kellogg (Mrs. Arthur Mansfield), Lina Beers Mansfield, Emily Terrill Booth (Mrs. Horace Beers), and Sophia Emily Beers (Mrs. William Kellogg).

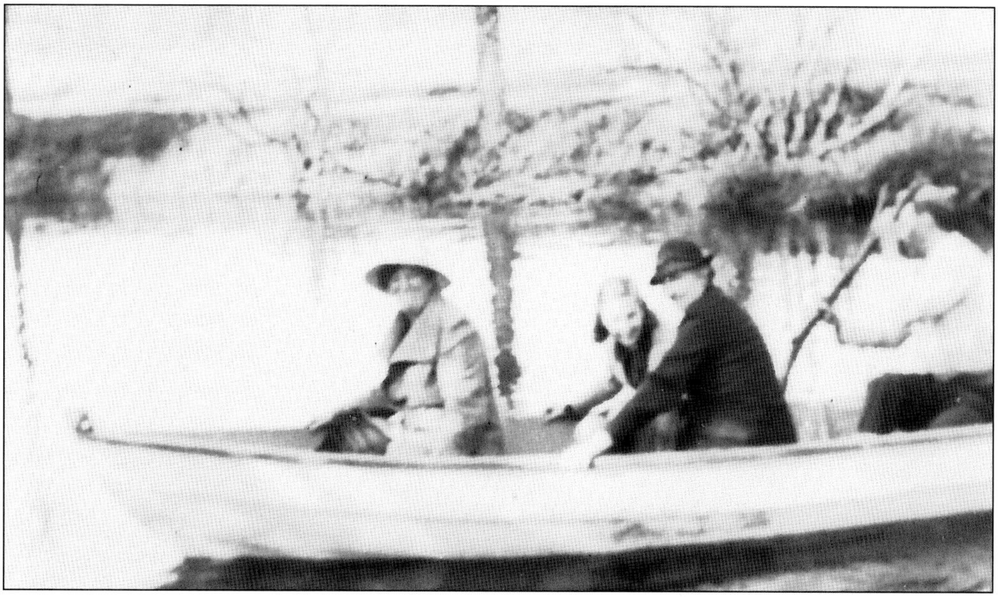

Boating on the Still River in the late 1930s, from left to right, are Josephine Pinckney, Sarah Carlson, Susan Beers Carlson, and Albert B. Lambert.

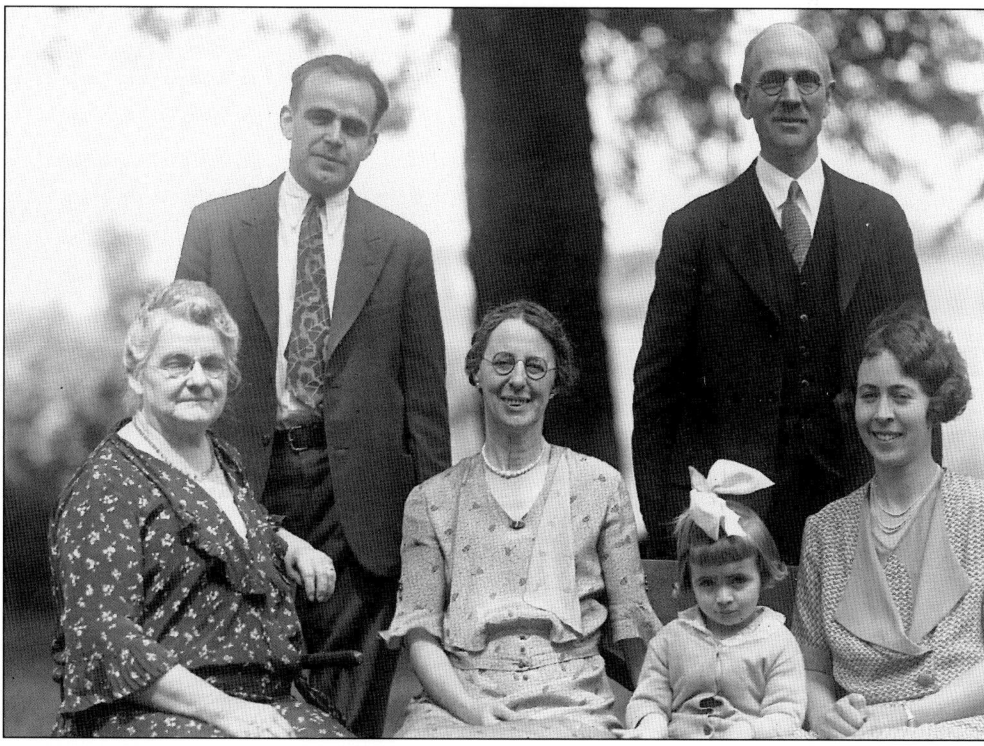

Members of the Terrill family are shown here, from left to right, as follows: (front row) Elinor Terrill, Mrs. Cronenberg, Janet Terrill, and Mildred A. Cronenberg Terrill; (back row) Stuart F. Terrill and Mr. Cronenberg. The Terrill family lived in the Obtuse District for many years. Brookfield's Civil War flag was kept at their family homestead until it was donated to the Brookfield Historical Society.

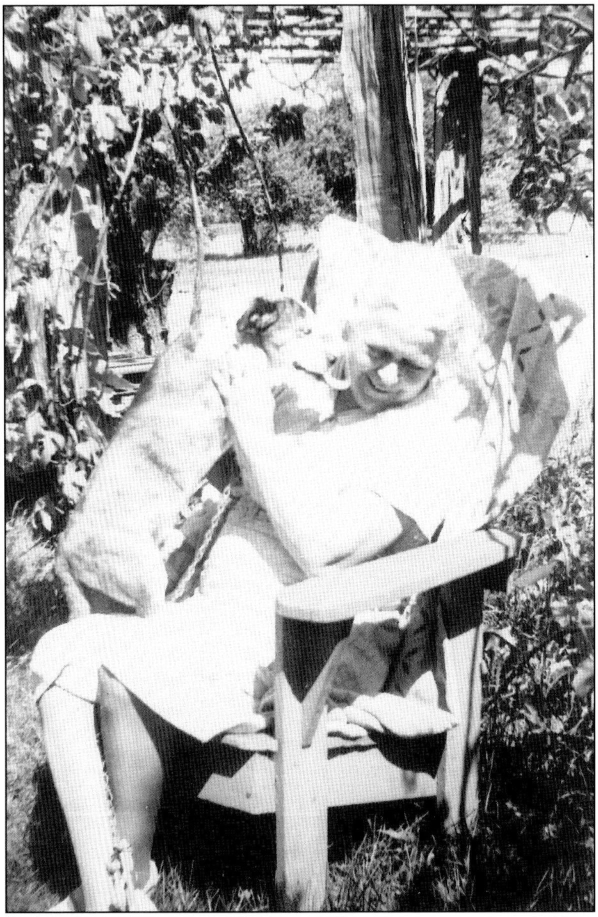

Mrs. Elizabeth Gamber was married to John W. Gamber. They lived in the Obtuse District. After she was widowed, she moved in with John and Delia Thornhill. She's seen here in 1934 with "Major."

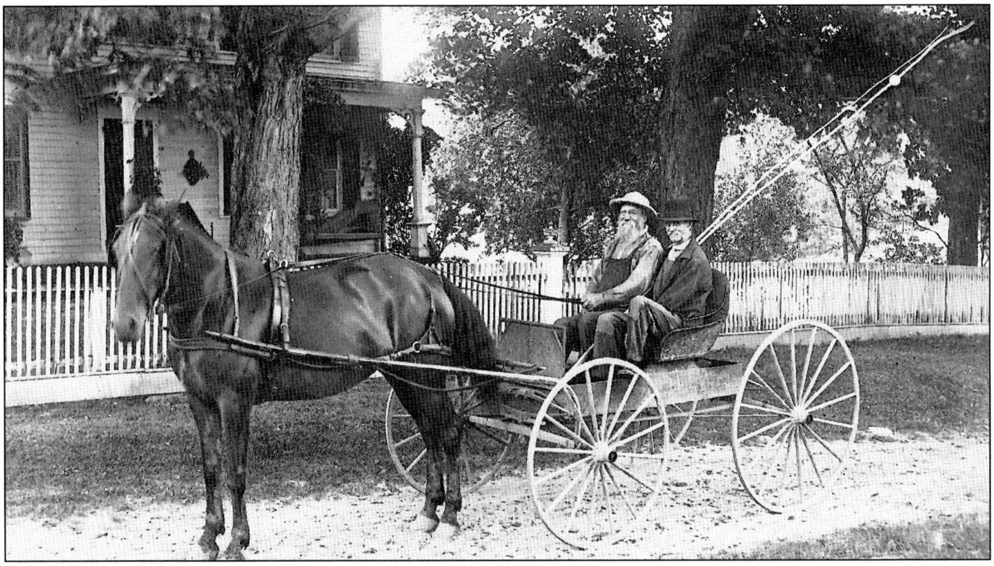

Shown in this 1915 photograph by Paul Fletcher Weld are Charles Hatch and his son. The photograph is titled "Going Fishing."

Mariam Morehouse poses with her four-year-old son, Daniel. His father was David Meeker Morehouse.

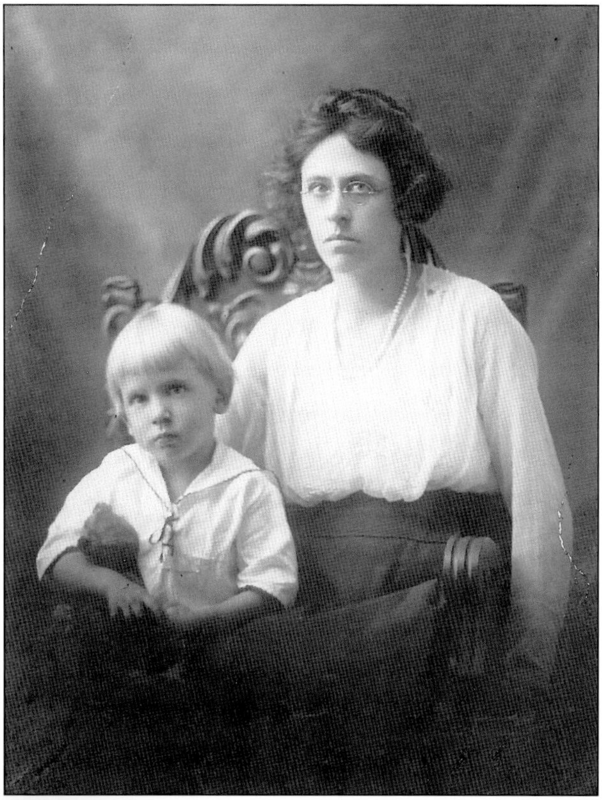

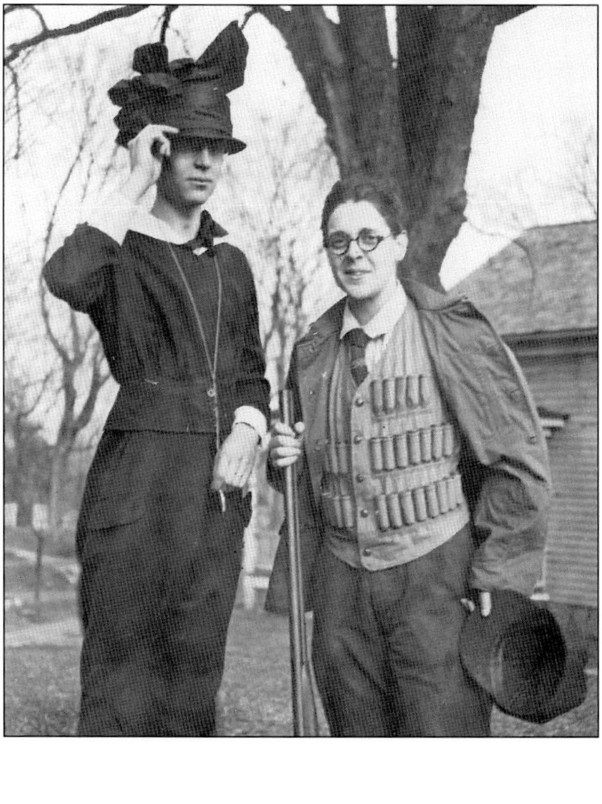

Lina Mansfield is seen here with her cousin, Ernest Mansfield. Ernest was the son of Howard and Edith Griffin.

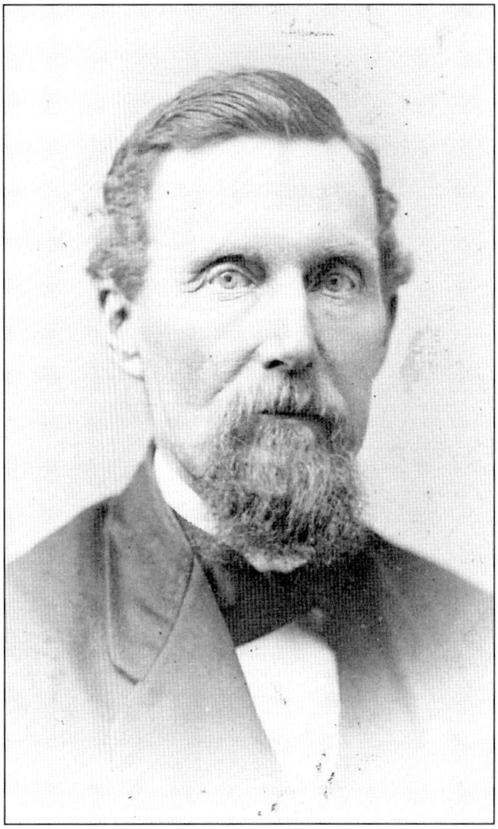

When Barzillai Buckley Kellogg built the brick house on Kellogg Street, it was located in New Fairfield. He was very active in New Fairfield and Brookfield.

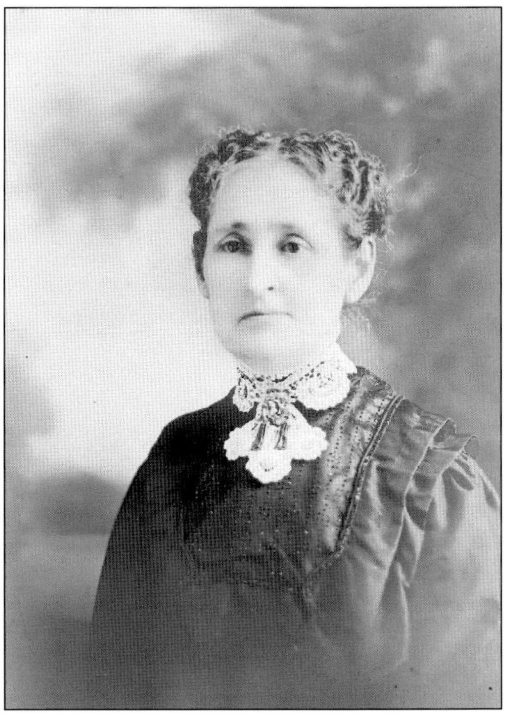

Sophia Emily Beers Kellogg was the daughter of Horace Beers. She married William, the son of Barzillai B. Kellogg.

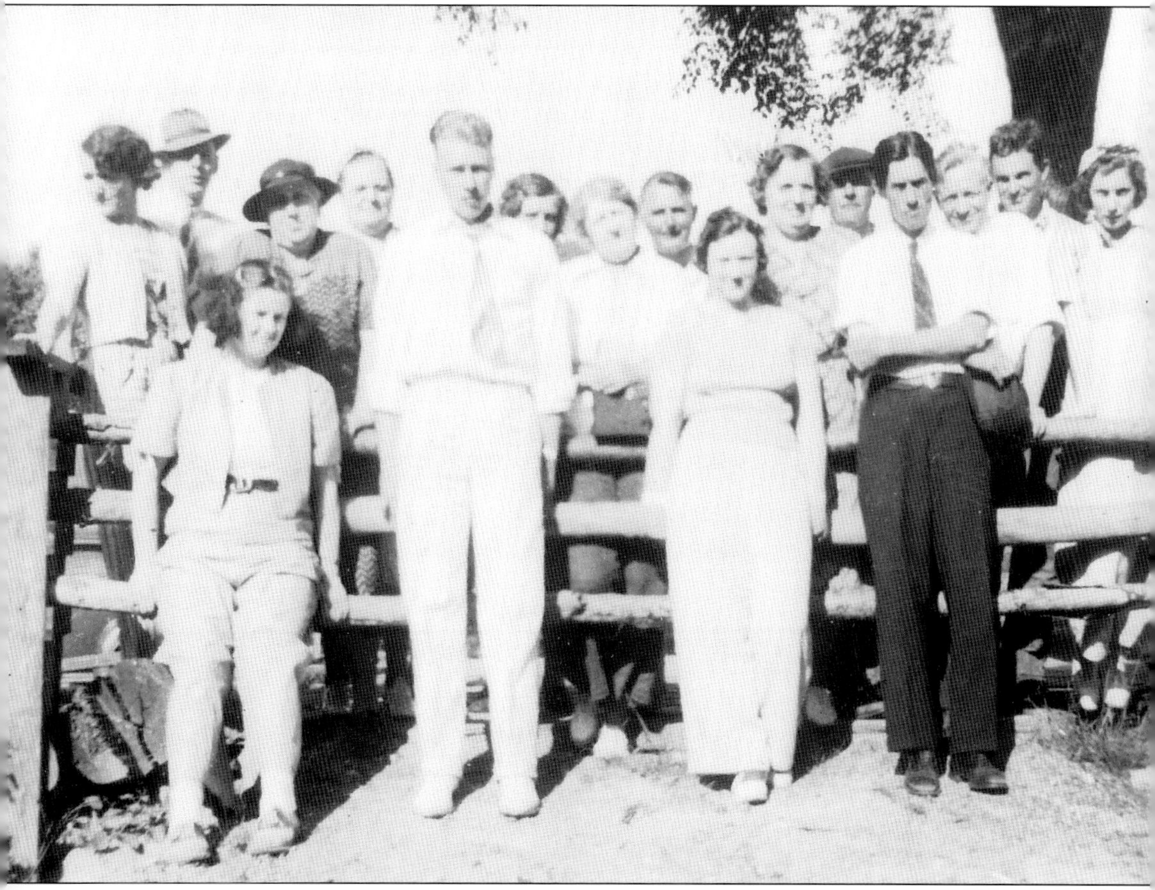

In the 1940s, a group calling themselves the Helping Hand Club was formed to participate in "worthwhile projects." Pictured here, from left to right, are as follows: (front row) Florence Thornhill, Paul Anderson, Esther and Frank Covill; (back row) Irene and George Hatch, Ellen Larson, Byron Ferry, Irene Danion, Alice Ferry, Ralph Danion, Delia Thornhill, John Thornhill, Walfred Johnson, Wesley, and Dorothy Elwood. The first meeting was held in the home of Mrs. John Thornhill.

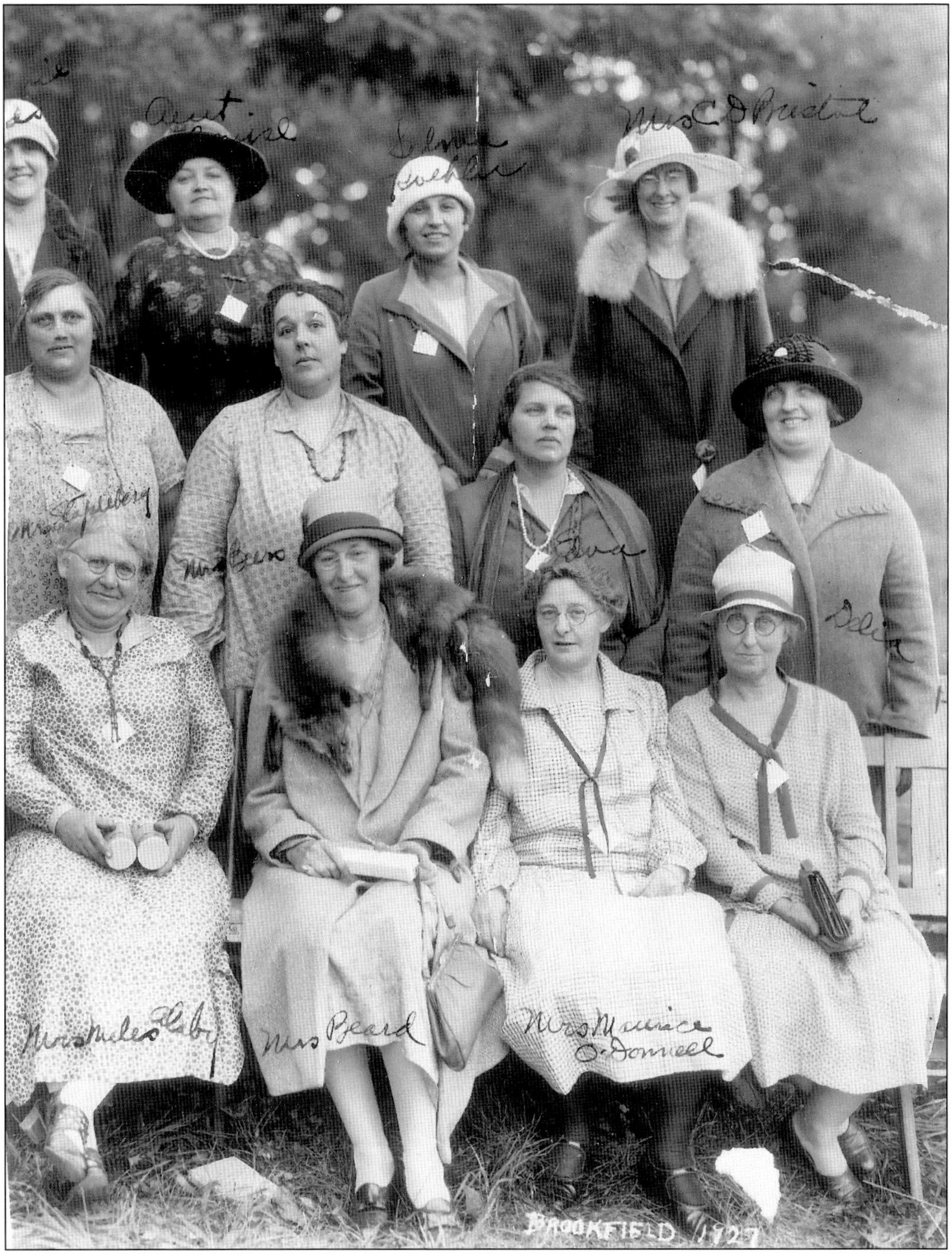

In 1921, this group of Brookfield women posed for a photograph. They are, from left to right, as follows: (front row) Mrs. Miles Alaby, Mrs. Beard, Mrs. Maurice O'Donnell, and unidentified; (middle row) Mrs. Stapleberg, Mrs. Beers, Edna Stansfield Martini, and Delia Thornhill; (back row) Mina Coords, Louise ?, Selma Koehler, and Mrs. C.D. Bristol.

On the left is Mary T. Haight, owner of the Old Post Road Inn in Brookfield Center. She lived in the old Peck Homestead, next door to the inn. Shown here with her is Hannah Eliza Weld, the hostess at the Old Post Road Inn.

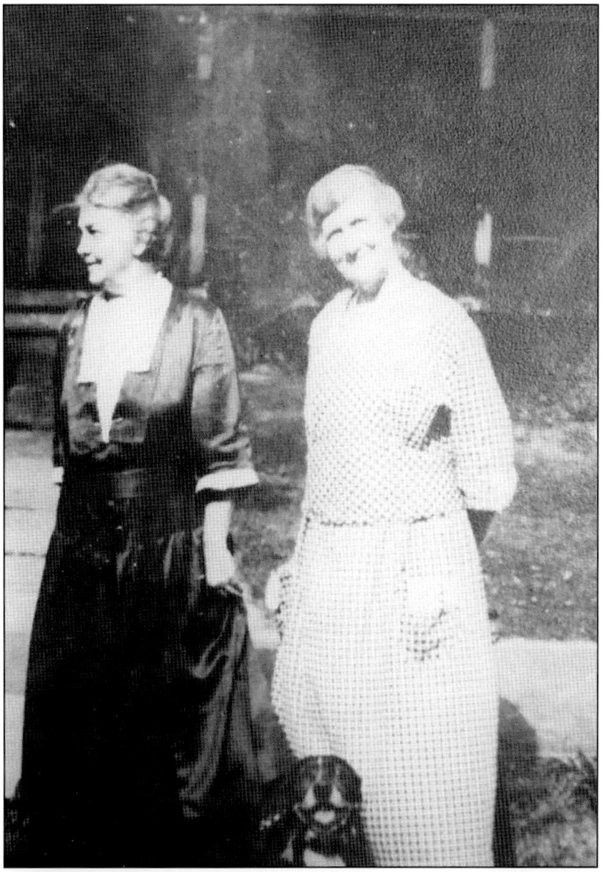

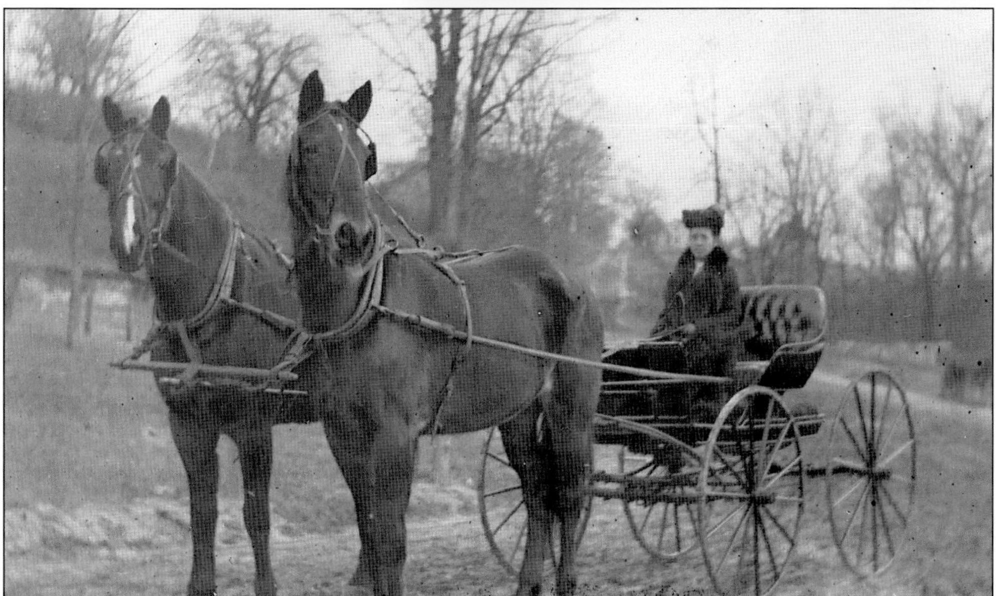

Out for a ride in her horse and buggy is Florence Emily Kellogg Mansfield, the daughter of Sophia and William Kellogg. She married Arthur S. Mansfield.

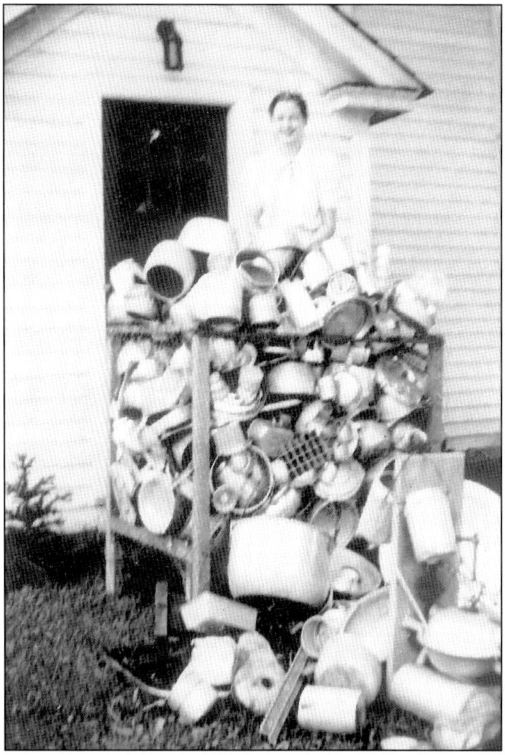

In 1941, Elizabeth Thornhill was the chairman of the scrap-metal drive in support of the war effort. The collection was in the front yard of the Thornhill's home. Shown here is her sister Florence.

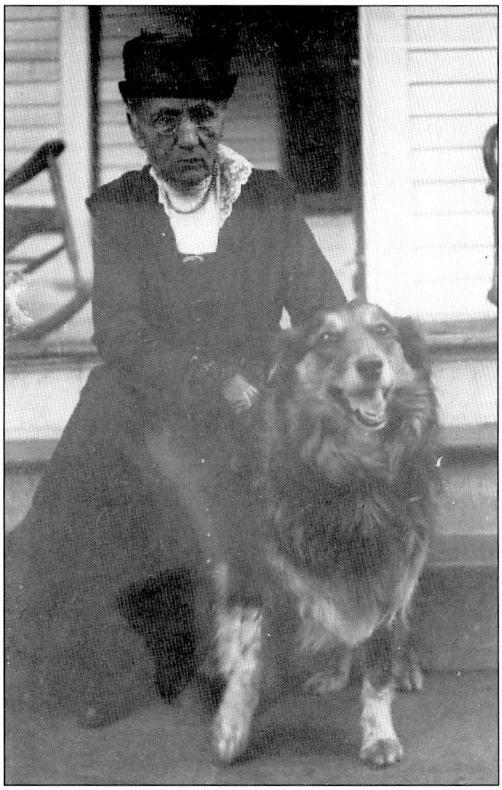

Daniel D. Joyce came to Brookfield in 1866. He purchased the Starr farm on Federal Road and married Sarah A. Clarke in 1865. Their only son was D. Clarke Joyce. In this 1916 photograph Sarah poses with "Prince."

Emily C. Hawley was the daughter of Henry B. and Ethel Skidmore Hawley. She was an author of many history books, including several on the history of Brookfield and the surrounding area, the Skidmore genealogy, and the Hawley family history. Her book *Annals of Brookfield* contains much of the early history of Brookfield and genealogies of the people of Brookfield.

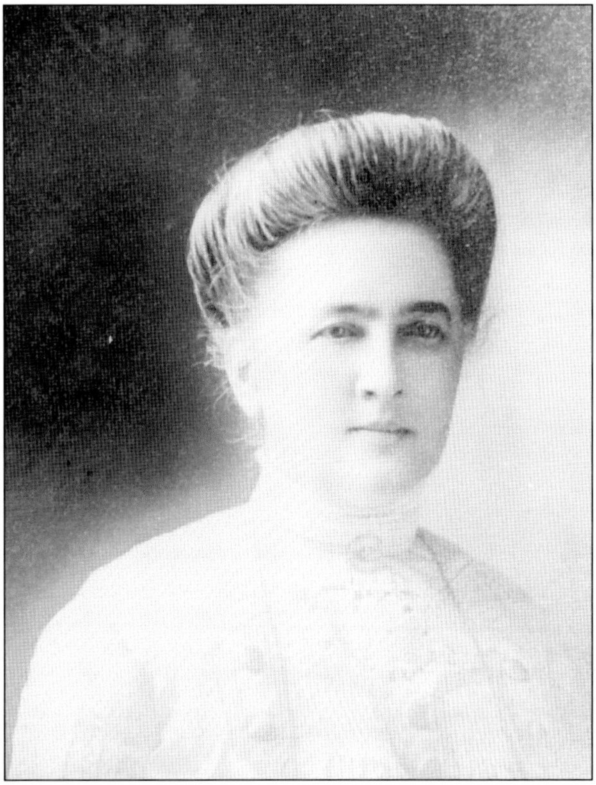

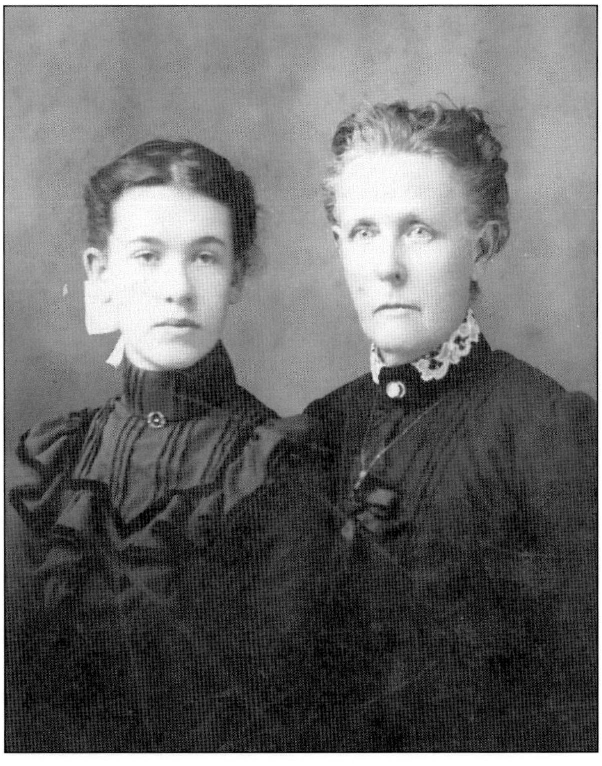

This is a 1902 portrait of Myrtle J. Russell and her aunt, Cynthia Russell.

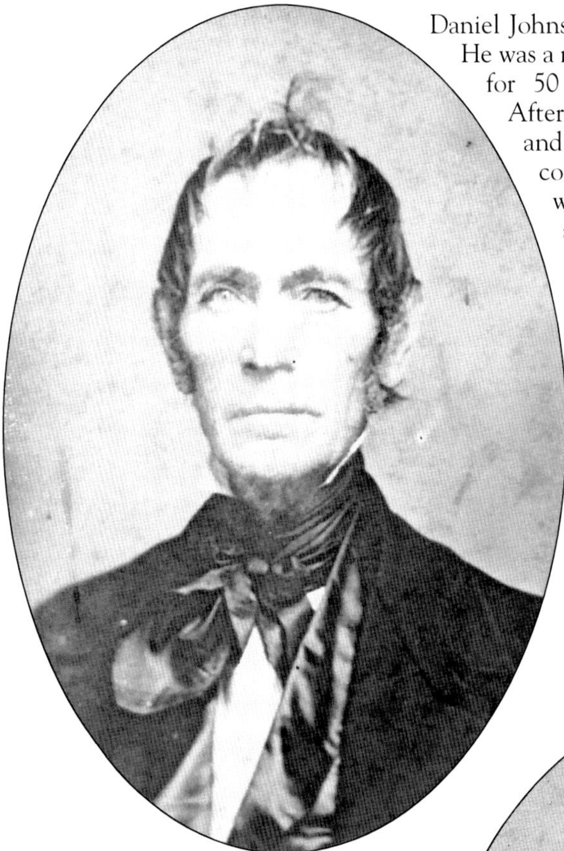

Daniel Johnson was born in 1788 and died in 1866. He was a merchant and tailor in Brookfield Center for 50 years. He married Lamina Wheeler. After his death, his shop was taken down and replaced with a store that was later converted to a home. In 1961, the house was taken down to make way for an addition and a parking lot for the town hall (formerly Center School).

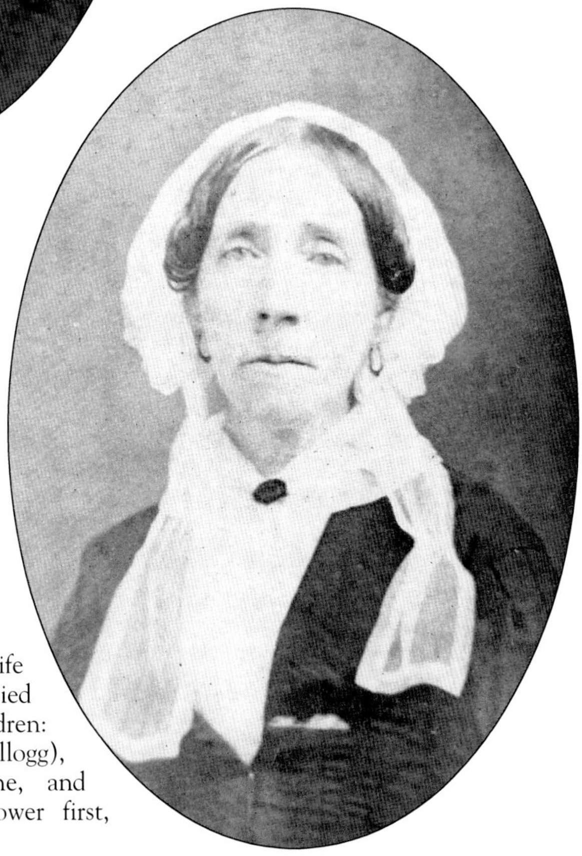

This is Lamina Wheeler Johnson, the wife of Daniel. She was born in 1796 and died in 1875. Together they had four children: Emeline (who married Barzillai B. Kellogg), Ason (twin of Emeline), Angeline, and Elizabeth (who married George S. Knower first, and then Henry Washburn).

Catherine Weadock lived in Brookfield. She was friends with the Mansfield family and took many trips with them.

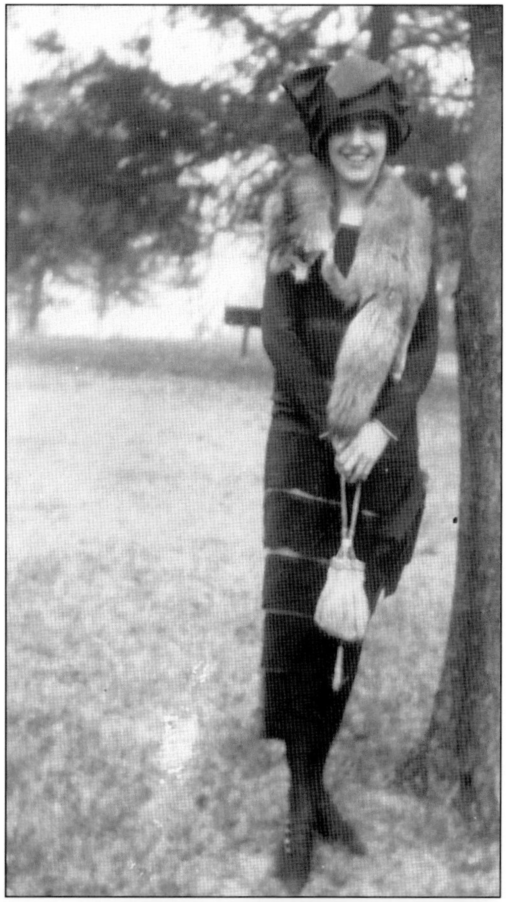

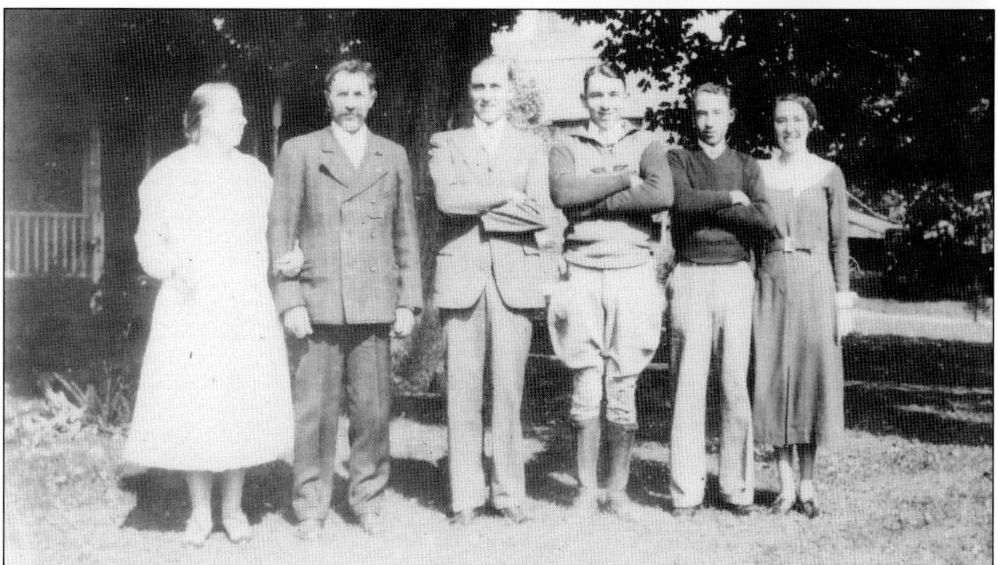

The Gurski family in shown front of their farmhouse on Obtuse Hill. They are, from left to right, Eva, Frank Sr., Harry, Frank Jr., Stanley, and Helen.

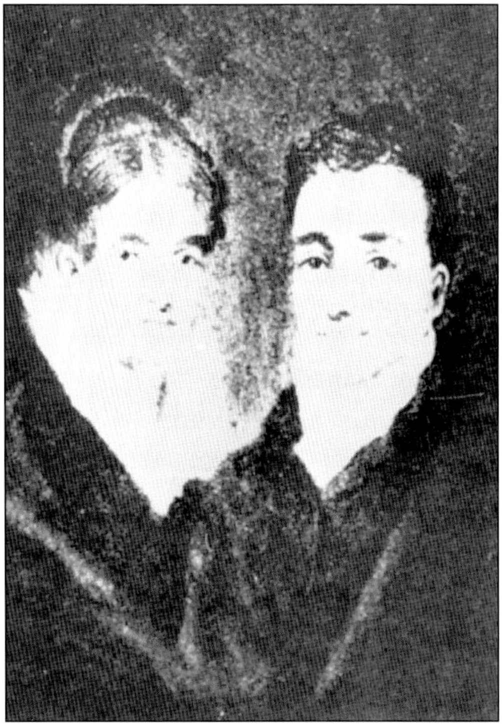

In 1819, Lucia Ruggles married Dr. Thomas Holman. They then left for the Hawaiian Islands as missionaries. Two years later they came back by way of China, making Lucia the first American woman to circumnavigate the globe. Dr. Holman died in Bridgeport, and Lucia returned home to Brookfield. She married Daniel Tomlinson and was the last survivor of the first group of missionaries to Hawaii.

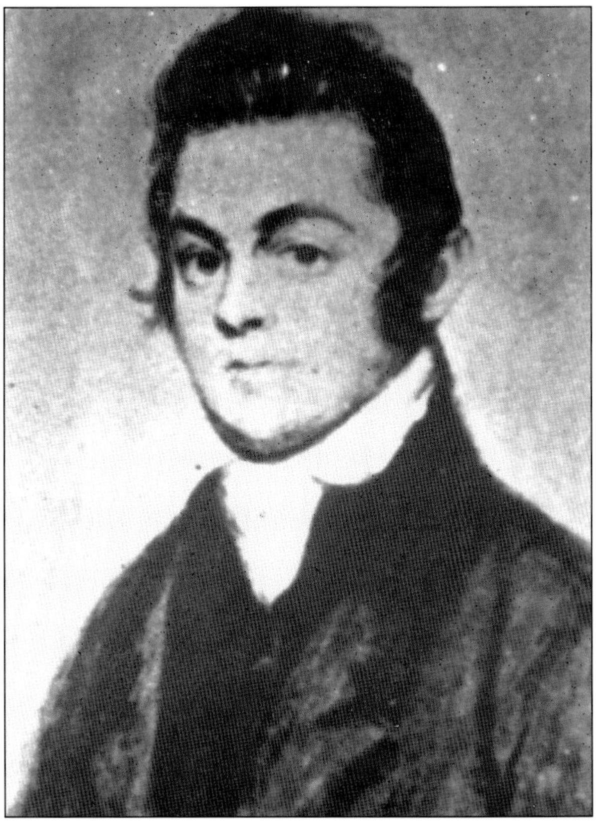

Samuel Ruggles, brother of Lucia, and his wife, Nancy, were also missionaries to the Hawaiian Islands in 1819. Samuel and Nancy were teachers and they help to write down the Hawaiian language. They stayed for about 15 years. They came back to Brookfield, but soon left for Fort Atkinson, Wisconsin, to be with their children. They both died in Wisconsin and are buried there.

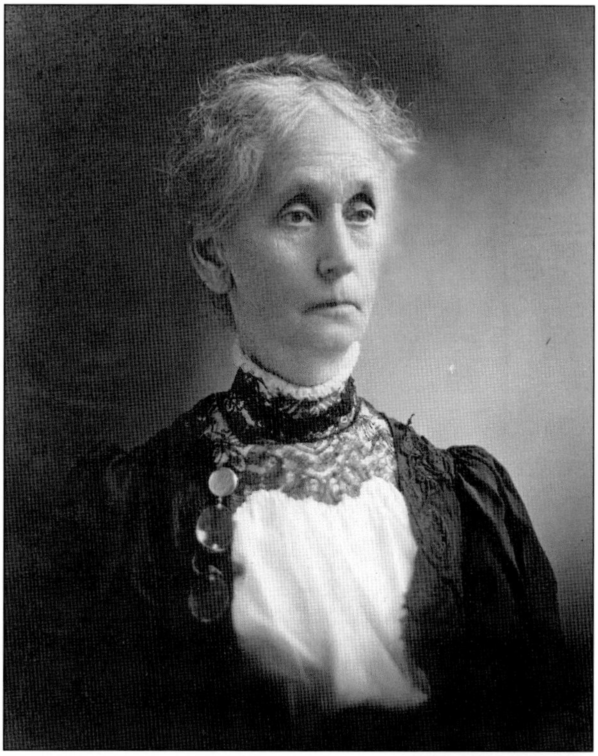

Florence Williams Sagendorf was the daughter of Dr. Amos and Sarah Holley Williams. She married John W. Sagendorf, and they had four children: Juliette, Florence, John, and Lucy.

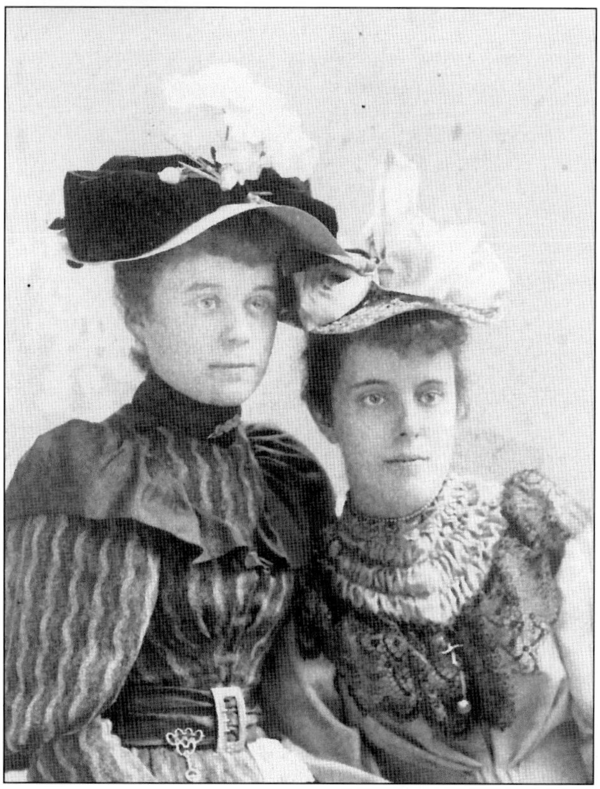

Clara Williams Blackman, the daughter of Charles and Georgina Metcalf Williams, is shown here with Nina Jackson. Clara married Claude B. Blackman, a dentist in New Milford, Connecticut.

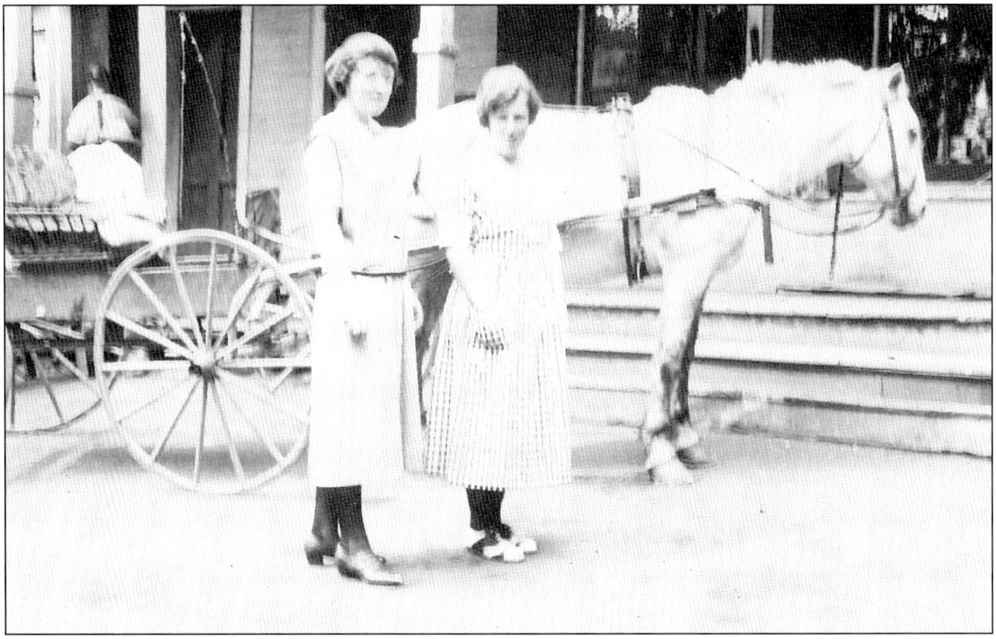

These two Brookfield women are standing in front of the Village Store on Whisconier Road.

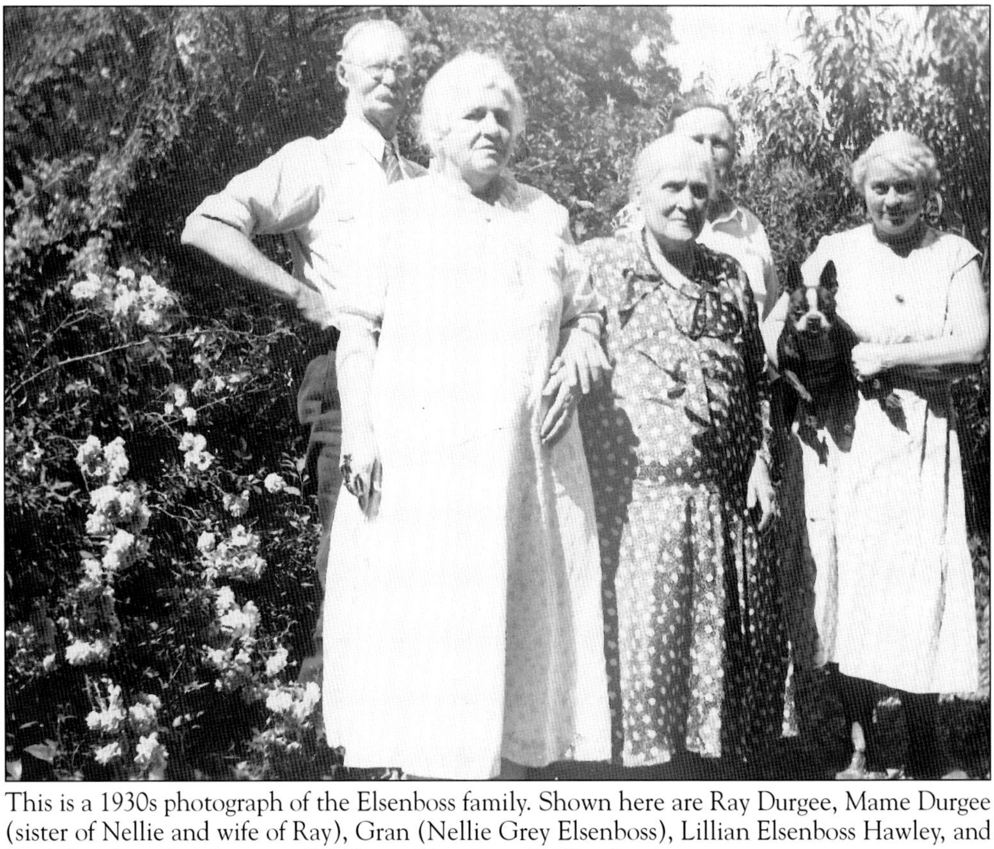

This is a 1930s photograph of the Elsenboss family. Shown here are Ray Durgee, Mame Durgee (sister of Nellie and wife of Ray), Gran (Nellie Grey Elsenboss), Lillian Elsenboss Hawley, and Paul Elsenboss Sr. (the son of Nellie and brother of Lillian).

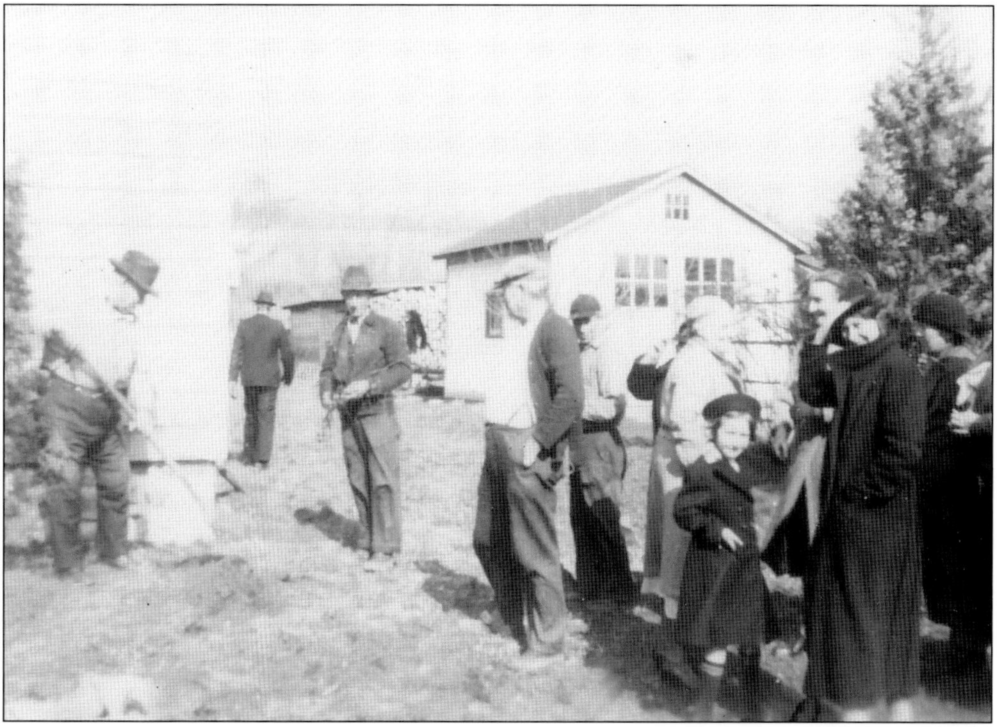

The Pokono Grange No. 191 was formed on December 30, 1920, with 32 charter members. For about six years, the meetings were held in Re-Joyce Hall. In 1926, the members purchased Hillcrest Hall on Whisconier Road. By 1958, they had built a new hall on Pocono Road. Here they are shown planting some trees at the hall.

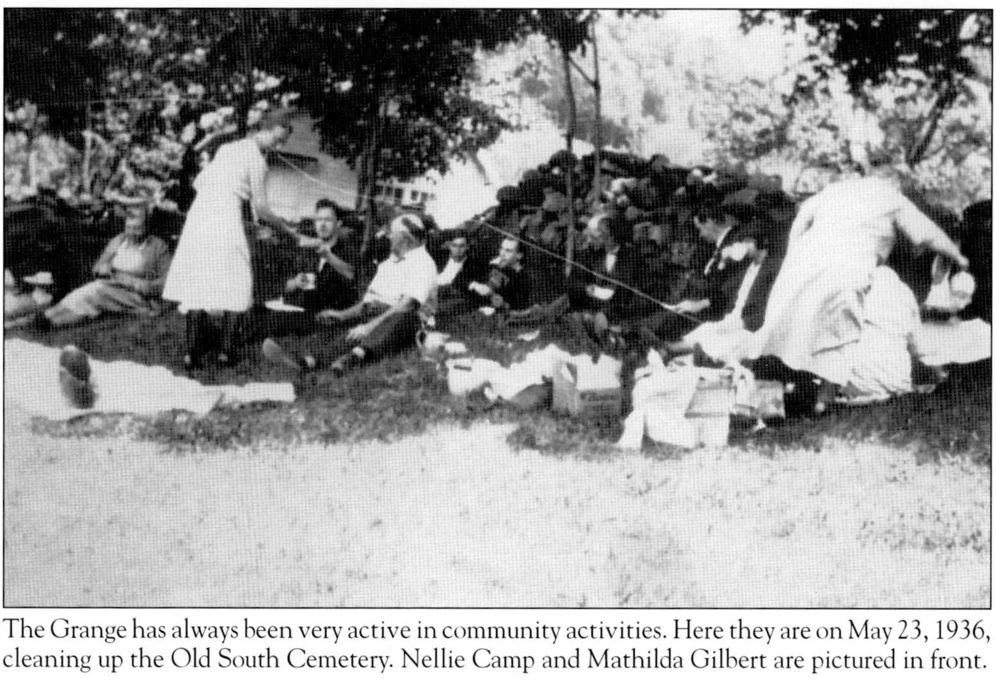

The Grange has always been very active in community activities. Here they are on May 23, 1936, cleaning up the Old South Cemetery. Nellie Camp and Mathilda Gilbert are pictured in front.

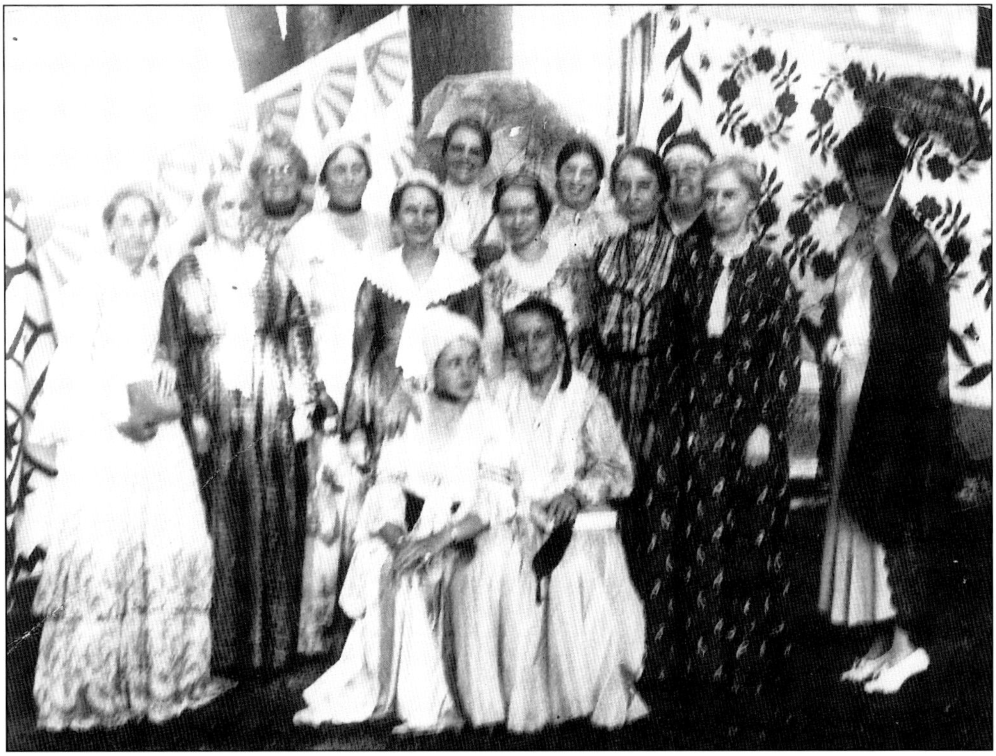

The Republican Women's Club poses for a photograph. Fourth from the left is Gertrude Platt, with Lenore just below her. Ruth Hawley is the fifth from the right, and third from the right is Gertrude Anderson.

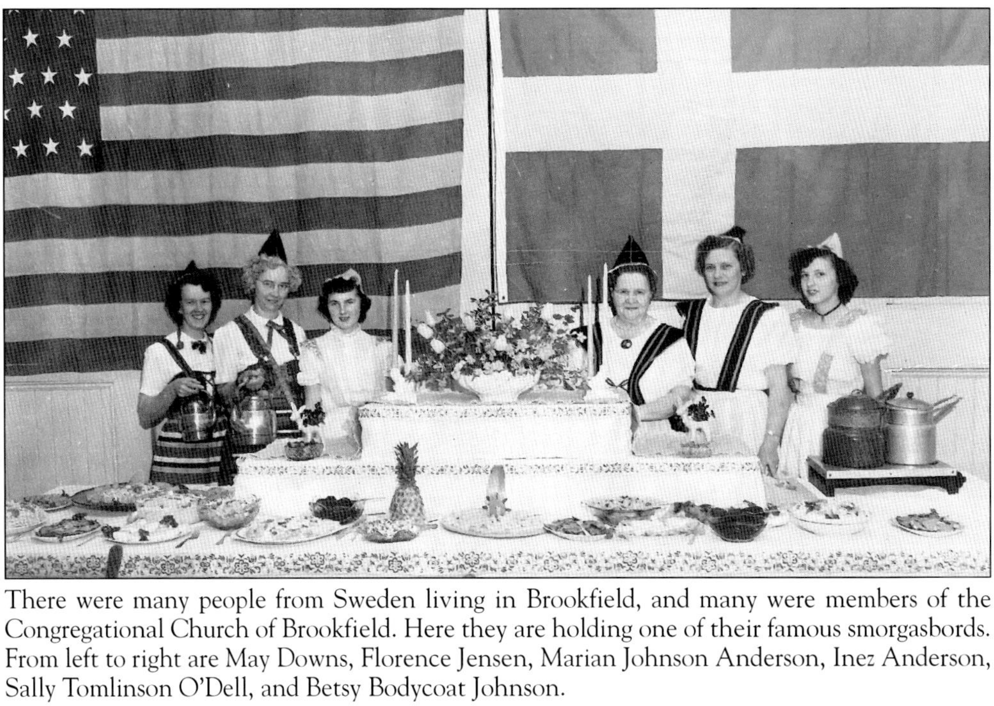

There were many people from Sweden living in Brookfield, and many were members of the Congregational Church of Brookfield. Here they are holding one of their famous smorgasbords. From left to right are May Downs, Florence Jensen, Marian Johnson Anderson, Inez Anderson, Sally Tomlinson O'Dell, and Betsy Bodycoat Johnson.

Dr. Homer Jones is seen here on vacation with his wife, Louise. He was born in Brookfield Center in 1866. A graduate of the University of the City of New York, he practiced medicine in New York City and Brooklyn, New York.

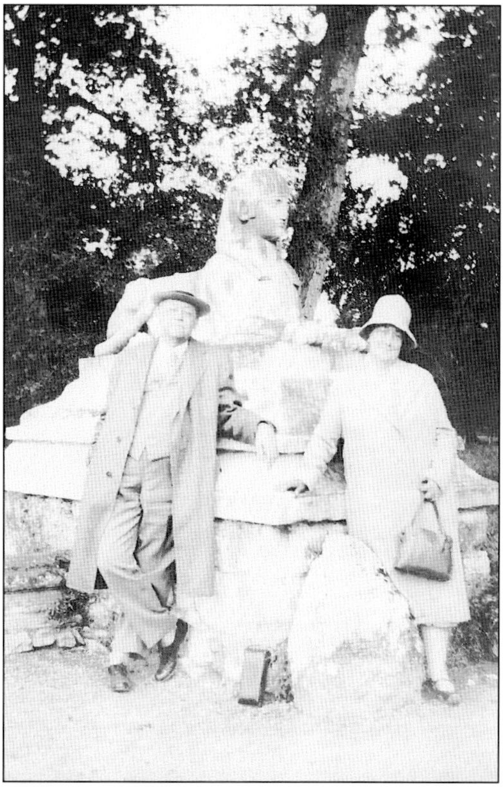

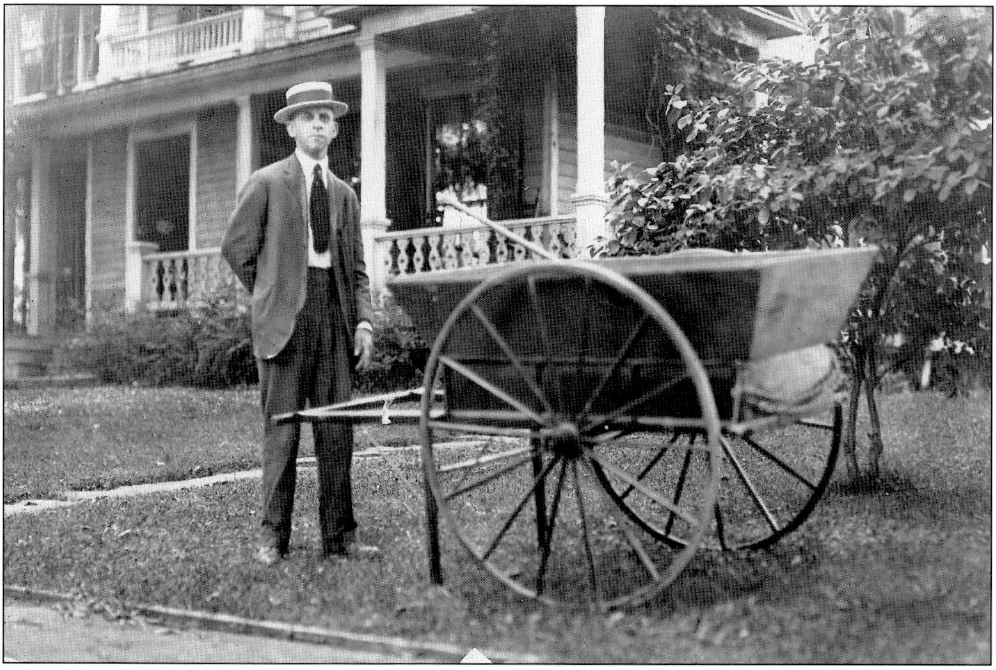

This is Willie Williams with his mail cart on Longmeadow Hill Road. He delivered mail and ran errands for people who lived in Brookfield Center. The house in the background was once the home of Rev. Henry D. Noble.

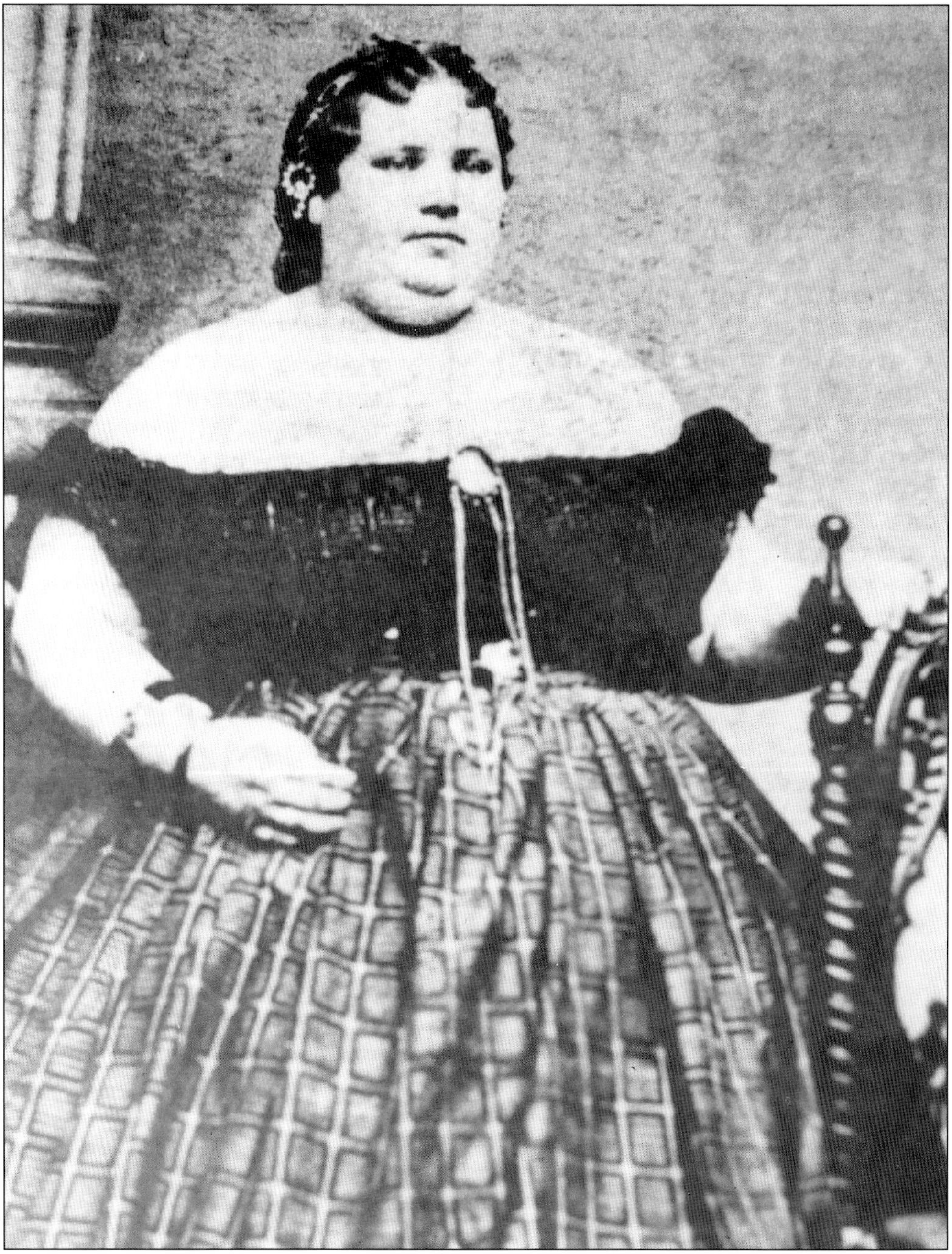

Sarah Jane Campbell Pishon was the first fat lady of the circus. She began her career in the Great American Museum owned by P.T. Barnum. At that time she was on exhibit with the original "Siamese Twins" and "Tom Thumb." She was born in Brookfield and died here. It is thought that P.T. Barnum probably saw her in the area, as he was from Bethel, Connecticut. Her mother, Sally, was a weaver and her father was Roderick Campbell. Sarah married a man by the name of Pishon, but no one knows anything about him. It was thought that he married her for her money. At one time, she weighed over 600 pounds. She died in 1864 at the age of 21 and was buried in Central Cemetery.